MEXICAN EVERYDAY

ALSO BY RICK BAYLESS

Rick and Lanie's Excellent Kitchen Adventures (with Lanie Bayless and Deann Groen Bayless)

Mexico—One Plate at a Time (with JeanMarie Brownson and Deann Groen Bayless)

Salsas That Cook (with Deann Groen Bayless and JeanMarie Brownson)

Rick Bayless's Mexican Kitchen (with Deann Groen Bayless and JeanMarie Brownson)

Authentic Mexican (with Deann Groen Bayless)

SEAFOOD SALAD TACOS WITH TOMATO, RADISH AND HABANERO

Rick Bayless
MEXICAN EVERYDAY

with Deann Groen Bayless

COLOR PHOTOGRAPHS BY CHRISTOPHER HIRSHEIMER

W. W. NORTON & COMPANY

NEW YORK © LONDON

Manufacturing by R R Donnelley, Crawfordsville
Book design by Chalkley Calderwood Pratt
Production: Andrew Marasia, Sue Carlson

ISBN 0-393-06154-X (hardcover)

W. W. Norton & Company, Inc., 500 Fifth Avenue, New York, N.Y. 10110

W. W. Norton & Company Ltd., Castle House, 75/76 Wells Street, London W1T 3QT

To Bob and Jewel Hoogstoel, who've warmly and lavishly shared their celebration of life's beauty with so many

Contents

Chapter 2: Contemporary Main-Dish Salads   92

Chapter 7: Desserts   298

ACKNOWLEDGMENTS

I am overwhelmed—humbled, really—as I survey the generosity of those who've helped put this book together. Deann, my wife of twenty-six years, offered copious amounts of insight, an editor's keen eye, a partner's steadfastness and encouragement and a producer's ability to bring the job to completion—beautifully and on time. Kirsten West left her inimitable touch on every page, having worked on these recipes from conception to perfection—testing, refining, retesting, rerefining. Maria Guarnaschelli, my editor of many years, asked the questions that led me to deeper, better and clearer material. Christopher Hirsheimer captured on film the genuine beauty of simple food, in large part, I believe, because her warm, generous spirit perceives beauty all around. Chalkley Calderwood Pratt designed an easy, elegant package for weaving together my words and Christopher's images, while Judith Sutton polished those words so they'd dance across the pretty pages. Doe Coover, great agent and great friend, stopped everything when I needed her, always making me feel I was her only author.

In my world of book deadlines and restaurant hubbub, Lanie, my fourteen-year-old, graciously puts up with unpredictable schedules, I hope because she knows I always carve out time for us to cook together. The ever-fabulous Jen Fite moves at lightning speed through the most complicated situations with hilarity and grace; I can't imagine how I'd get anything done without her organizing, advancing and campaigning for every project we tackle. Carlos Alferez, our partner and general manager of Frontera Grill/Topolobampo, and Brian Enyart, the managing chef, have afforded me, by their dedication and carefulness, the opportunity to invest countless hours in writing and testing, in order to bring the true flavors of Mexico to an ever-wider audience. Manny Valdes, JeanMarie Brownson and Greg Keller, my partners in Frontera Foods, our prepared foods company, have been generous supporters and tireless evangelists for wondrous Mexican flavors. Finally, to Rita Knorr, Sergio Rojas and Michael Horowitz, my longtime coaches in yoga, strength training and life, respectively, I owe an enormous debt of gratitude: you've offered just what I need to bring life into balance; you've opened the door to a whole new meaning of *fun*.

RICK GRILLING IN HIS LIVING-ROOM FIREPLACE

INTRODUCTION

Wᵉ've come to require a daily diet of vibrant flavors, haven't we? Tangy pad thai and Sichuan scorchers. Intricate Indian curries and herby-fresh Vietnamese spring rolls. Japanese wasabi-spiked sushi and Italian pasta arrabbiata with a good shot of garlic and chiles.

And lots of Mexican. Well, mostly our beloved Mexican-American tacos and burritos with salsa and sour cream, or, on occasion, a new Mexican-style pasta dish, say, infused with jalapeños and cilantro. But when we delve deeper than that simple—though admittedly charming and tasty—fare, there's an even more dynamic Mexican cuisine to be had. The cuisine that cooks in Mexico's heartland have perfected over centuries, born of native traditions, fused with Spanish know-how, and polished by generations of practiced hands.

Trouble is, the classic dishes those Mexican cooks have become famous for—the *moles, pipianes* and traditional braises of tomatoes and tomatillos enlivened with exotic herbs and chiles—typically require such an investment of time (for tracking down just the right ingredients, for preparation) that most of us consign them to the "special occasion" category. But special occasion dishes don't compose the whole of Mexico's regional cookbook:

our neighbor-country's cooks, many with fewer resources than we enjoy, have for centuries been living busy lives while daily putting three simple, full-flavored, *thoroughly Mexican-tasting* meals on the table.

That's where *Mexican Everyday* comes in. After cooking traditional and contemporary Mexican food for over twenty-five years—as a professional chef with a retinue of sous-chefs and as a father feeding a busy family—I think I've finally figured out how to get the most traditional, most complex and delicious flavor out of the fewest (and most easily accessible) ingredients in the least amount of time. (Which frequently means before my starving daughter has to go to dance class or play rehearsal or . . . you know the drill.) I applied that learning to an indispensable collection of Mexican classics, added in simple family favorites I've been fed by Mexican moms through the years and, in a few instances, wove together traditional ingredients into contemporary offerings. Then I compiled it all into a book that mirrors everyday eating at our house.

In broad strokes, the hub of this book is some fifty main dishes—most of them complete meals. I've bookended those entrées with a collection of plucky salad dressings and a few simple fruit desserts. (We usually toss together a salad to go with our main dish; dessert doesn't play a large role in our everyday eating.) In addition, there's a large selection on grilling—marinades, rubs, grilling skills for my favorite cuts and, of course, a robust collection of salsas to spoon on. And since grilled dishes cry out for rustic accompaniments, I've also included a selection of straightforward bean and rice preparations, plus a few simple vegetable salads that I think will capture your imagination.

It sounds as though the development of these recipes progressed along a straight path, but that's only partly true. Yes, over many years I have developed a deep understanding of Mexican ingredients and techniques that has equipped me for streamlining the classics. True, I've tasted (and jotted down recipes for) many simple dishes at kitchen tables all over Mexico. But it wasn't until I fully understood the crucial concept of *everyday* food—versus *weekend* food, *special-occasion* food, *feasting* food, however you want to brand it—that the framework for these recipes took form.

And the rather windy path to that clear understanding of everyday food, and the essential role it plays in our lives, took me through some unexpected terrain, through aspects of myself I'd rarely connected with. But as I navigated the various bends in my road, I began to notice a greater sense of well-being. I began getting healthier, more fit. Which means that, nowadays, I've become

accustomed to an almost identical interrogation from practically everyone I meet.

"How come," they all wonder out loud, blurt out loud, "you're so lean if you're a chef?"

It doesn't really take much reasoning to parse the thought process: A chef gains notoriety by making really delicious food. Delicious food is rich food—the stuff that makes us fat. And the more delicious the food, of course, the more we indulge. If you're a good chef, you . . . well, you should be at least *pudgy*.

Whether they'd admit it or not, I'd bet that most of my interrogators want to ask, What kind of freak *is* this guy? He spends all day in a great restaurant, surrounded by really good food, developing and tasting new dishes. Is he one of those weirdoes who's into self-denial? Doesn't he ever just sit down and dig in to the fruits of his own cooking? Does he have some kind of eating disorder?

Eating disorder? Are you kidding? Everyone who knows me will attest that I *love* to eat—from morning to night. I do it for a living. I do it for a hobby. I do it with friends and family, and when I'm alone. I'm always thinking about, and talking about, my next, or last, meal. Without trying to sound grandiose about the whole thing, I'm a chef because food and the people I share it with enrich my life with endless diversity and unexpected pleasures. From my youngest years, food has been my bridge to a full experience of life.

So, what's the deal with my leanness?

Abnormal metabolism or unique genetic makeup? I'm pretty sure that's not it, because I haven't always been lean. In fact, I was a Hostess-cupcake, *Gilligan's Island*–reruns, chubby adolescent—totally unathletic. Some of that adolescent chubbiness fell off naturally during my last high school years, but then slowly started coming back—bit by nearly unnoticeable bit. It's a common story: by my mid-forties, I'd accumulated at least twenty-five extra pounds—plenty noticeable on my average, 5-foot 9-inch frame.

That's when I rather accidentally found myself on the path that led to my uncovering the difference between the celebratory, succulent works of art our restaurant is known for and fresh, simple everyday food that satisfies the spirit's quest for deliciousness while providing the body with just what it needs to function at its peak.

When I was at my heaviest, several new ideas began percolating in my brain simultaneously. A friend started teaching yoga, and I found myself intrigued with her—yoga's—approach to the body and its connection to the spirit. I knew of yoga's purported stress-relief benefits and thought all that stretching could be a nice antidote to my fast-paced, late-night restaurant life. So I signed up to "dabble" in yoga, expecting little more than temporary detox. I'd never been able to stick with—let alone excel at—any physical activity.

Okay, I loved the relaxation I felt after the beginners' yoga class—who wouldn't? But about four months into it, just when I was expecting to flag, I hit a yoga groove that led to some unexpected changes in the way I thought about myself. It was as if my yoga practice was setting free some vision of my potential self. Longer, stronger, leaner, more lithe.

I liked it. In fact, I couldn't stop thinking about it. Problem was, my reflection in the mirror didn't match up with this inspiring new mental image. I looked lumbering and squatty. But knowing I'd uncovered something important about self-perception and yoga's potential as a tool for change, I was fired up to push myself past the yoga "dabble" to the real thing.

Essential Learning #1: **My weight reflects a mental picture I have of myself. For me, yoga challenged my body in directions I'd never considered—unlocking a welcome new image of myself, unlocking physical (even spiritual) potential I'd never considered.**

I made yoga progress little by little, tackling more and more vigorous approaches and demanding poses, though I certainly can't say my body was transforming itself as quickly as I'd imagined. That squatty heaviness snickered at my—by then desperate—attempts to slide my hands under my feet or sustain myself for more than a few seconds in a lunge position. Not only did I feel stiff and weak, but

I was trying to move around a fair amount of weight.

Which led me, in an uncharacteristically weak moment, to fleetingly consider the question, Is it possible for a person to sensibly get rid of extra weight *without* going on a diet?

Diets are something I've loudly railed against, having seen too much hype, too many unrealistic expectations, too many failures. I oppose them on (at least) two grounds—one nutritional, the other social. Most diets, after all, restrict what the dieter eats in quantity or variety, or both. Unrealistic quantity restriction frequently provokes the fear-of-starvation backlash (aka gorging), and narrowed variety not only becomes unsustainably boring, but it can be nutritionally unbalanced, even dangerous—unless you're treating a serious medical condition, which I'm not. Our species developed as omnivores, after all.

From a social perspective, diets can be isolating. I'd venture a guess that we've all known people who've used their diets as an excuse for not eating with the family, not going out with friends and, in extreme but sadly frequent cases, not partaking in holiday feasts. Food may be the fuel for the body, but it's also glue for the family, for the community.

I refused to go on a diet, but I decided I *could* take a closer look at what I was eating.

Like everyone, I've read a lot about the "empty calories" and growing portions in the American diet. I figured there must be some excess to cut out of my own diet—stuff I consumed without thinking, stuff I wouldn't really miss.

Since I'm not a "Yes, I'll super-size it," "Sure, I'll take fries with it" fast-food guy, I didn't have an easy target to start with. Until I landed on beverages. I was used to drinking sodas, sweetened "juice" drinks, mochas and coffee with cream, and I knew they were filled with a good amount of calories, "empty calories" most would say. So I devised this plan: on an everyday basis, I'd stick with water (sparkling or still), coffee (black) and tea (no sugar)—plus a glass of wine or a beer with dinner.

To tell the truth, I hadn't realized what I'd been missing. I turned my chef's training toward my beverage project and started doing tastings. I'd brushed past all the distinctive tastes of mineral waters, for instance. Not only did different coffee varieties offer a multiplicity of flavors, but different brewing methods from drip to press pot to espresso showed a different side of each coffee bean. And tea—I'm almost ashamed at how little I really knew about the wide world of black, semi-fermented and green teas, not to mention all the herbal flavors that were easily at my fingertips.

For all of my adult life, I've been a flavor junkie. Well, a flavor and texture and aroma junkie. Like most chefs, I get off on the smoky pungency of chipotle chiles or the crunch of jellyfish or the head-spinning fragrance of white truffles, but I discovered that beverages as simple as water, coffee and tea can provide endless thrills too.

That was the same time I started evolving toward another change—this time not in *what* I was consuming, just *how much*. I started cutting off a little part of my then-normal-size portions and pushing it toward the side of the plate. Ten percent to start with, then fifteen or twenty, maybe twenty-five. My goal certainly wasn't to starve myself, just to see what my body needed to feel full. I had to eat my food *slowly*—as slowly as you can in the fast pace of a restaurant environment—so that I wouldn't gobble mindlessly, quickly through the whole portion without questioning my hunger. And I realized I was practicing what I'd learned in yoga: listening to my body.

Over a few months, I weaned myself off about a quarter of what I'd been eating before, I lost ten pounds or so and I never felt hungry. Just good—and always ready for my next meal.

Essential Learning #2: **No matter what weight-loss diet plans promise, monitoring the *quantity* of food is essential to maintaining healthy weight. I hesitate to say it because it sounds so clinical, so undelicious, but the real truth is: I need to monitor the quantity of calories I consume—*calories*, because different foods have very different concentrations of calories (more below).**

I've always eaten some of everything—fruits, vegetables, grains, legumes, meats, fish, eggs, dairy, all kinds of fat—even though I've been keenly aware that all the diet gurus, if you got them together, would raise their voices into a cacophonous chorus that would denounce practically everything edible. All their contradictory barking had left me wondering if any of them could be trusted to elucidate nature's truths. Or, in fact, if such truths existed.

On the other hand, since I was in the process of scrutinizing what I was eating, should I consider making some choice changes? Should I turn away from my beloved fresh-baked corn tortillas because Dr. Atkins has convinced us that carbohydrates are bad for us? Should a plate of luscious pork *carnitas*, simmered until crispy in its own fat, be banished because of Dr. Ornish's fat-damning clinical studies? Should I avoid sugar and salt and coffee and commercially grown vegetables with their pesticide residues and . . . ? I began to feel overwhelmed.

So I chose what some might consider the gastronomic equivalent of a nose thumb, and I decided to eat a sensible amount of everything you find around the *perimeter* of the grocery store—the fresh ingredients that cultures have eaten for millennia, the unprocessed stuff.

Those are the foods a chef most likes to work with anyway, the ingredients we find so inspirational. They're piled high in traditional markets around the world. And "perimeter foods" have one very positive thing in common: practically all nutritional researchers recommend them. Most agree that a varied diet balancing fresh fruits, vegetables, meats, fish, poultry, dairy, grains and legumes is the healthiest diet for most people. Good nutrition is that simple, that easy to understand, that sensible.

As a chef, I use the *variety* I find on the grocery store's perimeter as my culinary challenge too. How can I simply prepare rutabaga, for instance, that will make it thrillingly delicious? Or chicken livers? Or skate wing? Sure, we all gravitate to certain favorite flavors and preparations, but I'm convinced that being dedicated to eating a wide variety sidesteps the potential Ping-Pong pull of nutritional debates and new discoveries.

(I dream of the day I'll be able to go into McDonald's and have the interaction go something like this:

Me: I'll take a quarter-pounder.

Them: Lamb, venison or beef?

Me: I think lamb, and some fries—what kind do you have?

Them: Taro, beet and potato.

Me: Taro sounds good—never had taro fries. What sizes do you offer?

Them: Sorry, only our normal small size— we're an *everyday* place. A sparkling juice to drink?

Me: Lamb, taro fries—no, I think I'll have a glass of Zinfandel.)

Essential Learning #3: Eating a wide variety of fresh ingredients is fundamental to nutritional fitness.

All this thinking about the fuel I was getting from different foods and beverages led me face to face with questions about foods I wasn't in control of. Meaning food I (or nature) didn't really make. Processed foods, prepared foods, fast foods. All of a sudden, I had an interest in knowing what exactly was in that granola bar I was in the habit of buying, that bottle of barbecue sauce, that Styrofoam carton of ramen noodles I kept on the shelf in case of emergency. It didn't take long to figure out that the granola bar snack was way more packed with calories (200, for one variety I've bought, a number I've now taught myself to look at) than an average apple (about 80 calories), say. And though the outcome should have been the opposite, it was the granola bar that frequently left me wanting more. It wasn't as satisfying, especially when the apple in question was from the farmers' market and filled with the distinctive perfume that only a locally grown, tree-ripened apple can have. Though I've never been a huge consumer of prepared, packaged or fast foods, I decided to make a bold step.

Essential Learning #4: Processed foods, many prepared foods and most fast foods have no place in *everyday* eating. As a believer in the resilience of the human body, I can't resist a Big Mac every once in a while (I'll even admit that I like that special sauce). I simply decided that such foods have no place in my everyday meals.

That's when my life's work—my work as a chef and cookbook author—took on a sharp new focus. That image of the grocery store's perimeter made me realize that the whole range of natural fruits, vegetables, grains, meats and fish has had nutritional staying power. In contrast, the recommendations of my nutritionist colleagues reflect—shall I say it?—a rather fledgling approach to the relationship between food and the human body. Though I admire the nutritionists' scientific approach, theirs is a new science, only having been around for a hundred and thirty years or so. Beginnings are always marked by regular "revolutions" in understanding.

The more mature perspective, it dawned on me, comes from traditional cultures that trace their roots back to antiquity. The traditional ways of eating, say, in the Mediterranean or Mexico, in China, Thailand or India. These are gastronomical approaches to nourishing large groups of people that developed over millennia, that focus on delicious flavor and that have stood the test of time. Though not developed based on a scientific model, they exemplify a tried-and-true approach that works for (and satisfies) the culture that developed it—day in and day out.

Now, I'm not talking about isolated dishes in these cuisines, but rather the whole kit and caboodle of how a culture eats from morning to night, on weekdays and weekends, through festivals and famines. That's where we discover the nutritional wisdom a culture has developed over centuries. With anything less than the whole picture, we run the risk of skimming off only the luxuriously rich dishes from other countries without including the simple preparations cooks use to balance them.

It's telling that if you remove from the world's traditional cuisines any influences of Western fast foods or industrialized or prepared foods, you see that most of them have developed more or less the same approach to nourishment—the grocery store–perimeter approach. They focus on a variety of simply prepared fresh foods for everyday eating. Modest amounts of deliciously seasoned food that balance the complex carbohydrates of fruits, vegetables, grains and legumes.

But a few days of that is enough, from most cultures' perspective. Human beings have a need to blow off the top—to feast, to party. Regularly. Big hunks of meat, lavish preparations, refined anything, luxuriously rich sweets. Even if it's just a feasting celebration of the weekend's arrival, abundant unique dishes seem even more special because of the simplicity of everyday nourishment.

It's that feasting our scientific approach to nutrition hasn't embraced yet. We put ourselves on diets (I think we can admit it: they're *bleak* diets) that lead us to judge everything we put in our mouths as "good" or "bad," that cause us to say that a break with their dietary proscription is "cheating."

Where does that come from? A blind faith in the wisdom of the relatively young field of modern nutrition? A puritanical heritage? An information overload that leaves us grasping for a couple of simple scientific principles we can hold on to?

Whatever the source, the fact is that we haven't been able to tackle the age-old simplicity of feasting. We've allowed the feasting-as-essential-to-good-health approach to be swept into the same dustbin as malnutrition and poor sanitation.

But that's just wrong. And we all know it . . . in our guts. So, many of us just eat defiantly. Willy-nilly and all the time. To the point that Americans have become the fattest people on earth.

Essential Learning #5: The world's most time-honored cuisines illustrate that: (1) everyday eating is best kept to deliciously seasoned simple preparations of natural ingredients (mostly unrefined and balanced among a variety of fruits, vegetables, grains, legumes and meat) served in moderate portions, and (2) fabulous feasts—once a week, or, for special occasions, more often—are an essential part of our healthy nourishment.

To say it another way, cuisines that have healthily nourished generation after generation have a pretty brilliant—but basic—way of putting essential foods together in the right proportions for everyday eating. Call it their foundation dishes. Yet those same cultures also realize that feasting is essential for a culture's aesthetic development, encouraging cooks to reach for new culinary heights. *And* that feasting is essential for cultural unity, bringing groups of people together around the table to share sustenance, culinary art, related histories. *And* that feasting is essential for the health of our bodies, allowing us the satisfaction of feeling thoroughly, completely full—with no need for midnight Häagen-Dazs raids.

A feast can make our spirits soar for days, while our bodies are regenerating themselves on everyday fare. In other words, no one ever got fat on a weekly feast, but missing that feast can leave you with strong cravings (both physical and spiritual) all week long.

Who can resist a strong craving?

I'd figured out how much food my body needed to maintain a weight that made me feel comfortable. I'd pared away calorie-rich processed foods (and extraneous stuff—like sodas and cream in my coffee—that I didn't really care all that much about) to allow me to eat more of what I really liked. And I'd gotten full swing into weekend and special-occasion feasting (noting that no matter how big the weekend feast, my weekly weigh-in number stayed just about the same).

I should have been totally satisfied, having found an equilibrium for myself, but a little fact of nature kept rearing its head to mock me. I knew that as each year passed, I lost a pound or so of muscle tissue. That's a fact of nature, of aging.

Now, to some, that may not sound like a big deal. Until you realize that muscle tissue (for most of us) pretty much gets replaced pound for pound by fat . . . and fat requires much less fuel (read: calories) to maintain than muscle does. Meaning that each year, to maintain my optimal weight, I would need to eat less. And that was a bummer. I wanted to have my cake and eat it too, so to speak. To maintain my weight and be able to eat the same amount I was enjoying.

My being completely bummed out by nature's unfairness came at about the time I decided I wanted to learn the yoga pose called forearm balance. Forearm balance is a little like a handstand, except that you perch upside down balanced on your forearms—like a sphinx with his legs straight up over his head. I just didn't have enough strength, and I knew it would take months—years?—of practice to develop it.

Yet I found something so compelling about yoga inversions—headstands, handstands and the like—that I was determined to master this one. I loved the freedom I felt in this flip-flopped, gravity-defying position.

So I bought some dumbbells, read some articles on strength training and made a resolution to augment my yoga with the strength exercises I'd need to sustain that inspiring posture.

My shoulders and arms responded immediately, and before I knew it, I was hovering in forearm balance and understanding a counter-fact of nature: I could maintain (even grow) muscle tissue by strength training, kind of *reversing* the flow of nature.

Well, I was feeling great—stronger, more energetic, confident (I could do *forearm balance*, for goodness sake!). And I was *really hungry*. I hadn't planned on that. *Hungry* as in *starving*. I'd read a lot about strength training—how aficionados eat five or six meals a

day, how they focus on a balance of protein, complex carbohydrates and fats for optimal muscle growth. I'd memorized their motto: you can't grow muscle without good food. Strength training was for me. Not only did I feel and look great, but the muscle I was growing (and not losing) was asking me, encouraging me, *requiring* me to eat more. It was the perfect exercise for a food lover. And as strength training enthusiasts point out, muscle burns fuel all day long—as opposed to the more limited fuel-burning potential of aerobic activities like jogging. Through the millennia, it seems, our bodies have become accustomed to some pretty rigorous, muscle-requiring work. Ironically, as the human race strives for more leisure, our bodies are telling us they're happiest with a steady dose of physical challenge.

Essential Learning #6: For us to be able to enjoy great food without gaining weight, our bodies need to burn as much fuel as possible. Though aerobic activity burns fuel, strength training can offer more: more control, healthier appearance and more fuel-burning-every-minute muscle.

There you have the six essential learnings of my past decade. I'd never suggest that they would mirror the experience you'd have had if you had accompanied me along the same path. Nor would I claim that they can provide the "aha!" that'll miraculously and quickly lead millions of Americans to a life of perfect health and happiness. No, my learnings can only serve as a starting point for understanding what works for you—*your* perfect balance of food (varieties, quantities and frequency of eating) and physical activity. For me, that balance involves frequent varied small meals steadied against a yoga and weight training practice, plus wonderful feasts once or twice a week. By listening to your body, you too will learn the right combination of foods, and how frequently to eat them; you'll learn how much physical activity you need—whether it's running on a tread-

mill, playing basketball, practicing tai chi or simply climbing the stairs instead of using the elevator.

I know my "each to his own discovery" approach may be disappointing to some. It's a far cry from the "14-Day Plan for Losing 30 Pounds," the "30-Day Promise of a Cover Model's Body." Instead, my "Food Lover's Guide to Healthy Living" begins simply with an invitation for you to listen to the truths your body and spirit can teach you.

Plus, of course, I am offering you a collection of full-flavored, everyday recipes. They will immediately convince you that simple, fresh, nutritionally balanced food can be compellingly delicious.

Now to the nuts and bolts of how I developed these recipes. First, I'll admit that for everyday meals, I'm not looking for exactly the same over-the-top gourmet experience I strive for in our restaurants. But I'm far too steeped in fine cooking to slide very far from that mark. So I developed a few guiding principles to employ when putting together Mexican dishes for my everyday cooking and eating repertory:

Select the right recipes: I've steered clear of *moles* (they're rich and complex and typically served only for special occasions in Mexico), except for the simple yellow and green ones. Red chile sauces, which I consider another crowning glory of the Mexican kitchen, sometimes require too much careful toasting, soaking, blending, straining and cooking to make them practical for simple meals—except when powdered dried chile can stand in for the pods or when a slow-cooker can offer the long-cooking richness that mitigates the need for otherwise time-consuming treatment of dried chile pods.

Pare back each recipe to its skeleton: Many Mexican classics have bells and whistles built in—wonderful if you have time to prepare them, but not essential if you don't. My approach here is to offer you each recipe's essentials, then to tag on traditional and contemporary suggestions for ways to embroider the basics. It adds an improvisational character to cooking (isn't that what most of us like about cooking?) and encourages seasonal and whimsical variations.

Streamline (but don't skip) the traditional roasting of ingredients for complex richness: Unlike other cooks looking for efficiency, I won't give up the rich flavor roasted garlic, onions, tomatillos and tomatoes give to most dishes, so I've figured out ways to do it quickly. Often I simply temper garlic's punch by microwaving unpeeled cloves for thirty seconds; that method brings out its sweetness, but it doesn't add much roastiness. For full flavor, I do a quicker version of my traditional in-the-skin dry pan-roast by pan-roasting *peeled* garlic, watching it very carefully to make sure it doesn't burn. Most tomatillos and tomatoes are roasted whole on a griddle in Mexico; my standard method in the United States is to roast them under a broiler. But for everyday cooking, especially when I'm doing a small amount and I'm pressed for time, I cut them in half and pan-

roast them quickly on the stovetop—no pre-heating, less equipment, half the time.

Buy smaller ingredients: Whether they're picked small (potatoes, green beans, spinach) or have been cut up for you (mushrooms, pineapple, cauliflower), smaller ingredients cook faster than larger ones. And for my everyday cooking, that no-brainer time-saving means a lot.

Maximize the use of kitchen equipment: Use your **broiler** for browning meat for a stew or braise, eliminating a messy step that requires constant supervision. Use a **slow-cooker** for making perfect beans and for developing the classic richness of Mexican braises without going through the time-consuming traditional ingredient preparation. Make rice in a **rice cooker**—no need to think about temperature adjustments or reheating. Rely on a **microwave** for steaming ingredients in the same bowl you'll mix them in, eliminating extra equipment and steps. Get comfortable using an **oil sprayer** (a good one is incredibly efficient in giving a light and even oil coating to skillets, baking dishes, tortillas and foods about to be grilled). You're probably already a **food processor** aficionado, but when you want a really smooth puree (especially of any sauce with nuts, seeds or most dried chiles), you'll need the fast blades and vertical orientation of a **blender**—a powerful one is worth its weight in gold. An **immersion blender** can be a really easy helper too if you're into salsas and soups.

While we're on the subject of kitchen

equipment, there's not much I couldn't cook without—except these few "necessities": a **grill** (gas is easy, charcoal more satisfying and, for me, more fun to cook on) with good heavy grates and a **perforated grill pan** or **basket** to hold small stuff; my **three principal knives** (chef's, paring, serrated); a pair of **kitchen scissors**; my **heavy 12-inch skillet** (it may seem very large to many of you, but it's the only pan in my kitchen big enough to do effective browning and simmering of a one-dish meal); and a **very hot stovetop burner**. I'm most efficient when I've got an easy-to-clean **garlic press**, a set of inexpensive **flexible cutting boards**, a sturdy **box grater** and an oh-so-fabulous **Microplane grater**.

Pantry Basics for Mexican Cooking

CHILES

◎◎◎◎◎◎◎◎◎◎◎◎◎◎◎◎◎◎◎◎◎◎◎◎◎◎◎◎

Chiles, Fresh

CHOOSING: Whether it's the small hot **serrano**, **jalapeño** or **habanero chiles** or the

Serrano and jalapeño chiles

Habanero chiles

larger milder **poblano**, **yellow/wax** or **Anaheim/New Mexico** chiles, always choose ones with unblemished, unwrinkled skin.

Poblano chiles

Yellow/wax and Anaheim chiles

STORING: In the refrigerator, loosely wrapped in a plastic bag so that they don't dry out, fresh chiles will last a week or so.

WHERE TO FIND: Well-stocked groceries, Mexican markets, online through melissas.com.

Chiles, Dried

CHOOSING: No matter where you buy them, never buy dried chiles that are brittle or crumbling—dried-out chiles have very little flavor. They should be pliable and, when you open the package, they should smell like spicy dried fruit. The wrinkled **anchos** and **pasillas** should be

Ancho chiles

Pasilla chiles

softer than the smooth-skinned **guajillo** and **árbol chiles**, and they should smell sweeter, more prune-like.

Guajillo chiles

Arbol chiles

STORING: In airtight containers, in a cool, dark place for 6 months or, preferably, in the freezer (to guard against any moth infestation) for a year or more.

WHERE TO FIND: Well-stocked grocery stores, Mexican markets, online through mexgrocer.com or gourmetsleuth.com.

Chiles, Ground

CHOOSING: Pure ground dried chiles (**anchos, guajillos, chipotles**) should smell spicy and a little sweet and have a vibrant, not dull, color.

STORING: In airtight containers, in a cool, dark place for 3 months or in the freezer for 6 months.

WHERE TO FIND: Well-stocked grocery stores, Mexican markets, online through mexgrocer.com or gourmet-sleuth.com.

Ground chiles

Canned chiles

Chiles, Canned and Bottled

CHOOSING: I've had good luck with the quality of San Marcos brand **chipotle chiles *en adobo*** (the ones packed in the tangy tomato sauce) and the La Costeña and Adelita brands **pickled jalapeños,** though many other brands are also of good quality. When buying pickled jalapeños, I don't recommend those processed with alum (which makes them crisp like a sweet pickle) or seasoned with sugar (which makes them taste like a sweet pickle).

STORING: On the shelf for a year or more.

WHERE TO FIND: Well-stocked grocery stores, Mexican markets, online through mexgrocer.com or gourmetsleuth.com.

VEGETABLES AND FRUIT

◎◎◎◎◎◎◎◎◎◎◎◎◎◎◎◎◎◎◎◎◎◎◎◎◎◎◎◎◎

Avocado

CHOOSING: Size has little to do with flavor, so choose the most economical. Just make sure the avocado is ripe or that you've planned long enough for it to ripen. Avocados don't ripen on the tree, so the crop is picked when it's mature and kept in cool storage, then moved into ripening mode (usually with warmer temperatures and a shot of ethylene gas) when ready to be sold. Mexican markets always have them ripe because they sell a lot of them and that's what their clientele demands. American supermarkets are often less accommodating to the guacamole maker—meaning you'll need to plan a week or so for a rock-hard avocado to come to soft ripeness. A fully ripened avocado will be soft at the round end (the fruit ripens from the pointy stem end down). A perfectly ripe avocado will be soft when firmly pressed; mushy means overripe, as does a loose pit shaking around inside. The vast majority of the avocados in the United States are the dark, pebbly-skinned Hass avocado, which has a rich, buttery flesh that is slower to darken than other varieties. (Both features make Hass avocados perfect for guacamole.) Other varieties, especially the globular Caribbean avocados found in Florida, have a less creamy flesh, darken rather quickly once cut and often can't be stored for very long once ripe.

STORING: Uncovered at room temperature until they are ripe (place them in a paper bag or fruit ripener to hasten ripening if you wish); fully ripened avocados can be stored, uncovered, in the refrigerator for several days.

Chayote

CHOOSING: In Mexican markets you'll often see the dark green spiny chayote, which Mexican cooks say tastes the sweetest; truth is, once you've wrestled those thorny spines off the beast, practically anything would taste sweet. For everyday cooking, I'd choose the easy, readily available, smooth, light green chayotes—make sure there are no blemishes.

Chayote

STORING: Unwrapped in the refrigerator for several weeks.

WHERE TO FIND: Well-stocked groceries, online through melissas.com.

Jícama

Jícama

CHOOSING: The smaller the jícama, the sweeter the flavor. Always choose jícamas that have smooth, unblemished skin.

STORING: Unwrapped (or at most very loosely wrapped in a plastic bag) in the refrigerator, jícamas will last for several weeks.

WHERE TO FIND: Well-stocked groceries, online through melissas.com.

Limes

CHOOSING: The widely available large green grocery store limes are perfectly delicious for everyday cooking. But if you have the chance to try the smaller yellow-when-ripe Mexican (aka key) limes, do it: they're tarter and more aromatic, meaning you'll experience a wonderful new range of lime flavor. Lemons don't grow in Mexico, though you can easily substitute their juice in any of these recipes; just know that they don't have the lime's strength of flavor.

STORING: Uncovered at room temperature for a few days; uncovered in the refrigerator for several weeks.

Mushrooms

CHOOSING: For many, a mushroom is only and always a white button mushroom. But why limit yourself when there's so much mushroomy deliciousness to take advantage of? Why not try the more complexly flavored **shiitake mushroom** or the

Shiitake mushrooms

delicate, beautifully textured **oyster mushrooms**? Always choose mushrooms

Oyster mushrooms

that look plump and firm—no shriveling or dullness of color.

STORING: In the refrigerator, loosely wrapped in a plastic bag so that they don't dry out, really fresh mushrooms will last about a week.

WHERE TO FIND: Well-stocked groceries, online through melissas.com.

Onions

CHOOSING: Nearly all the onions used in Mexican cooking are **white onions**, which taste very different (crisper, sharper) from yellow onions (aka Spanish onions).

STORING: Uncovered in a cool, dry, dark place, most onions will last for a month or so.

Plantains

CHOOSING: Though available in most well-stocked grocery stores, these cooking

bananas are most commonly found green—to slice and fry like potato chips or to steam and use as a starchy vegetable. If you're looking for sweet, ripe plantains—the ones whose yellow peel has been almost completely covered by black splotches—you'll probably have to go to a Latin market, where customers understand that the ugly, over-the-hill-looking fruits are sublimely delicious—wonderfully sweet balanced with just the right amount of thrilling tang. If you buy green plantains, expect them to take at least a week to ripen to full sweetness; if you buy yellow but still very firm plantains, expect them to ripen in several days.

STORING: Refrigerate plantains only once they're fully ripe (almost completely black and soft).

WHERE TO FIND: Well-stocked groceries, online through melissas.com.

Plantains

Sweet Potatoes, Mexican

CHOOSING: These reddish-purple tubers always look rough and just-dug when you find them in the market. Unless you notice deterioration or softening spots, the exterior roughness won't affect the white interior sweetness. In the United States, this root often goes by *boniato*, its name in the Caribbean Islands.

STORING: Uncovered in a cool, dark, dry place for several weeks.

WHERE TO FIND: In some well-stocked grocery stores, Mexican and Caribbean markets, online through melissas.com (they call them purple yams).

Tomatillos

Mexican sweet potatoes

Tomatillos

CHOOSING: Tomatillos typically come with their papery green husk still on—it protects them during storage. While my favorite tomatillo flavor comes from the medium-to-small tomatillos that have a purple blush, these tomatillos are typically only found in a handful of Mexican markets, farmers' markets and the gardens of true aficionados. Grocery stores sell large fully mature all-green tomatillos that have a fine flavor, but remember: the bigger the tomatillo, the more watered down the flavor will be. Though tomatillos can ripen to yellowish green, it's uncommon to find them that way in the markets; green offers the greatest citrusy tang.

STORING: Unwrapped in the refrigerator, tomatillos will keep for a month or more, as long as there is good air circulation and the husks don't wither.

WHERE TO FIND: Well-stocked groceries,

online through melissas.com.

Tomatoes, Canned

CHOOSING: Inexpensive canned tomatoes are often underripe and packed in water. Choose a respected brand packed in juice; Contadina and Hunt's tomatoes have come out well in several of our blind tastings, but my current favorite is Muir Glen organic (especially the fire-roasted) diced tomatoes. I like the richness and traditional Mexican flavor the fire-roasting gives.

STORING: On the shelf until opened; refrigerated in a covered storage container after opening.

Canned tomatoes

Tomatoes, Fresh

CHOOSING: The plum-shaped tomato called a saladette is a common variety for all-around use; it's meaty enough to use in cooking, juicy enough to make salsa. For the best experience, buy fresh-picked tomatoes at a farmers' market—as a general rule, choose round tomatoes for salsa, plum tomatoes for cooking. Off season, hothouse-grown tomatoes are usually better than ones that are picked green and then gassed to bring out the pinkish-red lure. Neither is particularly satisfying, so I lean toward dishes made with canned tomatoes in winter. Diced sun-dried tomatoes can be used to flavor guacamole and some versions of ceviche when good-tasting fresh tomatoes aren't available.

STORING: Though commonly kept in the refrigerator, tomatoes have remarkably more flavor if kept at cool room temperature (no higher than 65 degrees F, no lower than 50 degrees); the flavor difference is even more pronounced if the tomatoes have been ripened on the vine and never refrigerated. I refrigerate tomatoes only when they are so ripe that there is a risk of their spoiling.

HERBS AND SPICES

Achiote Seasoning

CHOOSING: This Yucatán-style seasoning paste of annatto (*achiote*) seeds, garlic,

Achiote seasoning

acid (vinegar, and/or citric acid), spices and salt is a challenge for most cooks to make from scratch. Though most of the brands imported from Yucatán are tasty, the ones I most often find are El Yucateco and La Anita.

STORING: At room temperature in a tightly closed container if using within a couple of weeks; refrigerated for up to a year.

WHERE TO FIND: Mexican markets, online through mexgrocer.com or gourmetsleuth.com.

Avocado Leaves

CHOOSING: Since anise-scented avocado leaves aren't widely available, you'll have to take what you find. Like bay leaves,

the best avocado leaves are whole and unblemished, with a hint of luster. Since the only avocado leaves that add flavor to food are from the wild Mexican avocado (all others are flavorless), make sure you get them from a source that knows what they're selling.

STORING: Room temperature, loosely wrapped in a plastic bag for 6 months.

WHERE TO FIND: Mexican markets, online through gourmetsleuth.com.

Avocado leaves

Banana Leaves

CHOOSING: Young, light green, thin fresh banana leaves are the most supple and easiest to work with, but they're usually only available in communities with a large banana leaf–using population (Thai,

Banana leaves

Filipino, Salvadoran, southern Mexican, for example). Most of us will only find the older, dark green, thicker frozen banana leaves, which, truthfully, do their job just fine in most preparations.

STORING: Fresh leaves can be stored loosely wrapped in a plastic bag in the refrigerator for a month or so. Frozen leaves can be stored in the freezer for about a year; defrost them at room temperature.

WHERE TO FIND: Some well-stocked groceries, Asian and Latin markets, online through melissas.com.

Cinnamon, Mexican

CHOOSING: This true cinnamon (our "cinnamon" is really powdered cassia bark, a

cinnamon relative with a very punchy flavor) is usually sold only in stick form. The sticks are made up of many thin layers of cinnamon bark (cassia sticks are one thick layer) that are soft enough to crumble into a spice grinder or into a mortar to grind. Mexican cinnamon has a more delicate, wonderfully flowery aroma.

STORING: Room temperature, in a tightly closed container for up to a year.

WHERE TO FIND: Mexican and other ethnic markets, online through mexgrocer.com or gourmetsleuth.com.

Mexican cinnamon

Epazote

CHOOSING: The fresh *epazote* you find in Mexican markets is often wilted looking,

Epazote

but that won't affect the herb's flavor in cooked dishes. So buy whatever you can find—always being on the lookout for the purple-tinged *epazote*, which I think has the most complex flavor. The dried *epazote* you find in Mexican markets is a medicinal (not culinary) herb, mostly consisting of the potency-packed stems.

STORING: After harvesting *epazote* from my garden or bringing home a large fresh-looking bunch from the store, I dampen several layers of paper towel, spread the herb branches into a single layer, roll up the whole affair and slip it into a plastic bag, then store it in the refrigerator for a week or so. Dried or frozen *epazote* leaves don't have much flavor.

WHERE TO FIND: In some well-stocked grocery stores, Mexican markets, online through herbchef.com.

Hoja Santa

CHOOSING: There are several different varieties of this very delicious, complexly flavored, anise-scented, large heart-shaped leaf—which probably won't mean much to you unless you're growing the stuff yourself. Take what you can get, choosing whole, umblemished leaves if there is an option.

STORING: To keep *hoja santa* fresh looking, layer leaves with pieces of paper towel, slide into a plastic bag and store in the

Hoja Santa

refrigerator. Though the leaves don't dry with much flavor, they can be successfully frozen; layer them with parchment or wax paper and seal in a freezer bag. Frozen leaves will be softer and look much darker than fresh ones, but that shouldn't affect their usefulness as a flavoring in cooked sauces.

WHERE TO FIND: You can buy an *hoja santa* plant through companionplants.com (search *Piper auritum)* or order the leaves online through herbchef.com.

Oregano, Mexican

CHOOSING: This oregano-scented member of the large New World verbena family (no, it's not related to Mediterranean oregano) is sold in Mexican markets in the whole leaf form (usually with stems as well). To use it, you'll have to pick out the stems and crush the leaves, giving it a very lively flavor. In well-stocked supermarkets, you'll find it cut into typical dried-herb bits.

STORING: Room temperature in a tightly closed container for up to 6 months.

WHERE TO FIND: In well-stocked groceries (occasionally, you have to read the fine print on oregano bottles to discover whether their contents are Mexican or Mediterranean oregano), Mexican markets, online through mexgrocer.com or gourmetsleuth.com.

MISCELLANEOUS

Beans, Dried and Canned

CHOOSING: Buy dried beans from a store that sells lots of beans (Mexican markets or grocery stores with a strong Mexican clientele are good bets), since old beans cook slowly and unevenly. The cooked canned beans offered by many brands (our current favorites are Joan of Arc and Bush's) have a true, clean flavor and are not broken up or mushy—meaning they are a good option for everyday cooking. Though many sources recommend buying unsalted beans, I think it's a mistake: beans need to be warm and given at least fifteen minutes to absorb salt. So, to speed along your cooking, buy salted beans.

STORING: Dried beans: at room temperature in a tightly closed container. For best results, use within 6 months of purchase.

Cajeta

CHOOSING: To my taste, the richest-flavored bottled *cajeta*, Mexico's famous *dulce de leche*–like caramel, is made with the traditional goat's milk. Bottled is generally thicker and stickier than homemade because the store-bought version usually contains glucose or corn syrup. Coronado brand is widely available and dependable.

STORING: At room temperature if using within a couple of weeks; refrigerated for longer storage.

Cajeta

STORING: Alongside the meat in your refrigerator for a week or so; chorizo can also be successfully frozen.

WHERE TO FIND: Many well-stocked grocery stores, Mexican markets, online through vvsupremo.com.

Crema, Mexican

CHOOSING: Some of the Mexican *cremas* (aka Mexican sour cream) on the market are simply American sour cream in a different package, meaning that they lack the rich creaminess of the real thing. Look for a domestically produced Mexican *crema* that is rich and creamy in texture and slightly nutty in flavor. Though

WHERE TO FIND: Well-stocked grocery stores, Mexican markets, online through mexgrocer.com.

Chorizo Sausage, Mexican

CHOOSING: This is not the cured, sliceable Spanish chorizo, but rather a fresh sausage that has to be cooked. Most Mexican markets with a butcher make their own, which frequently ensures a sausage with a unique character and, often, a little flavor-enhancing aging. I've tried many different regional and national brands, many of which are quite good. My current favorite brand is Supremo.

Mexican *cremas*

French *crème fraîche* is even richer and nuttier tasting than Mexican *crema*, it's closer in both texture and flavor than American sour cream; I buy it only occasionally for a treat, since it's usually very expensive. If my only option is American sour cream, I stir in a little milk to give it a softer, more easily spoonable consistency or, in cooked dishes, I replace *crema* instead with heavy cream.

STORING: In the refrigerator.

WHERE TO FIND: Some well-stocked grocery stores, Mexican markets, online through vvsupremo.com.

Hot Sauce

CHOOSING: Mexican hot sauces are typically richer in texture and less vinegary than Louisiana-style ones. Cholula brand is widely distributed here; Tamazula and Búfalo are a bit more complex to my taste.

STORING: At room temperature if using within a couple of weeks; refrigerated for longer storage.

WHERE TO FIND: Well-stocked groceries, Mexican markets, online through mexgrocer.com or gourmetsleuth.com.

Masa Harina (Tortilla Flour)

CHOOSING: There are a number of brands available, but many of them produce slightly gritty tortillas that are difficult to roll or fold without breaking—in general, a hazard of tortillas made from the powdered *masa harina* rather than the fresh-ground, paste-like *masa* that you can buy

Masa harina

at a tortilla factory and in some Mexican groceries. I've had the best luck with Maseca brand *masa harina*.

STORING: At room temperature for a month or so; sealed in a freezer bag and kept in the freezer for longer storage.

WHERE TO FIND: Many well-stocked grocery stores, Mexican markets, online through mexgrocer.com or gourmetsleuth.com.

Pumpkin Seeds

CHOOSING: For cooking, most Mexican cooks choose hulled seeds—which is good for us, since those are the ones most commonly found in our groceries and natural foods stores. To be at their best in a dish, pumpkin seeds need to be toasted; toasting changes both flavor and texture. You can buy toasted pumpkin seeds or toast them yourself: pour untoasted seeds into a dry skillet and stir regularly over medium heat for several minutes until all have popped from flat to roundish (they'll color slightly to golden in the process).

STORING: On the shelf in a tightly sealed container for a week or two; or in the freezer for longer storage.

WHERE TO FIND: Well-stocked groceries, natural foods stores, online through nutsonline.com.

Queso Fresco (Mexican Fresh Crumbling Cheese)

CHOOSING: Some manufacturers are making what they call *queso fresco* but it's really just a mild melting cheese like a Colby—very different from the non-melting, salty, fresh-tasting garnishing *queso fresco* that's used extensively to enliven dishes all over Mexico. *Queso fresco* is crumbly like feta, but not as creamy or briny; in a pinch, I've soaked feta to remove some of the brininess and used it as a substitute. Another substitute is the dry-pressed (not creamy) farmer's cheese; it will need to be salted. Some manufacturers give *queso fresco* names like *queso blanco* (white cheese—common in Caribbean and Central and

Queso fresco/queso añejo

South American neighborhoods) and *queso ranchero* (ranch-style cheese—think "cottage" cheese).

STORING: In the refrigerator, well wrapped in plastic, for a week or so; vacuum-packed *queso fresco* will last a week or two longer before it loses its fresh taste.

WHERE TO FIND: Some well-stocked grocery stores, Mexican markets, online through vvsupremo.com.

Queso Añejo (Mexican Aged Grating Cheese)

CHOOSING: Many of the domestic *quesos añejos* are rather bland, lacking the salty, nutty punch of the Mexican original, a punch that's necessary in a good grat-ing/garnishing cheese. Look for one that is imported from Mexico (the one from the town of Cotija is common—in fact, it's so common that many Americans think that *queso Cotija* is the legitimate name for all *queso añejo*). Or look for a domestic one that has a similar depth of flavor to Italian Romano. Or just use Romano. Or even Parmesan.

STORING: Though you can store *queso añejo* at room temperature for a few days, most of us keep it around for longer than that. Store it, well wrapped in plastic, in the refrigerator.

WHERE TO FIND: Some well-stocked grocery stores, Mexican markets, online through vvsupremo.com.

Salsa

CHOOSING: Most American salsas are more vinegary than their Mexican counter-parts. Choose a salsa that has fresh (preferably roasted) ingredients for the freshest flavor. And choose one with a defined chile flavor (green-tasting jalapeño and smoky chipotle are popular). Though the vast majority of salsas avail-able in the United States are made from tomatoes, green tomatillo salsa is not only tasty for dipping and doctoring, but it's very useful in cooking. The best are made with roasted tomatillos.

STORING: Refrigerate after opening.

Tostadas

CHOOSING: Buying these crisp-fried tor-tillas can be a huge time-saver, but some nationally distributed brands have a mealy texture and a stale taste. My first choice is always tostadas made by one of our local tortilla factories.

STORING: On the shelf sealed in a plastic bag for a week or two.

WHERE TO FIND: Some well-stocked gro-ceries, Mexican markets.

MEXICAN CINNAMON

MEXICAN
EVERYDAY

Salads and Other Easy-to-Make Sides

Simple, satisfying, stimulating: it's an everyday eating mantra worth repeating. One that, for me, means most meals consist of an enticing main dish and a lively salad—any one of a dozen different greens, a tantalizing dressing, maybe something aromatic or crunchy, depending on the availability of time and ingredients. A lettuce salad is certainly the easiest accompaniment that comes to mind, the eating of it slows me down enough to appreciate the pleasure I'm encountering and its freshness adds energy to the meal.

My trick for keeping a simple lettuce salad from becoming humdrum is mostly in the dressing. Good olive oil and vinegar make a perfectly fine dressing, but I think they need to be varied and embroidered to keep us all engaged—a very simple task when you look into it. Add a little cheese or mayonnaise or avocado, stir in some smoky chipotles or blend in roasted garlic and green chiles for depth and vigor.

And I bounce between a manageable variety of lettuces too. Romaine for easy crunch. Butter (Boston) lettuce for tender sweetness. Mesclun for intriguing variety. Frisée (curly endive) for toothsome chew. Salad spinach for sturdy, deep-green flavor. To make each salad the most satisfying, I riff on the strengths of the greens I choose for it. So I created for myself a variety of dressings. Then I made a list of greens—see pages 64–66—with notes about cool dressing matches and add-ins.

Greens show up as the accompaniment on my table more often than anything else, but they certainly don't have an exclusive. Simple vegetable salads work their magic, too: jícama salad (with watercress and lime) in January, when the new crop is in; green bean salad when the farmers' markets get rolling; sweet potato salad (with caramelized onions) for a picnic; chayote salad when you want something a little different; tomato salad, during the height of summer, with toasted red chile dressing; roasted pepper salad with Mexican *queso añejo.* I've streamlined their preparation to bring them within reach for everyday cooking.

Though most of the main dishes in this book are complete—no need for any accompaniment other than a salad—I think tacos, enchiladas and most of the grilled dishes, even some of the braises and sautés, cry out for beans or rice. So I've included my speediest versions of several bean and rice dishes in this chapter as well.

DRESSINGS

Classic *Vinagreta* for Five Moods

Vinagreta Clásica para Cinco Humores

◎ℋ◎ℋ◎ℋ◎ℋ◎ℋ◎ℋ◎ℋ◎ℋ◎ℋ◎ℋ◎ℋ◎ℋ◎ℋ◎ℋ◎ℋ◎ℋ◎ℋ◎ℋ◎

For me, the mood of a vinaigrette is set by the vinegar, and vinegars range from light and breezy rice vinegar to sweet and mellow balsamic vinegar, with elegant white wine vinegar and scrappy apple cider vinegar somewhere in between. Lime juice is another story, since you're changing from the determined confidence of vinegar's acetic acid to the carefree smiles of lime juice's citric acid. Once you've set the mood with a specific vinegar or citrus, the oil choice needs to go with that flow: I use rich-tasting olive oil with the boldest-flavored vinegars and a light vegetable oil (grapeseed oil is wonderful) for the lightest vinegars and with citrus. A mixture of rich and light works well for flavors that are in between. Salad greens play a role in all this moodiness too. Delicate mesclun greens taste young and fresh with a dressing that features white wine vinegar, rice vinegar or lime juice. The slightly bitter chew of frisée gets tamed with a balsamic–olive oil blend, while it roughhouses with an apple cider vinegar dressing. The congenial sweet crunch of romaine gets along with just about everything.

Makes a generous cup

3/4 cup vegetable oil, olive oil or a mixture
  of the two
1/4 cup vinegar (apple cider, white wine,
  balsamic or rice vinegar) or fresh
  lime juice
Salt

Combine the oil and vinegar with a scant teaspoon salt in a jar, secure the lid and shake to blend thoroughly. Taste and season with more salt if you feel the dressing needs it. (Remember that dressings should be highly seasoned.) Refrigerate until ready to use. Shake well immediately before use.

Riffs on *Vinagreta*

Here is a handful of single-ingredient add-ins to give your vinaigrettes a little intrigue:

◎ **GARLIC:** A single clove crushed through a garlic press is enough. For a mellower, richer garlic flavor, cut a slit in the side of 3 unpeeled garlic cloves, place in a microwaveable bowl, cover with plastic wrap and microwave them on high for 30 seconds. Break off the peels, then puree them with the remaining ingredients in a blender until smooth.

◎ **FRESH HERBS:** Thyme, basil, rosemary, cilantro and chives—especially the garlic chives that come up in my garden in the summer—are the herbs I rely on most to flavor simple vinaigrettes. They may be chopped and added to the other ingredients, or they may be blended in. One to 2 teaspoons is a good start for most herbs except chives, which can be added in more generous proportions.

◎ **PEPPER:** Adding about 1/2 teaspoon or more freshly ground black pepper gives a vinaigrette a very distinctive flavor. Maybe you think of pepper like salt—an unspoken seasoning whose presence almost goes unnoticed. For me that's not true. I'm steeped in traditional Mexican cooking, which doesn't use much black pepper (a pepper shaker/grinder is rarely found on a traditional Mexican table), so pepper in a vinaigrette is a noticeable, almost exotic flavor. I use several other kinds of pepper from time to time: white pepper (a robust-flavored variety that I buy in a Thai grocery), pink peppercorns, dried green peppercorns. Each adds a unique flavor.

◎ **MUSTARD:** This adds another unusual flavor to the Mexican kitchen, but one I love in vinaigrettes, especially with sturdier or spicier greens such as romaine, frisée and watercress. Choose coarse or smooth, depending on your aesthetic preferences—my daughter dislikes the little seeds in coarse mustard, while I rather like them.

Creamy *Queso Añejo* Dressing

Aderezo Cremoso con Queso Añejo

One of my favorite dressings for romaine or butter lettuce—simple, satisfying, a little creamy, a little cheesy. It's excellent, too, on any salad that contains tomatoes, cucumbers or roasted peppers.

Makes about 1 1/4 cups

3/4 cup vegetable oil, olive oil or a mixture of the two

1/4 cup very light vinegar (such as rice vinegar)

3 tablespoons mayonnaise

2 to 3 tablespoons grated Mexican *queso añejo* or other garnishing cheese such as Romano or Parmesan

Salt

Combine the oil, vinegar, mayonnaise, *queso añejo* and a scant teaspoon salt in a blender jar and blend until smooth. Taste and season highly with additional salt if necessary. Pour into a jar with a secure lid and refrigerate until ready to use. Shake well immediately before use.

Simple Riffs

Blending in 2 cloves of roasted garlic enhances the *queso añejo* flavor wonderfully. Chopped cilantro or chives are always welcome additions, as is a chopped chipotle chile *en adobo*.

Pickled Jalapeño Dressing

Aderezo Picante

◎❋◎❋◎❋◎❋◎❋◎❋◎❋◎❋◎❋◎❋◎❋◎❋◎❋◎❋◎❋◎❋◎❋◎

A bold dressing that benefits from the use of olive oil. It's perfect over cool steamed cauliflower or potatoes, sliced tomatoes or romaine tossed with slivered ham, thin-sliced onion and roasted peppers.

Makes about 1 1/4 cups

3/4 cup vegetable oil, olive oil or a
  mixture of the two
1/4 cup apple cider vinegar
1 canned pickled jalapeño, stemmed
1 tablespoon jalapeño pickling juice
Salt

Combine the oil, vinegar, pickled jalapeño, pickling juice and a scant teaspoon salt in a blender jar or food processor. Process until smooth. Taste and season highly with additional salt if appropriate. Pour into a jar, secure the lid and refrigerate until ready to use. Shake well immediately before use.

Simple Riffs

Any pickled chile will work, though a habanero will be very, very hot. A pickled yellow pepper will have a light floral quality that's very nice with roasted peppers. A couple of cloves of roasted garlic will add richness to the dressing.

Lime-Cilantro Dressing

Aderezo de Limón y Cilantro

◎✖◎✖◎✖◎✖◎✖◎✖◎✖◎✖◎✖◎✖◎✖◎✖◎✖◎✖◎✖◎✖◎✖◎✖◎✖◎

One of the most perfect balances of flavor—lime, cilantro and green chile. I like the richness added by using part olive oil. With or without the chile, it's a great dressing for light, tender greens (I love this dressing on butter lettuce and mesclun), or thinly sliced cucumbers, tomatoes and raw chayotes or a nicely textured mix of romaine, tomatoes and red onion.

Makes 1 1/4 cups

3/4 cup vegetable oil, olive oil or a
  mixture of the two
1/3 cup fresh lime juice
1/2 teaspoon grated lime zest (colored
  rind only)

1/2 cup (packed) roughly chopped
  cilantro
Fresh hot green chiles to taste (I like 2
  serranos or 1 jalapeño), stemmed and
  roughly chopped (optional)
Salt

Combine the oil, lime juice, lime zest, cilantro, chile and a scant teaspoon salt in a blender jar and blend until smooth. Taste and add more salt if you think it needs it, keeping in mind that dressings should be highly seasoned. Pour into a jar, secure the lid and refrigerate until ready to use. Shake well immediately before use.

Riffs on This Very Mexican Dressing

When I'm in Mexico, I'll make this dressing with herbs like *pipicha* or the saw-tooth cilantro often called *cilantrón* (available in Vietnamese groceries), or even the light-flavored *chipil*. The lime juice can, of course, be replaced by lemon, but it won't taste very Mexican. However, sour (Seville) orange, extremely popular in the Yucatán, is one of my favorite stand-ins for lime.

Roasted Garlic Dressing with Green Chile

Aderezo de Ajo Asado con Chile Verde

This is one of the most versatile dressings I make. The alluring aromas of roasted garlic and green chile are underscored by the sweet tang of balsamic vinegar. The combination balances nicely with robust Mexican flavors. It can dress anything from muscley frisée or sturdy romaine (grilled onions and radishes have gone into our roasted garlic–dressed romaine salad at Frontera Grill since the day we opened) to a salad of sliced tomatoes and cilantro. Olive oil is well appreciated in this dressing.

Makes about 1 cup

4 garlic cloves, unpeeled
Fresh hot green chiles to taste (I like 2 serranos or 1 jalapeño), stemmed
3/4 cup vegetable oil, olive oil or a mixture of the two
1/4 cup balsamic vinegar
Salt

Set a small dry skillet over medium heat. Lay in the unpeeled garlic cloves and the chiles. Roast, turning frequently, until soft and blotchy brown in spots, about 10 minutes for the chiles, 15 minutes for the garlic. Cool until handleable, then slip the skins off the garlic and roughly chop the chiles (no need to remove seeds).

Combine the garlic, chiles, oil, vinegar and a scant teaspoon salt in a blender jar or food processor. Process until smooth. Taste and season highly with additional salt if necessary. Pour into a jar and secure the lid. Refrigerate until ready to use. Shake well immediately before pouring out.

To Speed Up the Process

Though it doesn't give as sweet and roasty a flavor, you can combine the garlic (cut a slit in the peel of each first) and chiles in a microwaveable bowl. Cover with plastic wrap, poke a couple of holes in the top and microwave on high (100%) for 30 seconds, or until soft. Uncover and cool.

Simple Riffs

At Frontera we sometimes replace the balsamic with sweet sherry vinegar—worth seeking out. You could use red wine vinegar too, but you'll likely want to add a pinch of sugar. You can think of the roasted chiles as optional (sometimes I don't want any spice in my salad dressing) or as interchangeable with canned chipotle chiles *en adobo*.

Smoky Chipotle-Balsamic Dressing

Aderezo de Chile Chipotle, Hierbas y Vinagre Balsámico

◎✿◎✿◎✿◎✿◎✿◎✿◎✿◎✿◎✿◎✿◎✿◎✿◎✿◎✿◎✿◎✿◎✿◎✿◎✿◎

The sweet smokiness of the chipotle chile is buoyed beautifully here by the balsamic vinegar. Olive oil contributes wonderfully luxurious richness. Mexican oregano adds complexity. It's the perfect match to anything sturdy: crunchy romaine with red onion, frisée with bacon and goat cheese or a colorful mixture of grilled vegetables.

Makes 1 1/4 cups

3/4 cup olive oil, vegetable oil or a
  mixture of the two

1/4 cup balsamic vinegar

1 to 2 canned chipotle chiles *en adobo*

1 teaspoon chipotle canning sauce

1 teaspoon dried oregano, preferably
  Mexican

Salt

Combine the oil, vinegar, chiles, canning sauce, oregano and a scant teaspoon salt in a blender jar or food processor. Process until smooth. Taste and season with additional salt if you think it necessary, keeping in mind that all dressings should be highly seasoned. Pour into a jar, secure the lid and refrigerate if not using right away. Shake well immediately before use.

Chorizo Dressing

Aderezo de Chorizo

◎✼◎✼◎✼◎✼◎✼◎✼◎✼◎✼◎✼◎✼◎✼◎✼◎✼◎✼◎✼◎✼◎✼◎✼◎

Chorizo dressing will likely strike you as odd, until you think of bacon dressing on a spinach salad. There are so many flavors in chorizo (dried chiles, herbs, spices, garlic—not to mention the always-enticing flavor of cured pork) that a dressing made from it is over-the-top delicious. You just have to pair it with the right ingredients: salad spinach (garnish, as you would the bacon version, with sliced hard-boiled egg and red onion), steamed potatoes or green beans, sliced tomatoes. If you like spicy, replace part of the vinegar with the juice from a can of pickled jalapeños.

Makes about 1 cup

2 ounces fresh Mexican chorizo sausage, casing removed (a packed 1/4 cup)

2 garlic cloves, peeled and finely chopped or crushed through a garlic press

2/3 cup vegetable oil, olive oil or a mixture of the two

1/4 cup apple cider vinegar

1 teaspoon crumbled dried oregano, preferably Mexican

Salt

Place the chorizo in a small skillet and set over medium heat. Cook, stirring and breaking up clumps, until the sausage is browned and cooked through, 8 to 10 minutes. Add the garlic and stir for a minute, then remove from the heat.

Scrape the chorizo and garlic into a jar. Add the oil, vinegar, oregano and 1/2 teaspoon salt, secure the lid and shake until smooth. Taste and season highly with additional salt if necessary. Refrigerate until ready to use. Shake well immediately before dressing a salad.

If you want to use this as a warm dressing (as is common for spinach salad), microwave uncovered for 15 to 20 seconds, secure the lid and shake again.

Toasted Guajillo Chile Dressing

Aderezo de Chile Guajillo

Though not a classic dressing in Mexico, the red chile–infused flavor it imparts to vegetable salads—from fresh tomatoes to blanched chayote and roasted potatoes—is pure tradition. It's a fabulous dressing, though its rusty-red color doesn't enhance light green romaine as much as it does deep emerald watercress (great sprinkled with bacon and *queso añejo*).

Makes 1 1/4 cups

3/4 cup vegetable oil, olive oil or a mixture of the two

2 medium (1/2 ounce total) dried guajillo chiles (you can also use New Mexico chiles)

2 garlic cloves, peeled and cut in quarters

1/4 cup sherry vinegar (balsamic adds sweetness, champagne or white wine vinegar adds lightness, but the richness of sherry is my favorite)

Salt

Pour the oil into a small skillet over medium heat. While the oil is heating, break the stems off the chiles, tear them open and shake out all the seeds. Lay them in the oil, along with the garlic. Turn and stir continually until the insides of the chiles have lightened in color and they are toasty smelling, about 30 seconds (if the oil isn't too hot). Remove from the heat.

Transfer the chiles to a blender jar (leave the oil and garlic in the pan). Add the vinegar and a scant teaspoon salt and blend 30 seconds. When the oil and garlic are cool (5 to 10 minutes), add to the blender. Blend until smooth—it may take a minute or more. Taste and season highly with more salt if appropriate. Pour into a jar with a secure lid and refrigerate until ready to use. Shake well immediately before use.

A Few Riffs

At Frontera Grill, we love unrefined oils (Spectrum brand offers wonderful unrefined corn oil and peanut oil—available at natural foods groceries, they taste like what they're made of); there's no better place to let that corn oil shine than in this dressing. If guajillo chiles (or New Mexicos) are not available, substitute 1 to 2 canned chipotle chiles *en adobo*, but be warned that the dressing will be spicier.

◎ **RED CHILE FENNEL SALAD:** Braise trimmed, quartered small fennel bulbs in a covered pan in a 350-degree oven with a little olive oil, lime juice, salt and water until tender (at least 30 minutes). Cool, drizzle with the dressing and shower with chopped chives or green onions.

◎ **RED CHILE BEET SALAD:** Quarter baby beets, toss with olive oil and salt and roast until tender. Toss the hot beets with the dressing. Serve cool on a bed of watercress with crumbled goat cheese dotted all around.

Salsa Dressing

Aderezo Sabor a Salsa

I can't really imagine anyone in Mexico making this dressing—*Is it salsa? Is it dressing? What in heaven's name would you put it on?*—but I think it's really delicious. And easy, if you have a good-quality bottled salsa to pour into the blender with the lime, oil and cilantro. It's perfect over vegetables (from fresh tomatoes to braised artichokes) and tubers like potatoes and yuca, in fact everything except salad greens . . . unless you take the dressing in another direction by substituting green tomatillo salsa for the red tomato one. Be sure to choose a sturdy green like romaine, frisée or arugula (perhaps with some watercress tossed in).

Makes 1 1/2 cups

3/4 cup vegetable oil, olive oil or a mixture of the two
1/2 cup good-quality bottled tomato salsa
2 tablespoons fresh lime juice
1/4 cup chopped cilantro
Salt

In a blender jar or food processor, combine the oil, salsa and lime juice. Process until smooth. Pour into a jar and stir in the cilantro. Taste and season highly with salt (the quantity will vary depending on the saltiness of the salsa). Refrigerate, covered, until ready to use. Be sure to shake the jar's contents well before pouring it out.

Tangy Avocado Dressing

Aderezo de Aguacate

This creamy dressing is good tossed with a crunchy green like romaine. It's luxurious drizzled over—or used as a dip for—raw vegetables.

Makes 1 1/2 cups

1/2 cup vegetable oil, olive oil or a mixture of the two
3 tablespoons fresh lime juice
1 garlic clove, peeled and halved
1/2 cup mayonnaise
1 tablespoon Worcestershire sauce
1/2 ripe avocado, pitted and flesh scooped from the skin
1/2 cup (loosely packed) roughly chopped cilantro
Salt

Combine the oil, lime juice, garlic, mayonnaise, Worcestershire, avocado, cilantro and 3/4 teaspoon salt in a blender jar or food processor, along with 3 tablespoons cold water. Process until smooth. Taste and season highly with more salt if appropriate. Pour into a jar, secure the lid and refrigerate until ready to use. Shake well immediately before use—which should be within a day or so.

◎ **GRILLED OR ROASTED VEGETABLE SALAD:** In the summer, I quarter farmers' market baby vegetables (fingerling potatoes, golden beets, sweet turnips, pattypan squash), toss them with a little oil and salt and either grill them in a perforated grill pan or roast them in a hot oven until tender. When the vegetables are cool, I toss them with the dressing, adding extra cilantro and diced avocado, maybe a sprinkling of Mexican *queso añejo*. It's a perfect accompaniment to grilled fish.

◎ **CONTEMPORARY *ENSALADA RUSA*:** To bring this world classic, mayonnaise-dressed vegetable salad into the twenty-first century, cube, blanch and cool potatoes and carrots, then toss with the dressing, diced avocado and *queso añejo.* I still like to include the classic addition of peas; defrosted frozen peas are the easiest.

MY FAVORITE SALAD GREENS AND DELICIOUS COMBINATIONS

◎◎◎◎◎◎◎◎◎◎◎◎◎◎◎◎◎◎◎◎◎◎

1. Escarole

This green is a little less crunchy/chewy than frisée but has the same slight bitterness.

DRESSING: You'll want to balance that slight bitterness with naturally sweet dressings like Smoky Chipotle-Balsamic (page 58), Creamy *Queso Añejo* (page 52) and Roasted Garlic (page 56). Or take it head-on with Pickled Jalapeño Dressing (page 53).

DELICIOUS ADD-INS: I like to focus escarole's crunchiness by adding sliced cucumbers, radishes, raw red onion, even thinly shaved raw fennel or chayote, . . . then come back with the sweetness of smoked ham, goat cheese or blue cheese.

◎◎◎◎◎◎◎◎◎◎◎◎◎◎◎◎◎◎◎◎◎◎

2. Frisée/Curly Endive

This somewhat gnarly, frizzy-looking (my daughter, Lanie, calls it "spidery") green adds spunky character to a salad—once you get used to its slightly chewy crunch. If you're not really familiar with frisée (it's the green used to make the famous French *salade lyonnaise* with bacon, poached egg and croutons), be aware that it needs strong textures and flavors to balance its slightly bitter flavor.

DRESSING: I like to go bold and naturally sweet: Roasted Garlic (page 56), Smoky Chipotle-Balsamic (page 58), Chorizo (page 59) or Creamy *Queso Añejo* (page 52).

DELICIOUS ADD-INS: Again, choose ingredients that have a nice natural sweetness. And crunch. Bacon is both classic and delicious. Thinly sliced jícama, raw sweet turnip, red onion (raw or grilled), cucumber. I love to mix frisée with watercress and pea shoots—and sprinkle it with Mexican *queso añejo*.

◎◎◎◎◎◎◎◎◎◎◎◎◎◎◎◎◎◎◎◎◎◎

3. Salad Spinach or Asian (Spicy) Salad Mix

Though these greens have small leaves like mesclun, they're both less delicate. Plus, spinach is sweeter, Asian salad mix is spicier.

DRESSING: Roasted Garlic (page 56), Chorizo (page 59), Creamy *Queso Añejo* (page 52), Smoky Chipotle-Balsamic (page 58), Pickled Jalapeño (page 53), Lime-Cilantro (page 54)—these greens can pair with dressings that take them in many different directions.

DELICIOUS ADD-INS: Crispy bits of bacon are a no-brainer, as is red onion (raw or grilled), Mexican fresh cheese (*queso fresco*) or goat cheese crumbles, herb leaves or chopped chives (or green onions). A tiny dice of crunchy sweet turnip, jícama, carrot, daikon (or other radishes) or chayote is also good.

◎◎◎◎◎◎◎◎◎◎◎◎◎◎◎◎◎◎◎◎◎◎

4. Boston/Butterhead Lettuce

The very tender cupped palm-size leaves of this lettuce are light and sweet in flavor.

DRESSING: A naturally sweet dressing like Roasted Garlic (page 56) is a good match. If kept thin, the Creamy *Queso Añejo* (page 52) or Tangy Avocado Dressing (page 63) would also be very harmonious.

DELICIOUS ADD-INS: To add contrast to the delicate sweetness (without contrasting too starkly with the lettuce's tenderness), I suggest adding the leaves of fresh herbs, chopped chives (or green onions), very thinly

1 Escarole

2 Frisee/Curly Endive

3 Salad Spinach

4 Boston/Butterhead Lettuce

5 Watercress

6 Mesclun

7 Romaine Lettuce

sliced radishes and red onion or jícama; a little finely crumbled bacon is very good with Boston lettuce.

5. Watercress

Though this is technically a spicy herb, and some people don't like chomping on its thick but crunchy/juicy stems, I love it as a salad. Mexican food invites flavor and texture, both of which watercress gives in great abundance.

DRESSING: The stronger the better—Smoky Chipotle-Balsamic (page 58), Chorizo (page 59), Roasted Garlic (page 56), Pickled Jalapeño (page 53), Lime-Cilantro (page 54).

DELICIOUS ADD-INS: My favorites are sliced raw red onion, Mexican *queso añejo* and bacon. Mixing pea shoots into watercress adds a lighter, sweeter, less spicy flavor.

6. Mesclun

This mix of baby greens has become ubiquitous in the United States over the last decade or so. The real thing is delicate, herbal and tender—as is mâche, a green that's becoming more available and popular nowadays. But a lot of what we're seeing in our groceries these days is raised in hothouses and downright bland. The best I've tasted has come either from my own garden or from the farmers' market.

DRESSING: Roasted Garlic (page 56) is as full-flavored as I'd go; Lime-Cilantro (page 54) is a good all-around choice for mesclun greens.

DELICIOUS ADD-INS: Anything you combine with mesclun greens should be delicate—very thinly sliced radish, jícama, carrot, raw chayote (I cut these as thin as possible on a mandoline or shave them with a vegetable peeler). A few leaves of fresh herbs (including watercress) are wonderful with mesclun, plus, perhaps, a little dusting of Mexican *queso añejo* and chopped chives.

7. Romaine Lettuce

To me, this crunchy lettuce has a wonderfully light and sweet flavor that makes it a crowd-pleaser.

DRESSING: Because of its congeniality, it goes with every dressing in this book except the Toasted Guajillo Chile Dressing (page 60) and the Salsa Dressing (page 62) (unless it is made with green tomatillo salsa).

DELICIOUS ADD-INS: Romaine will partner with anyone who comes to the dance. A favorite salad of mine is romaine with lots of sliced radishes, grilled red onions and a shower of *queso fresco*, paired with the Roasted Garlic Dressing (page 56).

VEGETABLE SALADS

Tomato Salad with *Queso Fresco* (or Goat Cheese), Pan-Roasted Green Onions and Guajillo Chile Dressing

Ensalada de Jitomate con Queso Fresco, Cebollitas Asadas y Chile Guajillo

◎❊◎

My gut tells me that the most obvious approach to making a Mexican tomato salad is to recast chopped salsa ingredients—tomatoes, chopped green chiles, onions, cilantro and lime. It's so delicious, such a no-brainer, that I've probably done it a hundred times. But here's an alternative that focuses on the flavors of dried guajillo chiles, pan-roasted onions and fresh cheese. I only make this salad during the summer, when I can get local vine-ripe tomatoes—a rainbow of heirloom varieties— from my garden or the farmers' market. That's also when I find the kind of green onions called "knob onions," the ones with the one-inch bulbs at the end; many specialty farmers grow a red variety, which is even sweeter and more delicious.

Serves 4

For the Guajillo Chile Dressing

3/4 cup vegetable oil, olive oil or a mixture of the two, plus a little for the green onions

2 medium (1/2 ounce total) dried guajillo chiles (or New Mexico chiles), stemmed and seeded

2 garlic cloves, peeled and cut in quarters

1/4 cup sherry vinegar (balsamic adds sweetness, champagne or white wine vinegar adds lightness, but the richness of sherry is my favorite)

Salt

◎⌘◎

6 green onions, roots and wilted outer leaves removed

2 large (about 1 1/4 pounds total) ripe tomatoes, cored and sliced about 1/4 inch thick

About 1/2 cup (2 ounces) crumbled Mexican *queso fresco* or other fresh cheese such as goat cheese, or even blue cheese

Pour the oil into a medium-large (8- to 10-inch) skillet and set over medium heat. When the oil is warm, add the chiles and garlic. Turn and stir continually until the insides of the chiles have lightened in color and they are toasty smelling, about 30 seconds (if the oil isn't too hot). Remove from the heat.

Transfer the chiles to a blender jar (leave the oil and garlic in the pan). Add the vinegar and a scant teaspoon salt, then blend for 30 seconds. When the oil and garlic are cool (5 to 10 minutes), add to the blender; set the skillet aside without washing. Blend the dressing until smooth (which may take a minute or more). Taste and season with more salt if you think necessary. Pour into a jar and secure the lid.

Return the skillet to medium heat. Brush the onions with a little oil, then lay them in the skillet. Cook, turning regularly, until they become wilted and browned in places, about 3 minutes. Remove and slice crosswise at 1/4-inch intervals.

Arrange the sliced tomatoes on four salad plates. Sprinkle with salt (this is a good place for richly flavored, coarse-ground sea salt), then strew with the green onion.

Shake the dressing to combine thoroughly, then drizzle over the tomatoes. (Cover and refrigerate the remaining dressing for another salad.) Sprinkle with the cheese and serve.

◎ **THAT "SALSA" TOMATO SALAD:** Use the Salsa Dressing (page 62), Lime-Cilantro Dressing (page 54) or Roasted Garlic Dressing (page 56), replace the pan-roasted onion with a large roasted poblano pepper (peeled, seeded and chopped) and shower the salad with thin-sliced red onion and roughly chopped cilantro.

◎ **CHERRY TOMATO SALAD:** You can turn either one of the tomato salads into a cherry tomato salad (halving the tomatoes distributes the flavor better). I like a little watercress, torn arugula or frisée mixed in at the last moment.

JÍCAMA SALAD WITH WATERCRESS, ROMAINE AND LIME-CILANTRO DRESSING

Jícama Salad with Watercress, Romaine and Lime-Cilantro Dressing

Ensalada de Jícama con Berros, Cilantro, Lechuga Orejona y Limón

◎ℋ◎

This salad takes jícama on a different path from the red chile-lime one that most Mexicans gravitate to. I haven't added the sweet orange segments, either, or cucumbers that are part of most traditional jícama salads. Instead, I've kept the flavors fresh (lime, cilantro), bold (green chile, watercress) and crunchy (jícama and romaine). A tip: peel the jícama with a knife rather than a vegetable peeler—you'll go a little deeper, cutting away the tough layer just below the thin skin.

Serves 4

For the Lime-Cilantro Dressing

3/4 cup vegetable oil, olive oil or a mixture of the two

1/3 cup fresh lime juice

1/2 teaspoon grated lime zest (colored rind only)

1/2 cup (packed) roughly chopped cilantro

Fresh hot green chiles to taste (I like 2 serranos or 1 jalapeño), stemmed and roughly chopped (optional)

Salt

◎ℋ◎

1 medium (about 1 pound) firm, unblemished jícama, peeled and cut into sticks (1/4 inch is a good width, 2 inches a good length)

1 medium bunch watercress, large lower stems broken off (about 2 cups)

4 good-size romaine leaves, cut crosswise in 1/4-inch slices (about 2 cups)

Combine the oil, lime juice, lime zest, cilantro, chiles and a scant teaspoon salt in a blender jar. Blend until smooth. Pour into a jar and secure the lid.

In a large bowl, combine the jícama, watercress and romaine. Shake the dressing to combine thoroughly, then drizzle on about 1/4 cup. (Cover and refrigerate the remaining dressing for another salad.) Toss to combine. Taste and season with a little more salt if you think necessary. Serve right away.

Riffs on Jícama Salad

Arugula or mâche could replace the watercress, while cucumber could replace part of the jícama. A few toasted pine nuts are delicious sprinkled over the salad. If you're partial to fruit, add some diced mango; I'd stick with a simple lime *vinagreta* (page 49), which looks best on the fruit. A little crumbled Mexican *queso fresco* or goat cheese is really, really good on the fruit version of the salad.

Green Bean Salad with Red Onion and Salsa Dressing

Ensalada de Ejotes con Cebolla Morada y Aderezo Sabor a Salsa

◎✻◎✻◎✻◎✻◎✻◎✻◎✻◎✻◎✻◎✻◎✻◎✻◎✻◎✻◎✻◎✻◎✻◎

Green bean salads are no longer out of the ordinary—they're part of most good grocery store deli offerings nowadays. And I love them, but never as much as when I've made one myself from the little French beans (*haricots verts*) I find at my farmers' market, tossed with red onion slivers and dressed with salsa flavors. The salad is prettiest when you use bottled green tomatillo salsa, but tomato salsa has wonderful flavor too. By the way, this salad's great for picnics.

Serves 4

12 ounces (about 5 loosely packed cups) green beans, tops and tails broken off

For the Salsa Dressing

3/4 cup vegetable oil, olive oil or a mixture of the two

1/2 cup good-quality bottled salsa, preferably green tomatillo salsa

2 tablespoons fresh lime juice

1/4 cup chopped cilantro, plus more for garnish

Salt

◎✻◎

1 small red onion, thinly sliced

Scoop the green beans into a microwaveable bowl, sprinkle on a tablespoon or so of water, cover tightly with plastic and poke a few holes in the top. Microwave on high (100%) until the green beans are tender-crunchy, usually about 3 minutes. Uncover (careful: there will be trapped steam) and tip off any water. Let cool.

While the green beans are cooling, combine the oil, salsa and lime juice in a blender jar or food processor. Process until smooth. Pour into a jar and stir in the cilantro. Taste and season highly with salt (the quantity will vary depending on the saltiness of the salsa).

Add the onion to the cooled green beans. Shake the dressing to combine thoroughly, then drizzle on about 1/3 cup. (Cover and refrigerate the remaining dressing for another salad.) Toss to combine. Taste and season with additional salt if you think the salad could use it. Sprinkle with additional cilantro, and the salad's ready to serve.

A Few Riffs on Green Bean Salad

The green beans can be replaced by sugar snap peas or 3-inch sections of Chinese long beans. When I'm feeling adventurous, I shave a small head of raw fennel on the mandoline (or slice it very thin) and toss it in with the onion.

◎ **SUMMER SQUASH SALAD:** Grill 1/2-inch-thick slabs of summer squash (pattypans are great), cut them into strips and toss them with strips of roasted poblano or red bell pepper, the onion and dressing. This salad is particularly good with crumbled Mexican *queso fresco*.

◎ **LEEK SALAD:** Gently braise well-washed leeks (withered outer leaves and roots removed) in a little chicken or vegetable broth, lime juice and salt until tender; cool, then dress with the salsa dressing—use a tomatillo salsa.

Sweet Potato Salad with Caramelized Onions, Watercress and Guajillo Chile Dressing

Ensalada de Camote con Cebollas Caramelizadas, Berros y Chile Guajillo

◎✿◎✿◎✿◎✿◎✿◎✿◎✿◎✿◎✿◎✿◎✿◎✿◎✿◎✿◎✿◎✿◎✿◎✿◎

Think "potato salad." Then go to "sweet potato salad." Then replace the mayo with a rustic red chile vinaigrette sweetened with caramelized onions and balsamic vinegar. Really delicious, if a little unconventional. The nests of spicy watercress make the whole thing a little more salady, though they're not essential (and could easily be replaced with the likes of mâche, arugula or sliced romaine). If you seek out the white-fleshed purple-skin Mexican sweet potato—*camote morado*—you'll experience a sweetness and texture that's lighter than our orange-fleshed sweet potatoes. Feel free to sprinkle the finished salad with a little blue cheese.

Serves 8

For the Guajillo Chile Dressing

3/4 cup vegetable oil, olive oil or a mixture of the two

2 medium (1/2 ounce total) dried guajillo chiles (or New Mexico chiles), stemmed and seeded

2 garlic cloves, peeled and cut in quarters

1/4 cup sherry vinegar (balsamic adds sweetness, champagne or white wine vinegar adds lightness, but the richness of sherry is my favorite)

Salt

◎✿◎

1 large red onion, cut into 1/2-inch cubes

3 medium (about 2 pounds) sweet potatoes, peeled and cut into 1/2-inch cubes

2 very large bunches watercress

Pour the oil into a very large (12-inch) skillet and set over medium heat. When the oil is warm, add the chiles and garlic. Turn and stir until the chiles are toasty smelling, about 30 seconds (if the oil isn't too hot). Remove from the heat.

Transfer the chiles to a blender jar (leave the oil and garlic in the pan). Add the vinegar and a scant teaspoon salt, then blend 30 seconds. When the oil and garlic are cool (5 to 10 minutes), add to the blender; set the skillet aside without washing. Blend the dressing until smooth. Pour into a jar and secure the lid.

Return the skillet (it will have a light coating of oil) to medium heat and add the onion. Cook, stirring regularly, until soft and richly browned, 9 to 10 minutes. Add the sweet potatoes, 1/2 cup of the reshaken dressing and 1 teaspoon salt. Stir well. Cover and cook until the sweet potatoes are tender, about 10 minutes (a little longer if using white-fleshed Mexican sweet potatoes). Uncover, remove from the heat and let cool—most of the dressing will be absorbed into the potatoes. Taste and season with additional salt if appropriate.

Break the large stems off the watercress (you should have 8 loosely packed cups). Divide among eight plates, forming it into "nests." Scoop a portion of the sweet potato mixture into each nest. Drizzle a little dressing over the watercress. (Cover and refrigerate the remainder for another salad.) Serve right away.

Simple Riffs

Substitute Chorizo Dressing (page 59), Smoky Chipotle-Balsamic Dressing (page 58), Creamy *Queso Añejo* Dressing (page 52) or Roasted Garlic Dressing (page 56). If you are adventurous, make this salad from *malanga* or yuca (both of which are hard to peel and will take a little longer to cook than regular sweet potato). Easier, but perhaps no less adventurous, is to replace the sweet potato with parsnips or small sweet turnips.

◉ **ROASTED EGGPLANT SALAD:** Slice 2 medium (2 pounds total) unpeeled eggplants crosswise into 1-inch rounds. Brush with oil and sprinkle with salt. Lay in a single layer on a baking sheet. Brown 4 inches below a preheated broiler—about 3 minutes per side. Cool and cut into 1-inch pieces. Follow the Sweet Potato Salad recipe, adding the eggplant where sweet potato is called for. Toss everything together, remove from the heat after a minute or so and let cool before proceeding.

Chayote Salad with Tomato and Roasted Garlic Dressing

Ensalada de Chayote con Jitomate y Ajo Asado

◎✺◎✺◎✺◎✺◎✺◎✺◎✺◎✺◎✺◎✺◎✺◎✺◎✺◎✺◎✺◎✺◎✺◎

Most cooks overlook chayote because they think it's so bland. Truth is, there's a good amount of potential sweetness there—sweetness that needs to be concentrated during cooking. Blanching dissipates the sweetness, but steaming (or "microwave steaming," as I've called for in this recipe) brings it forward—as does roasting and sautéing. Reinforcing that sweetness with a little balsamic in the dressing, then jazzing up chayote's fuddy-duddy image with green chile, tomato and green onions, well, it's like giving chayote a set of this year's fashions from Banana Republic. For the most contemporary look, present the salad nestled into leaves of romaine, butter lettuce or watercress.

Serves 4

4 garlic cloves, unpeeled

Fresh hot green chiles to taste (I like 2 serranos or 1 jalapeño), stemmed

3 medium (about 1 1/2 pounds total) chayotes

Salt

3/4 cup vegetable oil, olive oil or a mixture of the two

1/4 cup balsamic vinegar

1 large (10-ounce) tomato, cored and cut into 1/4-inch pieces

2 green onions, roots and wilted outer leaves removed, cut crosswise into 1/4-inch pieces

Roast the unpeeled garlic and whole chiles in a small dry skillet over medium heat, turning frequently, until soft and browned in spots, about 10 minutes for the chiles, 15 minutes for the garlic. Set aside to cool.

CHAYOTE SALAD WITH TOMATO AND ROASTED GARLIC DRESSING

While the garlic and chiles are cooking, peel the chayotes, if you wish (the skin is so tender that peeling is optional). Cut in half lengthwise and pry out the pit. Cut the chayotes into pieces a little smaller than 1/2 inch. Scoop into a microwaveable bowl and sprinkle with a generous 1/2 teaspoon salt. Cover tightly with plastic wrap and poke a couple of holes in the top. Microwave on high (100%) until crisp-tender, usually about 5 minutes. Uncover and cool.

While the chayote is cooling, slip the skins off the garlic. In a blender jar, combine the garlic, chiles, oil, vinegar and 1 scant teaspoon salt. Blend until smooth. Pour into a jar and secure the lid.

Tip off any liquid that has collected under the cooled chayote. Add the tomato and green onions. Shake the dressing well, then drizzle on about 1/3 cup. (Cover the remaining dressing and refrigerate for another salad.) Toss to coat well.

The flavors are best if you let the salad stand a few minutes, tossing regularly. Taste and season with extra salt if appropriate. Divide among small plates and serve.

Riffs on Chayote Salad

In the winter, I like to replace the dressing with Toasted Guajillo Chile Dressing (page 60) and the tomatoes with sun-dried tomatoes. Thin-sliced red onion can always replace the green onion. And chopped cilantro or basil is always welcome.

◎ *PANZANELLA A LA MEXICANA:* If you use *half* the quantity of chayote and add 2 cups of lightly toasted cubes of crusty bread, cubed Mexican *queso fresco* and 3 tablespoons chopped parsley or cilantro, you'll have a salad reminiscent of Italian *panzanella.*

◎ **CHAYOTE SLAW:** Shred the raw chayote with a food processor or mandoline and toss it with the tomato, green onion and the dressing. You might shred cucumber or celery root to mix in with the chayote.

◎ **CHAYOTE "CARPACCIO" SALAD:** In Oaxaca, my friend Iliana de la Vega thin-slices lightly steamed whole chayote (I prefer to leave it raw when I make her salad) and dresses it with oil, vinegar and Oaxacan oregano (I typically use this roasted garlic dressing); a sprinkling of Mexican *queso fresco* (and, in my version, a little tuft of watercress) completes the dish.

Roasted Pepper Salad with Butter Lettuce and Creamy *Queso Añejo* Dressing

Ensalada de Chiles Asados con Lechuga Dulce y Queso Añejo

◎✺◎✺◎✺◎✺◎✺◎✺◎✺◎✺◎✺◎✺◎✺◎✺◎✺◎✺◎✺◎✺◎✺◎✺◎✺◎

The flavor of roasted peppers (aka chiles), in salads and beyond, echoes through the cooking of practically every country on earth. Mexico's cooks were likely the first to experience the compelling savor of roasted chiles (their culture was the first to domesticate large chiles) and, if served cool, the chiles were likely dressed with vinegar made from roasted hearts of agave—the *materia prima* of today's tequila. The recipe I'm offering you here is the simplest modern-day approach to good roasted pepper salad, weaving in the crunch of fresh red onion, nestling the roasty mixture into sweet lettuce, perfuming it with a little aged cheese. I can't imagine ever tiring of it. Or of the smell of roasting chiles.

Serves 4

1 1/4 pounds large fresh peppers (I like a mixture of 1 large poblano and 2 medium red bell peppers)

For the Queso Añejo *Dressing*

3/4 cup vegetable oil, olive oil or a mix of the two

1/4 cup very light vinegar (such as rice or champagne vinegar)

3 tablespoons mayonnaise

Salt

1/4 to 1/3 cup grated Mexican *queso añejo*, or other garnishing cheese such as Romano or Parmesan (divided use)

◎✺◎

1 small red onion, thinly sliced

1 head Boston/butterhead lettuce (or an equivalent amount of Bibb lettuce)

Roast the peppers over an open flame or 4 inches below a broiler, turning regularly until blistered and blackened all over, about 5 minutes for an open flame, about 10 minutes under the broiler. Place in a bowl, cover with a kitchen towel and let cool until handleable.

While the peppers are cooling, combine the oil, vinegar, mayonnaise and a scant teaspoon salt in a blender jar. Blend until smooth. Pour into a jar and stir in *2 to 3 tablespoons* of the cheese.

Rub the blackened skin off the peppers and pull out the stems and seed pods. Rinse the peppers to remove bits of skin and seeds. Cut into 1/4-inch strips and place in a bowl, along with the onion.

Shake the dressing to thoroughly combine, then drizzle the pepper mixture with about 1/3 cup of the dressing. Taste and season with salt, usually about 1/4 teaspoon.

Arrange a few lettuce leaves on each of four small plates. Scoop a portion of the pepper mixture into the center of each. Shake the dressing well and drizzle a little over the lettuce. (Cover and refrigerate the remaining dressing for another salad.) Sprinkle the lettuce and peppers with the remaining cheese, and the salad's ready to serve.

A Couple of Riffs on Roasted Pepper Salad

I think you'll like the salad made with Roasted Garlic Dressing (page 56) too, especially sprinkled with a little crumbled goat cheese or blue cheese. Boston lettuce can easily be replaced by romaine or even endive, if you like its natural bitterness.

◎ **ROASTED PEPPER–CHORIZO SALAD TACOS:** For picnics, you can skip the lettuce and make the salad with the Chorizo Dressing (page 59). Cook extra chorizo to sprinkle over the salad and pass warm tortillas (take them along in a small cooler chest, wrapped in steamy hot towels) for making tacos.

BEANS AND RICE

Home-Cooked Beans (Stovetop, Slow-Cooker or Pressure Cooker)

Frijoles de la Olla Tradicional o Moderna

My favorite beans are the ones that have gently bobbed about for hours in the slow-cooker—it keeps the liquid at just the right temperature for tender, creamy, intact morsels of earthy-sweet goodness. But the stovetop offers the same, if you keep the temperature low enough, use a heavy pot (preferably made of Mexican earthenware) and stir the beans from time to time. Or, if you're in a hurry (and making fried beans and don't care if the beans remain whole), you can fire up the pressure cooker. Many cooks in southern and Gulf-coastal Mexico match the rustic flavor of their beloved black beans with resiny *epazote* or anisey avocado leaves (*hojas de aguacate*); but not all cooks do, which means you can feel free to add one of them or not.

Makes 7 to 8 cups

1 pound (about 2 1/2 cups) dried beans (any *Phaseolus* bean will work, from white navies to reds and blacks—I'm not talking about lentils, garbanzos or favas here)

2 tablespoons rich-tasting fresh pork lard, vegetable oil or bacon drippings

1 medium white onion, roughly chopped

1 large sprig fresh *epazote* or 2 fresh or dried avocado leaves if cooking black beans (optional)

Salt

Spread the beans on a baking sheet and check for stones, dirt clods or anything else you wouldn't like to eat. Scoop into a colander and rinse. If using a slow-cooker, first pour the beans into a medium-large pot, pour in 2 quarts of water and bring to a rolling boil over high heat; then pour into the slow-cooker. For stove-top, pour the beans into a medium-large (4- to 6-quart) pot or a pressure cooker. Pour 2 1/2 quarts water into the pot or 2 quarts into the pressure cooker. Add the lard (or oil or bacon drippings), onion and, if using, the *epazote* or avocado leaves. (For best flavor, lightly toast the avocado leaves in a dry skillet.)

For the **slow-cooker**, allow at least 6 hours on high for the beans to become tender, though you can leave them cooking for up to 10 hours. For the **pot**, bring to a boil on high, then partially cover (unless you're using an earthenware Mexican bean pot) and reduce the temperature to low (the liquid should show a barely discernable simmering movement); the beans should be tender in 1 1/2 to 2 1/2 hours, depending on the variety and their freshness. You may need to replenish some of the water during stovetop cooking to keep the beans floating freely. For the **pressure cooker**, follow the directions that came with your model; in mine, cooking takes 25 minutes.

When the beans are tender, stir in 1 1/2 teaspoons salt and simmer for a few minutes longer. Taste and season with additional salt if you think the beans need it. Remove the *epazote* or avocado leaves, if using, and the brothy beans are ready.

To Soak or Not

Mexican cooks don't soak beans because they know that throwing out the soaking liquid isn't a very good idea. It doesn't do much to make them more digestible (only a steady diet of beans helps with that), and it makes the beans turn out pale in color and flavor.

◎ **TURNING A POT OF BEANS INTO DINNER:** Cut 1 1/2 to 2 pounds of boneless pork shoulder roast into 1-inch cubes. Spread on a baking sheet and slide close up under a hot broiler. In about 5 minutes, when the meat is brown, turn over and brown the other side. Transfer to a slow-cooker or large pot. Prepare the recipe as described, with the addition of the meat. Serve in deep bowls with salsa, a salad and warm tortillas.

Fried Beans

Frijoles Refritos

◎✳◎✳◎✳◎✳◎✳◎✳◎✳◎✳◎✳◎✳◎✳◎✳◎✳◎✳◎✳◎✳◎✳◎✳◎✳◎

Beans are a Mexican staple, which means, as it does for staples all over the world, that their preparation stays simple. They form the background for the bold diversity of Mexico's other flavors. So most cooks just want to add some garlic, plus a little tasty fat, and they're done. Some brown a handful of chopped onion before adding the garlic, but any other additions turn this ever-present staple into a dish in its own right.

The coarse mash of beans that this recipe yields (commonly, but mistakenly, translated as "*re*-fried beans," rather than *well*-fried beans) is more multipurpose than the homey bowl of brothy beans that's been offered at Mexican meals since the beginning of civilization. You can smear the mashed beans on soft tortillas when constructing tacos, or on crisp-fried tostadas for snacks or on crusty rolls when putting together a Mexican *torta*. Or you can simply spoon a dollop next to your enchiladas or grilled steak, sprinkle it with a crumbling of Mexican cheese if that appeals, and you'll be headed down one of the tastiest paths the human race has forged.

Makes 2 1/2 cups, serving 4 to 5

2 to 3 tablespoons rich-tasting fresh pork lard, vegetable oil or bacon drippings (use 3 tablespoons for creamier beans)

2 to 3 garlic cloves, peeled and finely chopped or crushed through a garlic press

3 1/2 cups home-cooked beans (see page 82) with just enough cooking liquid to cover
OR two 15-ounce cans beans

Salt

In a large (10-inch) skillet, heat the lard, oil or bacon drippings over medium. Add the garlic and cook, stirring constantly, until fragrant but not brown, about 1 minute. Add the beans. As the beans come to a simmer, coarsely mash them with a bean masher, old-fashioned potato masher or the back of a large cooking spoon. How smoothly you mash them is entirely a matter of personal preference—in most cases, I like them rather chunky. Cook, stirring nearly constantly, until the consistency of very soft mashed potatoes—expect about 10 minutes total cooking time. Taste and season with salt if you think necessary.

Mexican Cooks' Riffs on Texture and Flavor

In many places in Mexico, especially the southern and Gulf-coastal regions, black beans are cooked with toasted avocado leaves, then completely pureed in a blender or food processor and cooked until quite thick (often with a good amount of fat). I think of them as "bean butter," which should clue you in to their potential uses.

◎ **BEANS FOR DINNER:** A super-easy dinner starts with frying a packed cup (8 ounces) fresh Mexican chorizo sausage (casing removed), tipping off the excess fat, then adding the garlic and the beans. Cook until thickened, and serve with warm tortillas, a little salsa and a salad.

Quick Cowboy Beans

Frijoles Charros Rapidos

◎⌘◎⌘◎⌘◎⌘◎⌘◎⌘◎⌘◎⌘◎⌘◎⌘◎⌘◎⌘◎⌘◎⌘◎⌘◎⌘◎⌘◎

This is a quick version of the beans that are typically served in taquerías (and northern Mexican–style restaurants). Think of them as a smoky, spicy-as-you-want, super-satisfying version of plain-Jane brothy beans—they're perfect with tacos or grilled meats, really anything that's not cooked with a sauce.

Serves 4 to 6

4 thick slices bacon, cut into small pieces

2 garlic cloves, peeled and finely chopped or crushed through a garlic press

Half of a 15-ounce can diced tomatoes in juice (preferably fire-roasted)

3 1/2 cups home-cooked pinto beans (see page 82) with enough cooking liquid to cover

OR two 15-ounce cans pinto beans

1 or 2 canned pickled jalapeños—or more if you like spicy beans

Salt

1/2 cup chopped cilantro

In a large (4-quart) saucepan, cook the bacon over medium heat, stirring regularly, until crisp, about 4 minutes. Add the garlic and stir for a minute, then add the tomatoes with their juice. Cook, stirring regularly, for 3 to 4 minutes to blend the flavors. Add the beans, with their liquid, and simmer over medium-low heat for about 15 minutes.

While the beans are simmering, stem the chiles, cut in half lengthwise and scrape out the seeds. Chop into small pieces and add to the beans.

Taste and season with salt if necessary—if the beans you use were already seasoned, you probably won't need any more salt. Ladle into small bowls, sprinkle with the cilantro and serve.

A Couple of Easy *Frijoles Charros* Riffs

Replace the pickled jalapeños with a roasted poblano or red bell pepper (roast the pepper over an open flame or under a broiler, then peel, seed and chop). Or make a black bean variation: Replace the pickled jalapeños with 1 to 2 tablespoons ground ancho chile powder (add it with the garlic); this version is good with chopped *epazote* (add it with the tomatoes) instead of or in addition to the cilantro.

Gulf Coast–Style White Rice Pilaf

Arroz Blanco

◎✱◎✱◎✱◎✱◎✱◎✱◎✱◎✱◎✱◎✱◎✱◎✱◎✱◎✱◎✱◎✱◎✱◎✱◎✱◎

Though most lovers of Mexican-American cooking wouldn't believe it, a good portion of Mexico eats garlicky white rice, not the tomato-red preparation we've come to think of as "Mexican rice." It's prepared in the same style as the red version, first sautéing the raw rice so that the grains will cook up light and separate—the pilaf technique that came to Mexico via the Spaniards, who learned it from the Arabs, who brought it from cooks in the Mid-East. All of which sort of begs the question of authenticity, except that centuries of Mexicans have claimed this as their rice—mostly, I'm sure, because it's so good with so many of their dishes. I turn to this rice more than any other.

Serves 6 to 8

1 1/2 tablespoons vegetable or olive oil

1 1/2 cups white rice (I like the meatier texture of medium-grain rice)

1 small white onion, chopped into 1/4-inch pieces

2 garlic cloves, peeled and finely chopped or crushed through a garlic press

1 3/4 cups chicken broth

Salt

3 tablespoons coarsely chopped flat-leaf parsley, for garnish

Turn on the oven to 350 degrees and position a rack in the middle. Set a medium (3-quart) ovenproof saucepan over medium heat. Add the oil, rice and onion. Stir frequently until the grains of rice turn from translucent to milky-white, about 5 minutes—for the whitest rice, they shouldn't brown. Add the garlic and stir a few seconds, until fragrant, then add the chicken broth and 1 teaspoon salt (that's what I usually need when using a normally salted broth). Stir a couple of times, then let the mixture to come a full boil.

Cover the pan and set in the middle of the oven. Bake 25 minutes. Remove from the oven and let stand 5 minutes.

Fluff the rice with a fork and sprinkle with the chopped parsley.

◎ **WHITE RICE WITH PLANTAINS (AND BLACK BEANS):** This preparation—one of my favorite rice dishes—is common on Mexico's Gulf Coast. Cut a ripe plantain into roughly 1/4-inch cubes. Sauté it in the oil (you'll probably need a little more than is called for). Scoop onto paper towels to drain. Prepare the rice as directed, using the oil left in the pan. Add the plantain when fluffing the rice. Or go all the way and add a drained can of black beans to the rice along with the chicken broth—don't skip the plantain.

◎ **POBLANO RICE WITH HERBS:** Add 2 roasted poblanos (roast them over an open flame or under a broiler, then peel, seed and chop) and 1 teaspoon chopped fresh thyme or marjoram or crumbled dried oregano, preferably Mexican, along with the broth. This allows the flavor of the poblanos to permeate the rice during cooking. Or, to keep the poblanos more distinct, add them during the last few minutes of cooking, along with some corn kernels, if that appeals.

◎ **WHITE RICE IN A RICE COOKER:** When I need to keep rice warm for more than a few minutes before serving, I sauté the rice, scrape it into my rice cooker, add the remaining ingredients and let the cooker do the rest—no need for the oven.

Classic Mexican Red Rice

Arroz Rojo

◎✠◎✠◎✠◎✠◎✠◎✠◎✠◎✠◎✠◎✠◎✠◎✠◎✠◎✠◎✠◎✠◎✠◎✠◎

This is, more or less, the preparation that completes the expression "beans and" in Mexican kitchens, whether they're north or south of the Rio Grande/Rio Bravo. Mexican or Mexican-American, tomato-tinted rice offers just the right flavors to combine with practically anything the cooks make. When that classic tomato flavor weaves its way in gently from the addition of bottled tomato salsa, the kitchen craft becomes easier. Using the oven to finish the cooking means carefree, even, slow cooking (no burnt pot bottom or underdone rice grains). All you need is an ovenproof pan with a lid.

Serves 6 to 8

1 1/2 tablespoons vegetable or olive oil

1 1/2 cups white rice (I like the meatier texture of medium-grain rice)

1 cup bottled tomato salsa (or the substitute on page 62)

1 cup chicken broth

Salt

1 1/2 cups frozen peas

Turn on the oven to 350 degrees. Set a medium (3-quart) ovenproof saucepan over medium heat. Add the oil and rice. Stir frequently until the grains of rice turn from translucent to milky-white, about 5 minutes—don't worry if some of them brown.

Add the salsa, chicken broth and 1/2 teaspoon salt (that's what I add for normally salted salsa and salted broth). Stir a couple of times, then let the mixture come to a full boil.

Cover the pan and set in the middle of the oven. Bake 20 minutes. Uncover, add the peas and re-cover. Bake 5 minutes longer, then remove from the oven and let stand 5 minutes.

Fluff the rice, releasing the steam and mixing in the peas. You're ready to serve.

Just a Few of the Many Possible Mexican Rice Riffs

Halved garlic cloves, chopped red, white or green onion and sliced mushrooms can be sautéed with the raw rice. Cubed peeled carrots, parsnips, butternut squash, even Jerusalem artichokes or kohlrabi can go in with the salsa. Chopped snow peas or green beans can replace the peas. I really like to boost the flavor and texture of classic Mexican red rice with a roasted poblano (roast it over an open flame or under a broiler, then peel, seed and chop), fresh corn kernels and a handful of chopped cilantro, arugula or watercress leaves—all added along with the peas.

◎ **TURNING A POT OF RICE INTO DINNER:** In a medium-large (4- to 6-quart; 10- to 12-inch-diameter) heavy pot brown 8 chicken thighs (bone-in ones cook most evenly) in the oil over medium-high heat. Remove to a plate. Prepare the recipe as directed, nestling the browned chicken thighs into the pot when you add the broth.

◎ **RED RICE IN A RICE COOKER:** When I need to keep rice warm for more than a few minutes before serving, I sauté the rice, scrape it into my rice cooker, add the remaining ingredients and let the cooker do the rest—no need for the oven. Because peas don't hold well in a warm environment, though, I leave them out (or microwave them and stir them in just before serving).

2

Contemporary Main-Dish Salads

Since Mexican cuisine never developed an inventory of main-dish salads, the ones I've developed for this chapter come with no stories, no rich history of regional reflection to devulge. They present only unique poems of flavor, for which we've never developed more than a clumsy English vocabulary. So I'll simply let each one voice for itself the blend of satisfying traditional flavors in contemporary preparations that makes it so special, so what we like to eat. From a briefly marinated cilantro-salmon ceviche to a marriage of mango and avocado (with bacon, pumpkin seeds and fresh cheese) and a rib-sticking seared steak salad, these recipes are all gratifying and easy to prepare, gutsy without being heavy.

Roasted Poblano–Potato Salad with Flaked Tuna

Ensalada de Rajas, Papas y Atún

◎❊◎❊◎❊◎❊◎❊◎❊◎❊◎❊◎❊◎❊◎❊◎❊◎❊◎❊◎❊◎❊◎

Most cooks have their eye on the prize—taking that first bite of their delicious creation. For me, this dish offers considerably more, since its preparation fills the kitchen with the perfume of roasting chiles, one of the most intoxicating aromas imaginable. Stir them into a lightly dressed potato salad, and you've got a delectable treat to carry on a summer picnic. Add the flaked tuna, and you've got a full-flavored meal for any night of the week.

Serves 4

2 fresh poblano chiles

4 medium (about 1 pound total) red-skin boiling or Yukon Gold potatoes, each cut into 1/2-inch pieces

Salt

1/3 cup vegetable or olive oil

1 medium red onion, sliced 1/4 inch thick

3 tablespoons mild vinegar (I like rice or champagne vinegar)

1 teaspoon crumbled dried oregano, preferably Mexican

1/2 teaspoon ground black pepper

One 7-ounce can or pouch cooked tuna, drained if canned

1/2 cup chopped cilantro

Romaine, Boston/butterhead or Bibb lettuce, for serving

Roast the poblanos over an open flame or 4 inches below a broiler, turning regularly until blistered and blackened all over, about 5 minutes for the open flame, about 10 minutes for a broiler. Place in a bowl, cover with a kitchen towel and let cool until handleable.

Meanwhile, scoop the potatoes into a microwaveable bowl. Sprinkle with a teaspoon of salt and toss. Cover with plastic wrap and microwave on high (100%) for 4 to 5 minutes, until completely tender. Leave covered.

Rub the blackened skin off the chiles and pull out the stems and seed pods. Rinse the chiles to remove bits of skin and seeds. Cut into 1/4-inch strips.

Heat the oil in a large (10-inch) skillet over medium-high. Add the onion and cook, stirring frequently, until richly golden but still crunchy, 4 to 5 minutes. Remove from the heat and stir in the vinegar, oregano, black pepper and poblano strips. Stir well, then pour the mixture over the warm potatoes. Let cool to room temperature, then gently stir in the tuna and cilantro.

Arrange the lettuce leaves on dinner plates. Spoon a portion of the salad mixture down or into the center of the leaves. Drizzle any dressing that's collected at the bottom of the bowl over the greens, and serve.

A Few Riffs on Roasted Poblano–Potato Salad

The obvious stand-ins for poblanos are other fresh chiles, from red bells to Hungarian/bananas to cubanelles. Many yield less flesh than poblanos but can make a delicious salad. This is a wonderful place to feature farmers' market potatoes—I love fresh-dug banana fingerlings or the buttery-tasting Butterballs, anything but mealy baking potatoes, which tend to fall apart. Lime juice makes a nice alternative to the vinegar. And, of course, the field is wide open when it comes to options to replace the tuna—hot-smoked salmon, trout or other hot-smoked fish; grilled steak or roasted chicken; and crumbled *queso fresco*, goat cheese or blue cheese (the blue cheese is wonderful in combination with steak).

Avocado-Mango Salad with Fresh (or Blue) Cheese, Bacon and Toasted Pumpkin Seeds

Ensalada de Aguacate y Mango con Queso Fresco, Tocino y Pepitas Tostadas

◎✕◎✕◎✕◎✕◎✕◎✕◎✕◎✕◎✕◎✕◎✕◎✕◎✕◎✕◎✕◎✕◎✕◎✕◎✕◎

From the Mexican perspective, both buttery avocado and tropical mango derive beautiful benefits from chile, salt and lime, all three of which form a foundation for this salad's dressing, along with sautéed garlic's savory aroma and honey's mellowness. Add the crunch of toasted pumpkin seeds, the tenderness of Boston lettuce and the savory saltiness of crisp bacon and fresh Mexican cheese, and you have a compelling dish. It's the least substantial of my main-course salads—perfect for hot-weather appetites. Also, feel free to scale down the size of the portions so you can use this *delicia* as the first course for a special dinner. Or serve the large portions with grilled chicken breasts for a more robust meal.

Serves 4

4 slices bacon

1/2 cup hulled untoasted pumpkin seeds

1/3 cup fresh lime juice

1/3 cup vegetable or olive oil

2 garlic cloves, peeled

Fresh hot green chile to taste (I like a large serrano or a small jalapeño), stemmed (optional)

1 tablespoon honey

Salt

1 large head Boston/butterhead lettuce (or an equivalent amount of Bibb lettuce), leaves separated

2 large ripe avocados

2 ripe mangoes

A generous 3/4 cup coarsely crumbled Mexican *queso fresco* or mild blue cheese (Gorgonzola is great)

Cutting mango for salad

Arrange the bacon slices between a double layer of paper towels on a microwave-able plate. Microwave on high (100%) for 2 1/2 to 3 1/2 minutes, until crispy.

Pour the pumpkin seeds into a small skillet and set over medium heat. Once the first one pops, stir constantly until all have popped from flat to round, about 5 minutes. Scoop about one-third of the seeds into a blender jar and add the lime juice. Pour the remainder into a small dish.

Return the skillet to medium heat and measure in the oil. Add the garlic and optional chile. Cook, stirring regularly, until the garlic is soft and lightly browned, about 5 minutes. Scrape the oil, garlic and optional chile into the blender. Add the honey and 1/2 teaspoon salt. Process until smooth. Taste and season with more salt if you think necessary. (It should be highly seasoned.)

Divide the lettuce among four dinner plates. Pit the avocados, scoop the flesh from the skin and cut it into slices. Peel the mangoes, then cut the flesh from the pits. Slice to match the avocado pieces. Arrange the avocados and mangoes in the center of the lettuce. Drizzle the dressing over everything, then sprinkle with the cheese and the reserved toasted pumpkin seeds. Crumble the bacon and strew it over the top, and the salad is ready.

AVOCADO-MANGO SALAD WITH FRESH (OR BLUE) CHEESE, BACON AND TOASTED PUMPKIN SEEDS

A Few Simple Riffs

The bacon can be replaced with flaked hot-smoked salmon, eel, trout or other smoked fish. To make the salad vegetarian, leave out the bacon or replace it with pan-grilled onion slices. The pumpkin seeds can be replaced with pine nuts (they toast—and burn—much faster than pumpkin seeds). The luscious texture of mango works well with avocado, but so would ripe peaches or nectarines. The green chile could be replaced by ground hot red chile (like árbol)—sprinkle it over the salad rather than blending it with the dressing. Crumbled goat cheese is another good stand-in for the *queso fresco*.

OVER-THE-TOP CRAB-AVOCADO-MANGO SALAD: Sprinkle a generous portion of crabmeat over the avocado and mango before drizzling with the dressing.

Seared Rare Tuna Salad with Chayote Slaw and Guajillo Chile Dressing

Ensalada de Atún Asado-Crudo con Chayote Rallado y Aderezo de Chile Tostado

◎✖◎✖◎✖◎✖◎✖◎✖◎✖◎✖◎✖◎✖◎✖◎✖◎✖◎✖◎✖◎✖◎✖◎✖◎✖◎

Okay, I know this sounds like something off a fusion restaurant menu, but some fusion dishes lay the foundation for new classics. So buy a piece of meaty fresh tuna, shred some crunchy, sweet-tasting chayote and whip up the bold-tasting toasted chile *vinagreta*. You'll love the wonderful play of robust flavors and textures—a quick way to feel as if you've gone out to that cool new restaurant.

Serves 4

For the Guajillo Chile Dressing

3/4 cup vegetable oil, olive oil or a mixture of the two

2 medium (1/2 ounce total) dried guajillo chiles (or New Mexico chiles), stemmed and seeded

2 garlic cloves, peeled and cut in quarters

1/4 cup sherry vinegar (balsamic adds sweetness, champagne or white wine vinegar adds lightness, but the richness of sherry is my favorite)

Salt

◎✖◎

4 (about 1 1/4 pounds total) tuna steaks, not less than 3/4 inch thick

2 chayotes

About 4 cups (loosely packed) arugula, frisée leaves or thickly sliced romaine

A little chopped cilantro, to finish the salad

Pour the oil into a large (10-inch) skillet and set over medium heat. When the oil is warm, add the chiles and garlic. Turn and stir continually until the insides of the chiles have lightened in color, about 30 seconds (if the oil isn't too hot).

Remove from the heat and transfer the chiles to a blender jar (leave the oil and garlic in the pan). Add the vinegar and a scant teaspoon salt and blend for 30 seconds. When the oil and garlic are cool (5 to 10 minutes), add to the blender; set the skillet aside without washing. Blend the dressing until smooth—it may take a minute or more. Taste the dressing and season with more salt if you think necessary. Pour the dressing into a jar and secure the lid.

Return the skillet to medium-high to high heat. Sprinkle both sides of the fish with salt. When the oil-filmed skillet is really hot, lay the tuna in the pan. When brown, no more than 1 minute, flip and sear the other side. (The higher the heat, the more golden the crust—without overcooking.) Remove the skillet from the heat. Thoroughly shake the dressing, then carefully drizzle on about 3 tablespoons dressing (it may spatter a bit when it hits the hot pan). Turn the tuna in the dressing from time to time as it cools.

Peel the chayotes, if you wish (the skin is so tender that peeling is optional). Cut them in half lengthwise; pry out the pits. Shred through the coarse holes of a large grater or with a mandoline (finely shredded chayote looks sadly matted). Scoop into a bowl. Shake the dressing well, then toss the chayote with about 3 tablespoons dressing. Taste and season with salt, usually about 1/2 teaspoon.

Divide the greens among four plates, forming them into wide nests. Slice each piece of tuna in half crosswise on a bias and nestle the pieces in the center of the greens. Sprinkle with salt. Top each with a portion of the chayote salad. Drizzle the tuna and greens with a little dressing. (Cover and refrigerate the remaining dressing for another salad.) Sprinkle everything with cilantro, and dinner is ready.

Riffs on a Cool Salad

If you are fanatic about rare tuna, buy a single thick piece of tuna (not 4 steaks), cook it whole and slice it for serving. Thick pieces of any very fresh meaty fish (wahoo, ono, shark, swordfish) can be used to make this seared rare fish salad; or make it with halibut or salmon, which need more cooking. This salad is also good with Roasted Garlic Dressing (page 56) or Smoky Chipotle-Balsamic Dressing (page 58). The chayote slaw can be served as an accompaniment to many dishes. I love it with soft sun-dried tomatoes or sautéed mushrooms mixed in and crumbled toasted dried chile and Mexican *queso añejo* sprinkled over the top.

CEVICHE SALAD WITH AVOCADO, CILANTRO AND GREEN CHILE

Ceviche Salad with Avocado, Cilantro and Green Chile

Ensalada de Ceviche con Aguacate, Cilantro y Chile Verde

◎✵◎✵◎✵◎✵◎✵◎✵◎✵◎✵◎✵◎✵◎✵◎✵◎✵◎✵◎✵◎✵◎✵◎

Ceviches, the wonderful lime-marinated seafood cocktails of Latin American, are experiencing an evolution. In Mexico, for centuries ceviche has meant ultrafresh fish or shellfish that's preserved/marinated/"acid-cooked" in lime juice. But many modern chefs have broadened the concept to include practically any bold-flavored combination of seafood, vegetables, chiles, herbs, even fruit, that can be served as a cool appetizer or snack, usually with a bracing bolt of lime. My version here is pretty traditionally Mexican except that the fish in Mexico would likely be mackerel or kingfish, it would typically be marinated long enough to "cook" through and it would be served in a glass bowl or on a tostada, rather than nestled into greens. I've recently become enchanted with the Peruvian take on ceviche (the fish is marinated only moments before serving), especially since sashimi-grade fish (the top, okay-to-eat-raw grade) is becoming more common in our fish markets. Whatever your marinating preference, this salad is just the ticket on a warm summer night, served with crusty bread or crackers.

Serves 4

1 cup fresh lime juice

2 garlic cloves, peeled and roughly chopped

1 cup (loosely packed) roughly chopped cilantro

Fresh hot green chiles to taste (I like 2 serranos or 1 jalapeño), stemmed and roughly chopped

Salt

1 to 1 1/4 pounds sashimi-grade boneless, skinless fish (salmon, tuna and snapper are options you'll likely find), cut into 1/2-inch cubes

OR 1 to 1 1/4 pounds medium-to-small cooked shrimp

1 ripe avocado, pitted, flesh scooped from the skin, and cut into 1/4-inch cubes

1 large head Boston/butterhead lettuce (or an equivalent amount of Bibb lettuce), leaves separated

1 green onion, roots and wilted outer leaves removed, thinly sliced crosswise, or a little chopped cilantro, for garnish

In a blender or food processor, combine the lime juice, garlic, cilantro, chiles and 1 scant teaspoon salt. Process until smooth.

Scoop the fish into a large bowl. Pour the lime marinade over it and let it "cook" in the lime juice to suit your own taste: you can eat it right away (Peruvian-style) if you like raw fish, or let it "cook" for an hour or 2 if you like it more well-done; cooked shrimp need only a few minutes to soak up the flavor. (It takes about 4 hours to "cook" fish well-done in lime juice; if that is your desire, add the cilantro, chopped, just before serving to prserve its fresh color.)

Pour off half of the marinating liquid and set aside. Toss the avocado with the fish, then taste and season with additional salt if you think necessary.

Divide the lettuce among four dinner plates. Scoop a portion of the ceviche into the center of each arrangement. Sprinkle with the chopped green onion or cilantro. Drizzle some of the reserved lime marinade over the lettuce, and you're ready to serve.

Ceviche Riffs (Some for the Adventurous)

Practically any edible piscine morsel can be made into ceviche: Squid and baby octopus are favorites—I simmer both of them until tender (usually 20 to 30 minutes) before marinating them. Scallops are wonderful raw and barely marinated, as are sardines. Around Guadalajara, the fish markets offer ground fish for making ceviche to pile on little tostadas—it cooks through in a matter of minutes; if that appeals, look for ground fish for fish cakes in your local fish market. Avocado is just a start when it comes to add-ins: tomato, red or white onion, olives, cooked cactus (nopales), roasted poblano chile—these should get your creative juices flowing.

GRILLED CHICKEN SALAD WITH RUSTIC GUACAMOLE, ROMAINE AND *QUESO AÑEJO*

Grilled Chicken Salad with Rustic Guacamole, Romaine and *Queso Añejo*

Ensalada de Pollo a la Parilla con Guacamole Rústico, Lechuga Orejona y Queso Añejo

◎✿◎✿◎✿◎✿◎✿◎✿◎✿◎✿◎✿◎✿◎✿◎✿◎✿◎✿◎✿◎✿◎✿◎

Here's an offering to entice folks out of the "grilled chicken Caesar" rut. True, it starts with grilled chicken, but chicken that's redolent of roasted garlic, green chile, cilantro and lime, chicken that dances the *cumbia* with guacamole, crisp romaine and nutty aged cheese. The flavors are so captivating that you can get away without firing up the grill—this is a perfect place to put a stovetop grill pan to work.

Serves 4

For the Dressing

1/2 cup vegetable or olive oil, plus a little more for the onion

4 garlic cloves, peeled and halved

Fresh hot green chiles to taste (I like 2 serranos or 1 large jalapeño), stemmed and halved

1/2 cup fresh lime juice

3/4 cup (loosely packed) roughly chopped cilantro

1/4 teaspoon ground black pepper

Salt

◎✿◎

4 (about 1 1/4 pounds total) boneless, skinless chicken breast halves

1 medium white onion, cut into 1/2-inch slices

2 ripe avocados

2 medium romaine hearts, sliced crosswise into 1/2-inch-wide ribbons (about 8 cups)

About 1/3 cup grated Mexican *queso añejo* or other garnishing cheese such as Romano or Parmesan

Heat the oil in a small skillet over medium. Add the garlic and chiles and cook, stirring frequently, until the garlic is soft and lightly browned, usually 1 to 2 minutes. Pour the oil, garlic and chile into a blender jar or food processor. Add the lime juice, cilantro, black pepper and 1 scant teaspoon salt. Process until smooth.

Place the chicken breasts in a bowl and pour one-third of the garlic dressing over them, spreading it evenly over all sides.

Heat half the burners of a gas grill over medium-high (or start a charcoal fire and let it burn until the coals are covered with white ash but still quite hot, then bank the coals to one side). Lightly brush or spray the onion slices with oil; sprinkle with salt. Lay the chicken and onion directly over the heat of the grill. Sear the chicken on both sides, then move it away from the direct heat to finish cooking, usually about 5 minutes. Cook the onion until it is well browned, 3 to 4 minutes on each side. Chop the onion into small pieces and scoop into a bowl. Set the chicken aside to cool. (All of the grilling can be done in a grill pan on a stove over medium heat.)

Mashing guacamole for
Grilled Chicken Salad

Pit the avocados and scoop the flesh in with the onion. Add another one-third of the garlic dressing, then coarsely mash everything together with an old-fashioned potato masher, large fork or the back of a big spoon. Taste and season with salt, usually about 1/2 teaspoon.

Scoop the sliced romaine into a large bowl. Drizzle on the remaining garlic dressing and toss to combine. Divide among four dinner plates.

Scoop a portion of guacamole into the center of each plate. Cut each chicken breast into cubes and arrange over the guacamole. Sprinkle each plate with *queso añejo* (or its substitute), and you're ready to serve.

A Couple Riffs on This Great Salad

You can replace the grilled chicken with flaked hot-smoked salmon (I buy one that has a coarse black pepper coating). Watercress is a good addition to the romaine, or replace the romaine with a mixture of frisée and watercress.

Roasted Mushroom Salad with Spinach and Chorizo (or Bacon)

Ensalada de Hongos Asados con Espinacas y Chorizo (o Tocino)

◎✳◎✳◎✳◎✳◎✳◎✳◎✳◎✳◎✳◎✳◎✳◎✳◎✳◎✳◎✳◎✳◎✳◎✳◎

I love roasted mushrooms. They have a more rustic texture than their sautéed counterparts, as well as a more concentrated flavor. Here I've chosen to roast them with chorizo sausage and red onion, then toss the warm mixture with a nimble dressing of lime, olive oil and oregano. A warm spinach salad gone far south. To make the dish more substantial, crumble goat cheese over the finished salad, or serve it with a piece of good ripe cheese (and a crusty loaf of bread).

Serves 4

8 ounces fresh Mexican chorizo sausage, casing removed (1 packed cup) OR 8 thick slices bacon cut crosswise into 1/4-inch pieces

4 cups (8 ounces) sliced mushrooms, preferably shiitakes, oysters, chanterelles, hedgehogs or other full-flavored mushrooms, alone or in combination

1 large red onion, sliced about 1/4 inch thick

8 cups (about 8 ounces) salad spinach, long stems removed

3 tablespoons vegetable or olive oil

2 tablespoons fresh lime juice

1/2 teaspoon dried oregano, preferably Mexican

Salt

Heat the oven to 425 degrees; position a rack in the middle. Break the loose chorizo into small clumps on a baking sheet with sides, or scatter on the bacon pieces. Sprinkle the mushrooms and onion over the top, then slide into the oven. Stir after 10 minutes, breaking up any clumps of chorizo, then continue roasting until the onion is richly browned and the sausage or bacon fully cooked, about 10 minutes more.

While the mushrooms are roasting, scoop the spinach into a large bowl.

In a small microwaveable container, combine the olive oil, lime juice, oregano, 1/2 teaspoon salt and 2 tablespoons water. Heat on high (100%) in a microwave for 30 seconds.

When the roasted mushroom mixture is ready, sprinkle it over the spinach. Drizzle the warm dressing over the salad and toss to combine. Serve right away.

Riffs on Roasted Mushroom Salad

When I have time, I'll roast (then peel, seed and slice) a couple of poblano chiles to mix in. For a rich sweetness, replace the lime juice with balsamic vinegar; add a finely chopped canned chipotle chile or two to the dressing for smoky spiciness. That balsamic-chipotle dressing is really good on a salad that's half mushrooms, half cubed unpeeled eggplant, both roasted with the onion and chorizo.

Skirt Steak Salad with "Wilted" Greens, Tomato, Avocado and Lime

Ensalada de Arrachera con Lechugas Tibias, Jitomate, Aguacate y Limón

◎✖◎✖◎✖◎✖◎✖◎✖◎✖◎✖◎✖◎✖◎✖◎✖◎✖◎✖◎✖◎✖◎✖◎✖◎

For me, this is an incredibly satisfying dinner with a thick slice of the seven-grain bread from our local bakery. I love the extra-beefy flavor of skirt steak, the rustic chew of the frisée (salad spinach is also good) and the savory pleasure of the warm chipotle-infused dressing. The creamy avocado and ripe tomato don't hurt either.

Serves 4

1 medium-large head (8 ounces) frisée or escarole, root end cut off, the remainder cut into 2-inch sections OR 8 cups (about 8 ounces) salad spinach, long stems removed

2 medium-large (about 1 pound total) ripe tomatoes, cored and cut into 1/2-inch (or smaller) cubes

2 medium avocados, pitted, flesh scooped from the skin and cut into 1/2-inch (or smaller) cubes

1/4 cup plus 2 tablespoons vegetable or olive oil (divided use)

1 pound skirt steak (thicker "outer" skirt steak is most tender—it should already be trimmed of the exterior white membrane and surface fat)

Salt

Ground black pepper

2 to 3 garlic cloves, peeled and finely chopped or crushed through a garlic press

1/4 cup beef broth or water

1 canned chipotle chile *en adobo*, seeds scraped out and finely chopped

1/4 cup fresh lime juice

About 1/3 cup grated Mexican *queso añejo* or other garnishing cheese such as Romano or Parmesan

SKIRT STEAK SALAD WITH "WILTED" GREENS, TOMATO, AVOCADO AND LIME

Scoop the frisée (you should have about 8 cups) or spinach into a large bowl. Strew the chopped tomatoes and avocados over the top.

Set a very large (12-inch) heavy skillet over medium-high heat, and measure in *2 tablespoons* of the oil. Sprinkle both sides of the skirt steak with salt and pepper. Lay it in the hot oil and cook until it's about medium-rare, 1 to 1 1/2 minutes on each side. Remove to a cooking rack set over a large plate—this keeps the juices in the meat rather than running out onto the plate.

Turn the heat under the skillet to low. Add the garlic and stir for a few seconds, until very fragrant. Then pour in the broth (or water) and stir to release any browned bits on the bottom of the skillet (the liquid will quickly come to a boil). Turn off the heat and add the chile, along with the lime juice and the remaining *1/4 cup* oil. Season with salt (usually 1/2 teaspoon) and pepper (about 1/4 teaspoon is right for me).

Cut the skirt steak into roughly 3-inch lengths, then cut each piece across the grain into 1/4-inch strips. Add to the bowl with the frisée. Pour the warm dressing over the frisée and toss to coat thoroughly—the greens will wilt slightly. Divide among four dinner plates or large salad bowls. Sprinkle with the grated cheese and serve right away.

A Few Riffs on Steak Salad

Feel free to substitute boneless, skinless chicken breasts or thighs for the skirt steak. Or choose a 1- to 1 1/4-pound piece of flank steak and cook it whole (it'll take a few minutes longer than the skirt steak), then slice it across the grain (if the pieces are awkwardly long, cut them in half). When our local tomatoes aren't in season, I use sliced sun-dried tomatoes (my favorites are ones that have the texture of soft dried fruit, though drained oil-packed ones work well too). This is the perfect place for farmers' market greens like Japanese mizuna or shungiku greens, wild arugula, young dandelion and amaranth; a little watercress, young purslane and pea shoots are also fabulous additions.

◎ **BACON-AND-ONION STEAK SALAD:** This variation may be over-the-top for everyday eating, but I love bacon as much as skirt steak. Slice 2 thick pieces of bacon crosswise into 1/2-inch pieces. Scoop into a very large (12-inch) skillet, along with a sliced red onion and a tablespoon of olive oil. Fry over medium heat until the onion is richly browned. Scoop into a bowl, leaving behind as much fat as possible; use the skillet to fry the meat, as directed. Add the onion mixture to the salad along with the meat.

◎ **VEGETARIAN GRILLED EGGPLANT SALAD:** When I've got the grill fired up, I often grill extra things to serve for the next few meals: Cut 1 large eggplant and 1 large red onion into 1/2-inch slices, spray both sides of the slices with oil and sprinkle with salt. Grill over medium-high heat until browned and softening (this can be done in a grill pan or under a broiler). Cut the eggplant into strips. Make the dressing in a skillet as described, replacing the beef broth with rich vegetable stock and the lime juice with balsamic vinegar. I would leave the avocado out.

Lentil-Rice Salad with Ham, Cucumber, Red Onion and Herbs

Ensalada de Lentejas y Arroz con Jamón, Pepino, Cebolla Morada y Hierbas

◎✠◎✠◎✠◎✠◎✠◎✠◎✠◎✠◎✠◎✠◎✠◎✠◎✠◎✠◎✠◎✠◎

Lentils are the godsend bean for everyday cooking. They cook so quickly that you can toss them into the pot with rice and both will cook at the same rate. This warm combo is a tasty, nutritious side dish, playing earthy flavors against gentle sweetness, but turning it into a salad offers a multitude of delicious possibilities. Here I've chosen crunchy cucumber, savory roasted pepper and smoky ham, all enveloped in a rich chipotle dressing. But you can take the salad in many directions, including to your next picnic (I usually omit the spinach when I'm carrying it away from home).

Serves 4

Salt

2/3 cup lentils (choose green Le Puy or standard brown lentils—reds and yellows will fall apart during cooking)

1/2 cup rice (choose long-grain for the fluffiest salad)

For the Chipotle Dressing

3/4 cup vegetable oil, olive oil or a mixture of the two

1/4 cup balsamic vinegar

1 to 2 canned chipotle chiles *en adobo*

1 teaspoon chipotle canning sauce

1 teaspoon dried oregano, preferably Mexican

1 small red onion, thinly sliced

4 ounces ham, cut into 1/4-inch cubes (the better the ham, the better the dish; you need about 1 cup)

1 medium cucumber, peeled and seeded if you wish, cut into 1/4-inch cubes (you'll have about 1 1/4 cups)

1/2 cup sliced bottled roasted red pepper (or 1 medium red bell pepper, roasted, peeled, seeded and sliced)

4 cups (about 4 ounces) salad spinach, long stems removed

OR 1 small head (4 ounces) frisée, root end cut off, remainder cut into 2-inch sections

◎✠◎

Pour about 2 quarts water into a large (4-quart) saucepan and set over high heat. Add 1 tablespoon salt. When the water boils, sprinkle in the lentils and rice. Reduce the heat a little, but keep the water at a brisk boil, and cook until the lentils and rice are tender (no chalkiness inside) but show no signs of falling apart, about 15 minutes. Pour into a strainer set in the sink to drain completely.

Combine the oil, vinegar, chile, canning sauce, oregano and a scant teaspoon salt in a blender jar or food processor. Process until smooth. Scrape into a jar and secure the lid.

Scoop the lentil-rice mixture into a very large bowl, along with the red onion. Pour in about *1/4 cup* of the dressing and mix well. Let cool completely.

Add the ham, cucumber and roasted red pepper to the lentils and toss to combine. Taste and season with additional salt as necessary, usually about 1/2 teaspoon.

Scoop the spinach or frisée into a large bowl. Shake the dressing to thoroughly blend, then drizzle on about 3 tablespoons and toss to combine. (Cover and refrigerate the remaining dressing for another salad.) Divide the salad among four plates, roughly forming it into nests. Scoop a portion of the lentil salad in the center of each, and you're ready to eat.

A Few of the Many Possible Riffs on Lentil-Rice Salad

The Chipotle Dressing can be replaced by the Chorizo Dressing (page 59)—which might lead you to replace the ham with cooked chorizo too. Really, practically any of the dressings in the book will work here, each taking the flavors in a different but delicious direction. I'm particularly fond of using the Creamy *Queso Añejo* Dressing (page 52), made with lime instead of vinegar. A generous sprinkling of chopped cilantro makes a nice addition, no matter which dressing you've chosen. Boston lettuce makes a sweet-tasting replacement for the spinach or frisée, arugula a spicy one.

◎ **VEGETARIAN LENTIL-RICE SALAD:** Sauté a sliced onion in olive oil until richly brown (or grill it) and add in place of the ham.

◎ **TO SERVE RICE AND LENTILS AS A WARM SIDE DISH:** Boil the rice and lentils as I've described in the recipe, adding 3 garlic cloves (cut in half), several sprigs of fresh thyme and a couple of bay leaves. A couple slices of bacon, cut into small pieces, add a savory, smoky quality to the dish.

3

Classic Main-Dish Soups

Most Mexican midday meals (for the majority of Mexico, that's still the big meal of the day) start with a soup, a brothy soup chock-full of vegetables, usually made with a meat or poultry broth that's infused with herbs. The concept of multiple courses doesn't play much of a role in our modern everyday eating, so I've fused the idea of Mexican first-course soup with my one-main-dish idea to come up with five wonderfully delicious and completely satisfying main-dish soups.

Most everyone in North America knows about tortilla soup (though in Mexico it's actually not all that common), which I've always said makes a meal even when served in first-course portions. To the crunchy fried tortillas softening in a rich red chile–red tomato broth, enriched even more with a little melted cheese and avocado, we only have to add a little extra chicken to make the soup a meal. I've added chicken (or ham) to Mexico's ubiquitous first-course creamy corn soup too, moving it into the main-course category.

Practically every coastal restaurant in Mexico (and every seafood restaurant not on the coast) offers a rich seafood stew that's a dish of dreams. While I like to make an all-out cauldron of the stuff for parties, I've scaled the party version down to a few manageable steps for everyday eating. Mussels or clams add the right character to the broth, fish and potatoes add substance and dried red chiles, tomatoes and herbs add the dreamy intrigue.

Red chile *chileatole* is an indigenous soup in Mexico's Veracruz region; it's a wonderfully silky soup that, in the version I'm including here, matches red-chile earthiness with mushrooms, zucchini, chicken and the oh-so-Veracruz herb, *epazote*. Mushrooms are featured in many soups in central Mexico too, so I've included one of my favorites—a hearty vegetarian mix of woodland mushrooms with smoky roasted poblanos, potatoes, garlic and a dollop of cream. A nice beginning tour of Mexico's best soup pots, I'd say.

Creamy Corn Soup with Chicken (or Ham) and Poblano Chile

Crema de Elote con Pollo y Poblano

There's nothing more comfortable or common in Mexico than a creamy corn soup for everyday eating. The Aztecs were making corn soup when the Spanish arrived and tasted their first spoonful (Mexico is the birthplace of corn), but the preparation has certainly moved into the international domain. Corn is so friendly that it takes to each cuisine's local flavors—Mexico's being roasted poblano, which is magic with creamy corn. By simply adding chicken breast, I've turned this satisfying soup into a hearty meal.

Here's my low-tech tip for no-fuss cutting corn off the cob: Flip a small bowl upside down and set it in a very large bowl. Stand a husked ear of corn on the overturned bowl and use a sharp knife to shave the kernels off the cob. The kernels will fall around the overturned bowl so the bigger bowl catches them—which prevents your having to search out flying kernels in kitchen nooks and crannies. But if cutting kernels off cobs of fresh corn is more than you'll tackle, use frozen corn.

Makes a generous 6 cups, serving 4

1 large fresh poblano chile
1 tablespoon vegetable or olive oil
1 small white onion, sliced 1/4 inch thick
2 garlic cloves, peeled
3 cups corn kernels, preferably just cut from the cob (it takes about 5 ears of corn)
1 tablespoon cornstarch
1 quart milk
2 (12 to 14 ounces total) boneless, skinless chicken breast halves, cut into 1/2-inch cubes
OR 8 ounces ham, cut into 1/2-inch cubes
Salt
About 1/4 cup roughly chopped cilantro, for garnish

Roast the poblano over an open flame or 4 inches below a broiler, turning regularly until blistered and blackened all over, about 5 minutes for an open flame, about 10 minutes for the broiler. Cover with a kitchen towel.

Heat the oil in a medium (3-quart) saucepan over medium. Add the onion and garlic and cook until golden, about 7 minutes. Scoop up the onion and garlic with a slotted spoon, pressing them against the side of the pan to leave behind as much oil as possible, and transfer to a food processor or blender; set the pan aside. Add the corn, cornstarch and *1 1/2 cups* of the milk to the onion and garlic. Process to a smooth puree.

Set a medium-mesh strainer over the pan and work the pureed corn mixture through it. (You can skip the straining, but the skins of the corn kernels will give the creamy soup a coarse texture.) Return the pan to medium heat, and whisk frequently as the soup comes to a simmer.

When the chile is handleable, rub off the blackened skin. Pull out the stem and seed pod. Rinse the chile to remove bits of skin and seeds. Cut into 1/4-inch pieces.

Stir the chile pieces into the soup, along with the chicken or ham and the remaining *2 1/2 cups* milk. Simmer until the chicken is cooked or the ham is hot, about 5 minutes. Taste and season with salt, usually about 1 1/2 teaspoons. Serve hearty portions, with a sprinkling of the cilantro.

◎ **VEGETARIAN CREAMY CORN SOUP:** Replace the chicken with asparagus or zucchini, cut into 1/2-inch pieces.

◎ **SEAFOOD CORN CHOWDER:** Replace the chicken with an equal weight of peeled and deveined shrimp or a mixture of shrimp and crab (the crab should be added just before ladling up the soup). A sprinkling of crumbled crisp bacon, along with the cilantro, is really, really delicious.

Classic Tortilla Soup with All the Trimmings

Sopa de Tortilla

Like guacamole, tortilla soup has a place, I feel, in practically every collection of Mexican recipes. Especially everyday recipes. It's a filling, flavorful meal that can be made with little effort, but one that sings with an unmistakable Mexican harmony: Earthy dark pasilla chile. The softening crunch of toasty corn tortillas. Soul-satisfying broth. And creamy-rich avocado and cheese.

A note about the pasilla (sometimes called negro) chile: Its unique flavor defines tortilla soup in central Mexico. In Michoacán, in west-central Mexico, it's ancho chile. In your kitchen, it might turn out to be another chile, like New Mexico or even a little smoky chipotle (be forewarned that chipotle will make the broth quite spicy). Though for these everyday recipes I've relied heavily on the easier-to-use powdered dried chiles, finding powdered pasilla can be harder than finding the whole pod I've called for here. Should powdered chile be at your fingertips (be it powdered pasilla, ancho or beyond), replace the pod with about 1 tablespoon, added to the blender when pureeing the onion and garlic.

In Mexico, it's more common to crush toasted chile pods over the finished soup than to add chile to the base. You can follow that lead, or do both, as I do in my restaurants.

Makes about 10 cups, serving 6

1 large dried pasilla (negro) chile, stemmed and seeded

One 15-ounce can diced tomatoes in juice (preferably fire-roasted)

2 tablespoons vegetable or olive oil

1 medium white onion, sliced 1/4 inch thick

3 garlic cloves, peeled

2 quarts chicken broth

1 large sprig fresh *epazote*, if you have one

Salt

4 (about 1 1/4 pounds total) boneless, skinless chicken breast halves, cut into 1/2-inch cubes

1 large ripe avocado, pitted, flesh scooped from the skin and cut into 1/4-inch cubes

1 1/2 cups (6 ounces) shredded Mexican melting cheese (such as Chihuahua, quesadilla or asadero) or Monterey Jack, brick or mild cheddar

A generous 4 cups (about 6 ounces) roughly broken tortilla chips

1 large lime, cut into 6 wedges, for serving

Quickly toast the chile by turning it an inch or two above an open flame for a few seconds, until its aroma fills the kitchen. (Lacking an open flame, toast it in a dry pan over medium heat, pressing it flat for a few seconds, then flipping it over and pressing it again.) Break the chile into pieces and put in a blender jar, along with the tomatoes with their juice. (A food processor will work, but it won't completely puree the chile.)

Heat the oil in a large (4-quart) saucepan over medium-high. Add the onion and garlic and cook, stirring frequently, until golden, about 7 minutes. Scoop up the onion and garlic with a slotted spoon, pressing them against the side of the pan to leave behind as much oil as possible, and transfer to the blender; set the pan aside. Process until smooth.

Return the pan to medium-high heat. When it is quite hot, add the puree and stir nearly constantly until thickened to the consistency of tomato paste, about 6 minutes. Add the broth and *epazote*, if using. Reduce the heat to medium-low and simmer for 15 minutes. Taste and season with salt, usually about a generous teaspoon (depending on the saltiness of the broth).

Just before serving, add the chicken to the simmering broth. Divide the avocado, cheese and tortilla chips among the serving bowls. When the chicken is done, usually about 5 minutes, ladle the soup into the bowls. Pass the lime separately.

Contemporary Riffs on the Tortilla Soup Theme

Goat cheese can replace the melting cheese. Rotisserie or grilled chicken can stand in for the raw chicken breasts (add it at the last second). Ditto for grilled duck breast or confit-style legs. Blue corn tortilla chips are delicious, though perhaps not as pretty.

◎ **VEGETARIAN TORTILLA SOUP:** Use vegetable broth instead of chicken broth and omit the chicken. Or replace the chicken with 1/2-inch cubes of firm tofu (I like to cut 1/2-inch slices and sear them in my grill pan, then cut them into cubes before adding to the soup).

◎ **TORTILLA SOUP WITH GREENS:** Add a couple handfuls of sliced chard leaves (or practically any other green) to the soup along with the chicken. Tougher greens like collards and kale should be added before the chicken; soft ones like spinach or arugula should go in when the chicken is half-done.

Red *Chileatole* with Mushrooms, Chicken and Zucchini

Chileatole Rojo de Pollo

◎✵◎✵◎✵◎✵◎✵◎✵◎✵◎✵◎✵◎✵◎✵◎✵◎✵◎✵◎✵◎✵◎✵◎

This is the savory red chile soup of Veracruz that welcomes everything from tropical root vegetables like yuca and *camote morado* (white sweet potato) to wild lobster mushrooms and the substantial flower blossoms from exotic trees like *colorín*. My everyday version captures the sweet earthiness of red chile (plus the traditional pungency of *epazote*, if you have it) and uses it to envelop easy-to-get mushrooms, chicken and zucchini. If you have a batch of ancho puree on hand, use 2 tablespoons in place of the ancho powder.

Makes 6 cups, serving 4

1 tablespoon vegetable or olive oil

1 small white onion, sliced 1/4 inch thick

2 garlic cloves, peeled

2 tablespoons ground ancho chile powder (available from national companies, such as McCormick, Mexican groceries and internet sites)

1 1/2 tablespoons *masa harina* (Mexican corn "flour" for making tortillas—look for it in well-stocked groceries)

4 cups chicken broth

8 ounces mushrooms (I love shiitakes here), stemmed and sliced 1/2 inch thick (you'll have 3 generous cups)

1 medium zucchini, cut into 1/4-inch cubes

1 large sprig fresh *epazote* (or flat-leaf parsley)

2 (10 to 12 ounces total) boneless, skinless chicken breast halves, cut crosswise into 1/2-inch-thick strips

Salt

In a medium (3-quart) saucepan, heat the oil over medium. Add the onion and garlic and cook, stirring regularly, until golden, about 7 minutes. Scoop up the onion and garlic with a slotted spoon, pressing them against the side of the pan to leave behind as much oil as possible, and transfer to a food processor or blender; set the pan aside. Add the chile powder, *masa harina* and *1 1/2 cups* of the chicken broth. Process to a smooth puree.

Set the saucepan over medium-high heat. When it is quite hot, add the puree. Stir nearly constantly until the mixture comes to a boil and thickens slightly. Add the remaining *2 1/2 cups* stock, the mushrooms, zucchini and *epazote* (or parsley). Simmer 10 minutes.

Add the chicken strips and simmer until the chicken is cooked, about 5 minutes. Taste and season with salt, usually about 1 teaspoon (depending on the saltiness of the broth). Ladle the soup into bowls, and you're ready to serve.

Riffs on the Red *Chileatole* Theme

Once you've got the traditionally flavored base simmering, the rest is up to your imagination and resources. You can easily make this soup vegetarian, replacing the chicken broth with vegetable broth and omitting the chicken. And you can vary the vegetables—and the meat, for that matter. I usually try to combine at least two vegetables with contrasting tastes and textures. Potatoes with green beans (great with chicken), sweet potatoes with shiitake mushrooms (great with pork), chayote with nopal cactus (great with shrimp). When using nopal cactus, I typically cut the cleaned pads into 1/2-inch squares and sauté them in a little oil; they will release their sticky juice into the skillet, but it will evaporate as the nopales cook. When they're dry, they're ready to add to the soup.

Red Chile Seafood Soup

Caldo de Mariscos

◎✠◎✠◎✠◎✠◎✠◎✠◎✠◎✠◎✠◎✠◎✠◎✠◎✠◎✠◎✠◎✠◎✠◎✠◎✠◎

Making seafood soup may sound as if there's a special occasion in the offing, but that no longer has to be true. With the wide availability of fresh seafood, this version of Mexico's beloved, and easily varied, coastal soup—even with its supertraditional robust roasted red chile flavor—is within anyone's reach. Chicken broth provides a rich background, shellfish add that delicious taste of the sea and *epazote* gives a classic Gulf Coast flavor, though it's not essential. (*Epazote* is available in some well-stocked groceries and Mexican markets, and it's very easy to grow in pots or small garden plots.)

Makes about 3 quarts, serving 6

2 tablespoons vegetable or olive oil

3 (3/4 ounce total) dried guajillo chiles, stemmed, seeded and torn into large pieces

One 15-ounce can diced tomatoes in juice (preferably fire-roasted)

1 large white onion, chopped into 1/4-inch pieces

2 garlic cloves, peeled

6 cups chicken or fish broth

4 medium (about 1 pound total) red-skin boiling or Yukon Gold potatoes, each cut into 8 pieces

2 large sprigs fresh *epazote*, if you have them

Salt

1 pound mussels, scrubbed and debearded if necessary
OR 2 pounds clams, scrubbed

1 pound fish fillets (I like halibut, mahimahi or catfish), cut into 1-inch cubes

About 1/2 cup roughly chopped cilantro, for garnish

1 lime, cut into 6 wedges, for serving

Heat the oil in a medium (5- to 6-quart) soup pot over medium. Add the chiles and stir-fry until they have changed color slightly and are toasty-fragrant, 30 seconds to a

RED CHILE SEAFOOD SOUP

minute. (Don't overtoast the chiles, or the soup will be bitter.) Scoop up the chile pieces with a slotted spoon, pressing them against the side of the pot to leave behind as much oil as possible, and transfer to a blender jar; set the pan aside. (A food processor will work, but it won't completely puree the chile.) Pour the tomatoes, with their juice, into the blender.

Add *two-thirds* of the onion and all the garlic to the pot. Cook over medium, stirring frequently, until golden, about 7 minutes. Meanwhile, scoop the remaining onion into a strainer and rinse under cold water; set aside to use as a garnish. Use your slotted spoon to transfer the onions and garlic to the blender, and process until smooth.

Set a medium-mesh strainer over the pot and work the tomato-chile mixture through it. Return the pot to medium-high heat and cook, stirring frequently, until reduced and thick, about 6 minutes. Add the broth, potatoes and *epazote* (if you have it). When the mixture comes to a boil, reduce the heat to medium-low and simmer until the potatoes are tender, usually about 15 minutes. Taste and season with salt, usually a generous 1 1/2 teaspoons.

Just before serving, raise the heat to medium-high and add the mussels or clams and fish. Boil briskly until the bivalves have opened, usually about 4 minutes.

Ladle into large bowls. Sprinkle generously with the cilantro and the remaining onion. Serve your steaming bowls of beauty with the lime wedges passed separately for each person to squeeze in *al gusto*.

Riffs on the Seafood Soup Theme

The fish and shellfish can easily change to include practically any seafood you can lay your hands on. Here are my general guidelines: Mussels or clams add complexity to the soup, so I always try to include them. Shrimp and scallops are good for meaty sweetness. Most medium- or large-flake fish can be used in this dish. (Fish with a fine flake, like sole or small flounder, tend to fall apart in the soup, and strong-flavored fish, such as mackerel, bluefish and salmon, can overwhelm the flavors of the broth.) If you want to use crabmeat, add it just before you serve the soup so it doesn't disintegrate.

The potatoes can be replaced by cubes of chayote (I don't even peel them), 1-inch lengths of green beans, peas or corn (use the same weight). Or replace them with a drained 28-ounce can of hominy to make a dish similar to the *pozole de mariscos* that's popular on Mexico's west coast.

Mushroom-Potato *Crema* with Roasted Poblanos

Crema de Hongos y Papas con Chile Poblano

◎✱◎✱◎✱◎✱◎✱◎✱◎✱◎✱◎✱◎✱◎✱◎✱◎✱◎✱◎✱◎✱◎✱◎✱◎✱◎

This soup shows off the natural affinity between earthy mushrooms and earthy potatoes. Too much of a good thing can, sometimes, lead to lost luster, which is why I like the deep-green spice of roasted poblanos in this soup. And the aromatic flecks of cilantro. And, of course, the sweet bits of corn. If I want to gild this beautiful lily, I'll cook a small handful of chopped bacon until crisp and add it to the soup just before serving.

Makes a generous 6 cups, serving 4

4 medium (about 1 pound total) red-skin boiling or Yukon Gold potatoes, cut into roughly 1-inch pieces

3 garlic cloves, peeled and halved

6 cups chicken or vegetable broth

1 large fresh poblano chile

8 ounces mushrooms (I like shiitake or oyster mushrooms), sliced 1/4 inch thick (you'll have about 3 cups slices)

1 scant cup corn kernels (they can be frozen or ones you've cut off 1 to 2 large ears)

1 large sprig fresh *epazote* (you can substitute a big sprig of fresh thyme, or leave the herb out all together)

1/4 cup plain yogurt, heavy cream or sour cream

Salt

About 1/4 cup roughly chopped cilantro, for garnish

Scoop the potatoes and garlic into a medium (3-quart) saucepan, pour in *half* of the broth and set over high heat. When the liquid boils, reduce the heat to medium and simmer briskly until the potatoes are tender, about 15 minutes.

While the potatoes are cooking, roast the poblano over an open flame or 4 inches below a broiler, turning regularly until blistered and blackened all over, about 5 minutes for an open flame, about 10 minutes for a broiler. Cover with a kitchen towel. Let cool until handleable.

Rub the blackened skin off the chile and pull out the stem and seed pod. Rinse the chile to remove bits of skin and seeds. Cut into 1/4-inch pieces.

When the potatoes are tender, use an immersion blender to puree the soup base (or blend in several batches in a food processor or a *loosely covered* blender draped with a kitchen towel and return to the pan). Add the remaining *half* of the broth, the mushrooms, poblano, corn and *epazote* (or thyme, if using). Simmer for 10 minutes over medium heat.

Just before serving, scoop about 1/2 cup of the hot soup into a small bowl. Mix in the yogurt, cream or sour cream. Stir the mixture back into the pot, then taste and season with salt, usually about 1 1/2 teaspoons. Ladle the soup into bowls and sprinkle with the cilantro. Soup's on.

Riffs on the Potato-Mushroom Soup Theme

Though my version of this soup is vegetarian when made with the vegetable broth, it doesn't have to be. Ham, ham hocks, bacon and chorizo are all wonderful in the soup—start with about 4 ounces. As is crab. The corn can be easily replaced by other vegetables that offer a contrast in taste and texture: small fresh fava beans (my favorite), peas, 1-inch lengths of green beans. Use about the same volume measure. And I love the soup made with half potatoes and half parsnips or young turnips, or rutabaga.

◎ **FOR THE ADVENTURER:** Use bacon drippings to sauté a heaping cup of cubed cleaned nopal cactus pieces until all their liquid has evaporated; add them, with bacon, just before serving.

4

Quick Meals from the Grill: Seasonings, Salsas and Skills

The aromatic goodness of food cooked over a flame or coals is one of a small handful of universally embraced flavors. Each country has a way to distinguish its grilled foods, however—rubs, marinades, condiments, grilling methods. In this chapter, I'm going to outline for you Mexico's grill-side manner, starting with a few very useful dry rubs and marinades that focus on chiles and spices. The next layer is classic salsas (with plenty of ideas for freewheeling variations to suit your mood or resources). Then I put it all together with get-started notes on marinating, grilling and serving ten of my favorite foods, all in the Mexican style, of course.

Though most of my grilling is a mix-and-match improvisation of seasonings, condiments and grills, I am including five Mexican classics from the grill to give you a full picture of how Mexican cooks have evolved their grilling style. There's a southern Mexican grilled steak with smoky salsa and sweet plantains, a grilled chicken with the traditional Yucatecan *escabeche* spices, a central Mexican pork *adobado* with red guajillo chile salsa, a Sinaloa-style roadside whole chicken with grilled green onions and the Caribbean-Mexican *achiote*-grilled fish *tikin xik* with roasted tomato salsa. Though not a complete list of Mexico's celebrated grilled dishes, they offer a broad range of flavors and styles to spark your own improvisations.

Though I'm a self-admitted grill geek—I think I was at seven unique,

can't-do-without-'em grills last I had the courage to count—I tested
these recipes on a good gas grill with three burners and on a kettle-
style charcoal grill. Every grill cooks slightly differently, so feel your
way through a recipe, thinking about the rich color or degree of doneness you're looking for rather than temperature knob adjustments or
the timing I've given. I can cook a good meal on practically any grill
(though the less sophisticated ones require a lot more monitoring and
moving of the food) if it has a decent grill grate. Thin little chrome-
plated grill grates make grilling more difficult; sturdy (preferably cast-
iron) grill grates make the job much easier.

RUBS AND MARINADES

Garlicky Ancho Chile Rub

Adobo Seco de Chile Ancho

◎❊◎❊◎❊◎❊◎❊◎❊◎❊◎❊◎❊◎❊◎❊◎❊◎❊◎❊◎❊◎❊◎

This easy dry rub—similar to what's used on ribs in the American Southwest—is more robust (and less tangy) than the classic spreadable ancho chile Adobo Marinade on page 140. It shows its best profile on grilled red meats, but a light sprinkling is welcome on practically anything. If you have a small food processor (or washable "spice" grinder), chop the garlic in it, then add the remaining ingredients and pulse until combined.

Makes 1 cup

4 cloves garlic, peeled and finely chopped or crushed through a garlic press

1/3 cup ground ancho chile powder (available from national companies such as McCormick, Mexican groceries and internet sites)

4 teaspoons brown sugar

1 teaspoon dried oregano, preferably Mexican

1/2 teaspoon ground cumin

4 teaspoons ground black pepper

Salt

In a bowl, stir together the garlic, ancho powder, brown sugar, oregano, cumin, pepper and 5 teaspoons salt until thoroughly blended. Scoop into a container, cover and store in the refrigerator for up to a month or more.

Smoky Chipotle Rub

Adobo Seco de Chile Chipotle

The flavors of this dry rub are similar to those of the Garlicky Ancho Chile Rub (page 137), with one exception: the sweet smokiness from the chipotle powder makes it perfect for anything made with pork or with roasted root vegetables (potatoes, carrots, sweet potatoes).

Makes 1 1/2 cups

4 garlic cloves, peeled and finely chopped or crushed through a garlic press

1/2 cup mild paprika (one of the smoked paprikas would be more than welcome)

1 1/2 tablespoons ground chipotle chile powder (available from national companies such as McCormick, Mexican groceries and internet sites)

1 tablespoon sugar

2 teaspoons ground black pepper

Salt

In a bowl, stir together the garlic, paprika, chipotle powder, sugar, pepper and 2 1/2 tablespoons salt until thoroughly blended. Scoop into a container, cover and store in the refrigerator for up to a month or more.

Garlic-Lime Marinade

Adobo de Ajo con Limón

◎✤◎✤◎✤◎✤◎✤◎✤◎✤◎✤◎✤◎✤◎✤◎✤◎✤◎✤◎✤◎✤◎✤◎

A lot of Mexican grilled beef gets seasoned with little more than a squeeze of lime and a generous sprinkling of salt. That approach can produce thoroughly delicious results, especially if you're tasting the beef in a salsa-splashed steak taco late in the evening while standing within earshot of a sizzling street stall somewhere along Mexico's coast. This version translates those street-vendor flavors into an easy-to-use, bright (but wonderfully balanced) marinade that is good on virtually everything from beef to fish. A final tip: if you're using this marinade on fish, adding a little grated orange zest (the colored rind only) is really good.

Makes 3/4 cup

6 garlic cloves, unpeeled

1 fresh serrano chile

1/4 cup vegetable or olive oil

Salt

1/2 cup fresh lime juice

Heat a small skillet over medium. Roast the unpeeled garlic and chile in the dry skillet, turning occasionally, until both are blackened in spots and soft, about 10 minutes for the chile, about 15 minutes for the garlic. Cool, then pull the stem off the chile and the papery skin from the garlic.

Place the chile and garlic in a blender or food processor, add the oil and a scant teaspoon salt and process. With the machine running, dribble in the lime juice. Store in a sealed container in the refrigerator for up to a week or so.

Adobo Marinade

Adobo de Chile Ancho

◎❊◎❊◎❊◎❊◎❊◎❊◎❊◎❊◎❊◎❊◎❊◎❊◎❊◎❊◎❊◎❊◎

This simple version of the punchy, rich red chile seasoning is as much at home on a meaty steak as on a piece of fish; and adobo-marinated chicken is a Mexican benchmark of flavor. Modern cooks have slathered adobo on sweet potatoes, heirloom potatoes and mushrooms just before roasting or grilling. If you have access to ancho chile pods, plus a few extra minutes preparation time, you can create an even more harmonious flavor by replacing the 1/3 cup ancho powder with 1/3 cup ancho puree (see page 141); decrease the water to 1/3 cup and increase the salt to a generous teaspoon. When using the puree, there is no need for the final 10-minute simmering.

Like most marinades, this will keep for a long time, and though it contains "preserving" ingredients like vinegar, salt, red chile, garlic and sugar, it will stay fresh longest if you store it in the refrigerator.

Makes about 3/4 cup

1 tablespoon vegetable or olive oil

4 garlic cloves, peeled and finely chopped or crushed through a garlic press

1/3 cup ground ancho chile powder (available from national companies such as McCormick, Mexican groceries and internet sites)

2 tablespoons vinegar (apple cider vinegar is common in Mexico)

1 teaspoon dried oregano, preferably Mexican

1/2 teaspoon sugar

Salt

In a small saucepan, heat the oil over medium. Add the garlic and stir until fragrant but not browned, about 1 minute, then add the ancho powder, vinegar, oregano, sugar, 3/4 teaspoon salt and 3/4 cup water, whisking to combine thoroughly. Simmer over medium-low heat for about 10 minutes to blend the flavors and eliminate the raw ancho taste. Allow to cool to room temperature, then scrape into a jar and cover. Refrigerate for up to a month or more.

ANCHO PUREE WITH WHOLE CHILES

Makes 3 cups

Stem and seed 8 (about 4 ounces) dried ancho chiles. Toast them a few pieces at a time on a dry skillet over medium, pressing them flat against the hot surface for about 10 seconds with a metal spatula until they are aromatic and have lightened in color a little on the inside; flip and toast the other side. Place the chiles in a bowl, cover with hot water, weight with a plate to keep them submerged and let soak for 30 minutes.

Drain the chiles, discarding the water. Transfer to a blender or food processor and add 2 cups water. Process to a smooth puree. (If the mixture won't go through the blender blades, add a little more water.) Scrape into a jar and secure the lid. Store in the refrigerator for up to 3 months.

Yucatecan Garlic-Spice Marinade

Adobo de Escabeche

◎✤◎✤◎✤◎✤◎✤◎✤◎✤◎✤◎✤◎✤◎✤◎✤◎✤◎✤◎✤◎✤◎✤◎✤◎

This exotic mix of flavors, reminiscent of those from North Africa, shows up in two forms in Mexico's Yucatecan markets: a dry packet of spices that cooks elaborate on with vinegar, garlic and, often, oil; and a seasoning paste (there called a *recado*) that cooks dilute with more vinegar (or lime) and sometimes oil. Either way, the mixture has the alluring aroma of cinnamon and cloves, the spicy pungency of black pepper and the mellowness of fragrant roasted garlic. This has become an iconic seasoning for Yucatecan chicken, fish and thin-cut steaks, but I have another suggestion: it's an outstanding salad dressing for tomatoes, grilled green beans or steamed chayote that can be made by mixing a couple of tablespoons of the marinade with an additional 2 tablespoons vinegar and an additional 1/3 to 1/2 cup oil.

Makes about 1/2 cup

1 head garlic, broken into individual
   cloves (expect about 12 cloves)

1/3 cup vegetable or olive oil

6 tablespoons vinegar (apple cider
   vinegar is common in Mexico)

A pinch of ground cloves

1/2 teaspoon ground black pepper

1/2 teaspoon ground cinnamon, preferably Mexican *canela*

1 teaspoon dried oregano, preferably
   Mexican

1/2 teaspoon sugar

Salt

Cut a slit in the side of each garlic clove. Place them in a microwaveable bowl, cover with plastic and microwave on high (100%) for 30 seconds. Cool until handleable, then slip off the papery husks.

One by one, drop the garlic cloves into a running blender or food processor, letting each get thoroughly chopped before adding the next. Stop the machine, remove the top and add the oil, vinegar, spices, herb, sugar and 1/2 teaspoon salt. Re-cover and process until the mixture is as smooth as you can get it. Scrape into a small jar, cover and refrigerate for up to a month or more.

CLASSIC SALSAS

Chunky Fresh Tomato Salsa

Salsa Mexicana

◎✠◎✠◎✠◎✠◎✠◎✠◎✠◎✠◎✠◎✠◎✠◎✠◎✠◎✠◎✠◎✠◎✠◎✠◎

If you're comfortable and efficient with a knife, the flavors of Mexico's quintessential, eponymous salsa (often called *pico de gallo* on our side of the border) can be on your table at a moment's notice. But not everyone is a knife wizard, so I devised this version, which uses the food processor for the garlic, green chile, cilantro and half the tomatoes—meaning that a very good fresh tomato salsa is within everyone's easy reach. Green onions are the easiest to cut (they are the only onion my daughter likes to chop), but feel free to use white or red onion if that's what's available or appealing. At our restaurants, we only make this salsa when ripe local tomatoes are in season.

Makes 2 cups

1 garlic clove, peeled

Fresh hot green chiles to taste (I like 2 serranos or 1 jalapeño), stemmed and halved

2 medium-large (about 1 pound total) ripe round tomatoes

1/3 cup (loosely packed) roughly chopped cilantro

1 large green onion, roots and wilted outer leaves removed, chopped into small pieces

1 tablespoon fresh lime juice (or light-flavored vinegar)

Salt

Drop the garlic and chile pieces one at a time into a running food processor, letting each get finely chopped before adding the next. Turn off the processor and remove the lid. Cut 1 tomato in quarters and add it to the food processor, along with the cilantro. Pulse 4 to 6 times, until you have a coarse puree. Scrape the mixture into a bowl.

Cut the other tomato into 1/4-inch pieces and add to the bowl, along with the green onion. Taste and season with lime juice (or vinegar) and salt, usually a generous 1/2 teaspoon. This salsa is best if eaten within an hour or two, but it will keep for a number of hours in the refrigerator.

Riffs on *Salsa Mexicana*

Chopped raw tomatillos can replace some of the chopped tomato. The cilantro can be replaced or augmented by pungent herbs like Mexican *pipicha*, *pápalo* or *hoja santa*, or saw-tooth cilantro (aka *raurau* in Asian markets). Any of the lemony or anisey herbs, from lemon verbena to lemon balm to anise hyssop, give the salsa a special character. I love the addition of avocado, cucumber and jícama—but not necessarily all at once. The same goes for crisp apple or pear or ripe mango, peach or nectarine.

◎ **ONE OF MY FAVORITE SHRIMP DISHES:** For four people, heat a wok (or a very large skillet) over medium-high. Drizzle in a little olive oil, then add 1 1/4 to 1 1/2 pounds peeled, deveined shrimp. Stir-fry until half-cooked, about 2 minutes, then douse with the salsa. Stir-fry for another couple of minutes, until the shrimp are just cooked through. Sprinkle on a little extra lime juice and chopped cilantro.

◎ *BISTEC A LA MEXICANA*: Make the salsa without the lime juice. For four people, heat a wok (or a very large skillet) over medium-high. Drizzle in a little olive oil, then, in 2 batches, stir-fry 1 1/4 to 1 1/2 pounds thin-cut beef (buy *bistec* at a Mexican grocery or 1/8-inch-thick sandwich steaks—salt before cooking). Remove to a plate when lightly browned, leaving behind as much oil as possible. Stir-fry the salsa until reduced—this can take up to 10 minutes. Add about 1/2 cup water or beef broth, return the browned meat to the pan and bring to a boil. Serve, passing quartered limes and extra chopped green chile and cilantro, if you wish.

Rustic Roasted Tomato Salsa

Salsa de Molcajete

Okay, I'll admit that I've used the word *molcajete* rather loosely here, since a *molcajete* is the long-surviving volcanic-rock mortar that's still used in a Mexican kitchen to grind the ingredients for this kind of salsa. No, using a food processor doesn't turn out *exactly* the same salsa in less time. But it can get pretty close, especially if you take time to roast the garlic and chiles and use fire-roasted canned tomatoes. A tip: most tomatoes need the jazzy lift of lime juice or vinegar, so plan on using it.

Makes about 2 cups

2 fresh jalapeño chiles (or 4 serranos, 1 or 2 habaneros or practically any fresh chiles)

3 garlic cloves, unpeeled

1/2 cup finely chopped white onion

One 15-ounce can diced tomatoes in juice (preferably fire-roasted)

1/3 cup (loosely packed) roughly chopped cilantro

A teaspoon or so of fresh lime juice or cider vinegar (optional)

Salt

Set a small skillet over medium heat. Lay the chiles and garlic in the skillet and dry-roast until soft and blotchy black in spots, about 10 minutes for the chiles, about 15 minutes for the garlic.

While the chiles and garlic are roasting, scoop the chopped onion into a strainer and rinse under cold water. Shake off the excess water and pour into a medium bowl.

Pull the stems off the roasted chiles and peel the papery skins off the garlic. Scoop them into a food processor and pulse until they are finely chopped. Add the tomatoes, with their juice, re-cover and pulse a few more times, until the mixture is as coarse or smooth as you want your salsa to be.

Pour the tomato mixture into the bowl with the onion. Add the cilantro and stir

Rustic Roasted Tomato Salsa

thoroughly. Thin with a little water if necessary to give the salsa an easily spoonable consistency. Taste and season with the lime juice or vinegar, if using, and salt, usually about 1/2 teaspoon. If not using within an hour or two, cover and refrigerate.

Note: If you're not planning to use the salsa within a few hours, wait until you're ready to serve to add the onions and cilantro.

Using Fresh Tomatoes

When time and resources (meaning vine-ripe local tomatoes) are on my side, I make this salsa with fresh tomatoes: I roast 1 1/2 pounds (3 medium-large) tomatoes (I especially like the high-acid, flavor-packed heirlooms like Zapotec Pleated or Costoluto Genovese; seeds for both are available from Seeds of Change) close up under a hot broiler until blistered and blackened in spots, then flip them over and roast the other side. Peel off the skin, chop them and use them in the salsa.

Riffs on Roasted Tomato Salsa

A variety of herbs besides cilantro can be worked in here, but basil, fresh oregano and the like make the salsa taste Italian—not necessarily a bad thing, just not what I'm usually after. Beans haven't been a common addition to salsa in Mexico (that started on our side of the border), but I've seen it there several times recently; you can, of course, go all the way to the Southwestern classic: corn and bean salsa, which usually has more than a little vinegar added. Fruit salsas are also not common in Mexico (though showing up some now), but are classic to the U.S. Southwest (usually made with peaches and, again, more than a little vinegar). If I add fruit to this salsa, it's usually mango (roasting the peeled and diced mango on a nonstick baking sheet in a 400-degree oven for a few minutes until brown makes it even more delicious); lime juice and finely grated zest (colored part of the rind only) add delicious punch. Cranberries (raw or cooked), apples, pears and jícama also make good additions.

◎ **SALSA CHICKEN:** The easiest main dish in this book: Brown 4 chicken breasts or 8 thighs (boneless, skinless are okay, but not as tasty) on one side in a little oil in a large (10-inch) skillet over medium-high heat. Flip them over, add the salsa, cover and simmer over medium-low until cooked through. Great with rice and a salad.

Smoky Chipotle Salsa with Pan-Roasted Tomatillos

Salsa de Chipotle con Tomate Verde Asado

◎❀◎❀◎❀◎❀◎❀◎❀◎❀◎❀◎❀◎❀◎❀◎❀◎❀◎❀◎❀◎❀◎❀◎

I've been smitten with chipotle salsa ever since the first time I tasted it on a crusty sandwich (*cemita*) in a Pueblan market stall thirty years ago. It's three simple ingredients in perfect balance: the smoky spice of chipotle chiles, the lively sweet-edged tang of roasted tomatillo and the alluring complexity of roasted garlic. I like chipotle salsa spooned on practically everything except ice cream, though I'm particularly fond of it with grilled fish or chicken or beef or . . . here I go again.

Makes about 1 1/4 cups

3 garlic cloves, peeled

4 medium (about 8 ounces total) tomatillos, husked, rinsed and cut in half

2 canned chipotle chiles *en adobo* (or more, if you like really spicy salsa)

Salt

Set a large (10-inch) nonstick skillet over medium-high heat (if you don't have a non-stick skillet, lay in a piece of foil). Lay in the garlic and tomatillos (cut side down). When the tomatillos are well browned, 3 or 4 minutes, turn everything over and brown the other side. (The tomatillos should be completely soft.)

Scoop the garlic and tomatillos into a blender jar or food processor, along with the chiles and 1/4 cup water. Process to a coarse puree. Pour into a salsa dish and cool.

SMOKY CHIPOTLE SALSA WITH PAN-ROASTED TOMATILLOS

Thin with a little additional water if necessary to give the salsa an easily spoonable consistency. Taste and season with salt, usually a generous 1/2 teaspoon.

Riffs on Chipotle Salsa

You can replace the tomatillos with roasted tomatoes (two 4-ounce plum tomatoes, roasted like the tomatillos, or half a drained 15-ounce can of fire-roasted tomatoes), but keep in mind that the tomato will tip the flavor toward sweet rather than tangy. A little cilantro, fresh thyme or parsley is always welcome, as is green or white onion—especially if it's grilled. A splash of mescal (or the less-smoky tequila) makes a *borracha* (drunken) salsa that's dynamite. Instead of pureeing the chiles, you can finely chop them and add them to the pureed (green) base; they'll show up as little red flecks, and the salsa will be less smoky.

◎ **EASY CHIPOTLE SAUTÉ:** In a very large (12-inch) skillet, sauté 1 sliced white onion with 1 to 1 1/4 pounds cubed boneless skinless chicken breast, pork tenderloin, steak, shrimp or firm tofu until well browned. Add the salsa and stir-fry until everything is done as you like; dribble in a little water if the sauce is too thick for you. This is really good sprinkled with chopped cilantro.

Fresh Tomatillo Salsa

Salsa Cruda de Tomate Verde

This is my default salsa when time is of the essence: toss everything in the blender, turn it on and enjoy the fresh-fresh tang of tomatillo salsa. But serve it within an hour or so—after that, the flavors start to fade. If you want to add a little white onion, as many cooks in Mexico do, chop it separately, run it under cold water to minimize its pungency and stir it into the blended salsa. The salsa is reminiscent of one of those relishy mint chutneys frequently found in Indian restaurants.

If raw garlic isn't your thing, poke a hole in the side of 2 cloves of unpeeled garlic and microwave them for 30 seconds. Peel and add to the blender or processor. They'll add a mellower, sweeter flavor.

Makes 1 1/2 cups

4 medium (about 8 ounces total) tomatillos, husked, rinsed and quartered

1 large garlic clove, peeled and quartered

Hot green chiles to taste (I like 2 serranos or 1 jalapeño), stemmed and roughly chopped

1/2 to 2/3 cup (loosely packed) roughly chopped cilantro

Salt

Combine the tomatillos, garlic, chiles and cilantro in a blender jar or food processor. Add 1/4 cup water and a generous 1/2 teaspoon salt. Process to a coarse puree; if using a blender, begin blending on low, at first pulsing to get the mixture moving evenly through the blender blades. Pour into a salsa dish and thin with a little more water if necessary to give the salsa an easily spoonable consistency. Taste and season with additional salt if you think necessary. Serve within an hour.

Riffs on Fresh Tomatillo Salsa

Replace or augment the cilantro with: (1) lemony herbs like lemon balm, lemon verbena or a little finely sliced kaffir lime leaf; (2) finely grated citrus zest (colored part of the rind only) from kaffir or key limes or from lemons (Meyer lemon zest is particularly good); or (3) unexpected herbs like basil, flat-leaf parsley, fennel fronds (the green feathery "leaves"), mint or *hoja santa*.

◎ **SPICY CILANTRO SCRAMBLED EGGS:** In a very large (12-inch) skillet, heat 3 tablespoons oil over medium-high. When hot, add the salsa and stir until reduced and thick, about 4 minutes. Add 8 eggs (beaten to mix the yolks and whites) and stir slowly, scraping all the way across the bottom of the pan, until the scrambled eggs are as done as you like. Top with more chopped cilantro and serve right away.

Roasted Tomatillo Salsa

Salsa de Tomate Verde Asado

◎✹◎✹◎✹◎✹◎✹◎✹◎✹◎✹◎✹◎✹◎✹◎✹◎✹◎✹◎✹◎✹◎✹◎✹◎

I f all-raw tomatillo salsa is all light-fresh-immediate, roasted tomatillo salsa is richer and more settled, balancing freshness with the sweet caramel of pan-roasting. I love the way it perks up grilled steak tacos or makes a black bean tostada a dish to dream about. And a soft tortilla full of chorizo sausage and browned potatoes plays incredibly well with roasted tomatillo salsa. You can make the base of this salsa in advance—as much as several days. But I'd advise you to add the cilantro (finely chop it) and onion when you're ready to serve.

Makes 1 1/2 cups

4 medium (about 8 ounces total) tomatillos, husked, rinsed and halved

2 large garlic cloves, peeled

Hot green chiles to taste (I like 2 serranos or 1 jalapeño), stemmed and roughly chopped

About 1/3 cup (loosely packed) roughly chopped cilantro

1/2 small white onion, finely chopped

Salt

Set a large (10-inch) nonstick skillet over medium-high heat (if you don't have a nonstick skillet, lay in a piece of foil). Lay in the garlic and tomatillos, cut side down. When the tomatillos are well browned, 3 or 4 minutes, turn everything over and brown the other side. (The tomatillos should be completely soft.)

Scrape the tomatillos and garlic into a blender or food processor and let cool to room temperature, about 3 minutes. Add the chiles, cilantro and 1/4 cup water. Blend to a coarse puree. Pour into a salsa dish and thin with a little additional water if necessary to give the salsa an easily spoonable consistency.

Scoop the chopped onion into a strainer and rinse under cold water. Stir into the salsa. Taste and season with salt, usually about 1/2 teaspoon.

Riffs on Roasted Tomatillo Salsa

Though it's common and easy to use small hot green chiles in this salsa, one of my favorite versions includes a whole roasted/peeled/seeded poblano chile, coarsely pureed with the other ingredients. It may sound like heresy to Mexican cooks, but a dash of Worcestershire, balsamic vinegar or coarse-grain mustard is good in this salsa. If I'm serving the salsa with something off the grill, I'll slow-grill a large green onion or two (or just a slice of white onion), chop it and add it in place of the raw onion. To underscore the tomatillo's natural citrusy tang, I sometimes add a little fresh lime juice. (For more citrus, and herb, ideas, see the Riffs on Fresh Tomatillo Salsa, page 153.) Or go full-bore fruity and stir in finely chopped pineapple, apple or pear.

◎ **PASTA WITH ROASTED TOMATILLOS AND CHICKEN OR SALMON:** Put on a pot of water to boil, then make the salsa, without letting the ingredients cool. Boil 12 ounces pasta (fusilli or shells are good choices) in salted water until al dente. Drain, reserving 1/4 cup of the cooking liquid. Return the pasta to the pot, and add the salsa, the reserved cooking liquid and 2 cups coarsely shredded cooked chicken or salmon—I usually buy rotisserie chicken or pepper-coated hot-smoked salmon that's easy to flake. Sprinkle on a generous cup grated Mexican *queso añejo* or Parmesan, toss and serve with chopped cilantro, extra cheese and a few wedges of lime for each hungry eater to add to his or her liking. Wonderful at room temperature for a picnic.

Toasty Arbol or Guajillo Chile Salsa

Salsa Roja de Chile de Arbol o Guajillo Asado

◎✸◎✸◎✸◎✸◎✸◎✸◎✸◎✸◎✸◎✸◎✸◎✸◎✸◎✸◎✸◎✸◎✸◎✸◎

With the first bite of this salsa, you know you're not in Kansas anymore. The vivid red of American bottled salsa has been transformed here into an earthy rusty red. The typical American sweetness gets jazzed with tomatillo brightness. And our thick and chunky, perfect for chips, gives way to light and nearly smooth. This is a classic, spicy Mexican salsa that's meant for drizzling over tacos, tostadas, eggs and anything from the grill. When made from árbol chiles, the salsa is very spicy.

Makes 1 cup

2 tablespoons vegetable oil

16 (1/4 ounce total) dried árbol chiles, stemmed, or 2 (1/2 ounce total) dried guajillo chiles, stemmed

3 garlic cloves, peeled

4 medium (about 8 ounces total) tomatillos, husked, rinsed and cut in half

Salt

Measure the oil into a large (10-inch) skillet and set over medium heat. Roll the árbol chiles between your fingers to loosen the seeds, then break them in half and shake out as many seeds as will come out easily. Or, if using guajillos, tear them open and sweep out the seeds with your fingers. Lay the chiles in the hot oil. Turn constantly until they're aromatic and have changed color slightly, about 30 seconds. With a slotted spoon, scoop the chiles into a blender jar, leaving behind as much oil as possible.

With a paper towel, wipe out the oil from the skillet (no need to wash it). Set the skillet over medium-high heat and lay in the garlic and tomatillos (cut side down). When the tomatillos are well browned, 3 or 4 minutes, turn everything over and brown the other side. Scoop into the blender jar and add 1/2 cup water. Blend until nearly smooth. Pour into a salsa dish and cool.

Thin with a little additional water if necessary to give the salsa an easily spoonable consistency. Taste and season with salt, usually about 1/2 teaspoon.

Riffs on *Salsa Roja*

Though I love the rich flavor that oil-toasting gives the chiles, dry pan-toasting (the chiles, garlic and tomatillos) is a common variation. Practically any small dried chile can be (and has been) used to make this salsa: the little round nutty-tasting cascabels; smoky dried chipotles, moritas or moras; the very hot pequíns or tepíns; regional chiles like the onzas, catarinas, costeños—the list could go on for pages.

◎ **SPICY BAKED CHICKEN WITH MANGO:** For even cooking, I usually choose either 8 thighs or 4 breast halves, with bones and skin intact for best flavor and texture. Lay the chicken skin side up in a single layer in a baking pan. Pour the sauce over the chicken, then scatter a peeled, diced large mango (or 3 diced pitted peaches or nectarines) over the sauce. Bake at 400 degrees until just cooked through, about 20 to 30 minutes for breasts, 30 to 40 minutes for thighs. Remove the chicken to a serving platter. Spoon the fat from the sauce. Add 1 tablespoon honey to the sauce and stir, mashing the fruit into the sauce. Spoon it over the chicken and serve.

Roasted Fresh Chile Salsa

Salsa de Chile Fresco Asado

◎✕◎✕◎✕◎✕◎✕◎✕◎✕◎✕◎✕◎✕◎✕◎✕◎✕◎✕◎✕◎✕◎✕◎✕◎

You can think of this salsa as a not-too-smooth fresh green version of your typical bottled rusty-orange hot sauce—fresh chiles replace dried ones, fresh lime juice replaces vinegar. The sweet roasted fresh chiles add richness, plus a power-house of heat should you choose a chile like cayenne or habanero. The not-too-hot jalapeño is a good chile to start with, as you're getting to know this approach to salsa; its natural, juicy sweetness makes a salsa that's well rounded and utterly delicious—a favorite of market-stall cooks in Guadalajara. In its pure simplicity (no additions, no riffs), this salsa is one of my favorites too.

Makes 1/2 cup

4 ounces fresh hot green chiles (about 4 medium jalapeños, 16 medium serra-nos, 2 medium-hot banana/Hungarian wax or 12 medium green or yellow-orange habaneros—really *any* small hot chile)

4 garlic cloves, peeled

2 tablespoons fresh lime juice

Salt

Turn on the broiler and adjust the rack to its highest level. Break the stems off the chiles, cut them in half lengthwise and lay them, cut side down, on a small baking sheet. Scatter the garlic cloves among the chiles.

Slide under the broiler and roast until the chiles are soft and blotchy black in places, about a minute or two. Scrape the chiles and garlic into a blender or food processor and add the lime juice and 1/4 cup water. Process until nearly smooth.

Pour into a small bowl or salsa dish and thin with a little additional water if necessary to give the salsa an easily spoonable consistency. Taste (cautiously) and season with salt, usually about 1/2 teaspoon. Cover and refrigerate (for up to 5 days) if not using right away.

◎ **SPICY STEAK AND POTATOES:** For two lovers of green-chile spiciness, cut 2 medium-large (10 to 12 ounces total) red-skin boiling or Yukon Gold potatoes into quarters and scoop into a microwaveable bowl. Sprinkle with 1/2 teaspoon salt, cover and microwave on high (100%) until tender, about 4 minutes.

Prepare your charcoal or gas grill—you want the fire medium-hot. Mix 2 tablespoons oil with half of the salsa (best made with jalapeños for this preparation) and smear over your favorite steak—I like 10 to 12 ounces of rib-eye. Toss the potatoes with a little oil. Lay the steak and potatoes on the grill (I put the potatoes in a grill basket) and cook until done as you like, turning from time to time.

Guacamole Three Ways: Simple, Herby or Luxurious

Guacamole Tres Estilos

◎❀◎❀◎❀◎❀◎❀◎❀◎❀◎❀◎❀◎❀◎❀◎❀◎❀◎❀◎❀◎❀◎❀◎

I gave up looking for "the one best guacamole" years ago, because "the best" is only *the best* for a particular moment, a particular set of ingredients, a particular group of people and the role it plays in their eating or snacking. That's why I've written this recipe in stages. I want you to have an easy-to-follow guide for making the perfect guacamole for a multitude of uses, a variety of occasions. So I start with the simplest perfect mash of avocado, garlic and salt (I know many cooks in Mexico who think that adding anything but those two ingredients to avocados is the first step on the road to ruin). This guacamole is a delicious condiment to spread on sandwiches or grilled meat tacos that are served with salsa. Adding cilantro and lime to the basic guacamole gives it the pizzazz to stand alone, as a topping for crispy tacos or tostadas, or even as a dip. Green chile, white onion and red tomato—do I need to point out that those are the colors of Mexico's flag?—create a chest-thumping, look-at-me guacamole that's perfect with a bowl of chips at a party where the music's turned up and there are lots of laughs.

Makes 1 1/4 to 1 1/2 cups

2 medium ripe avocados

1 garlic clove, peeled and finely chopped
  or crushed through a garlic press

Salt

To make it herby, add:

2 tablespoons chopped cilantro

About 1 tablespoon fresh lime juice

To make it luxurious, also add:

Fresh hot green chile to taste (I like 1
  serrano or 1/2 to 1 jalapeño), finely
  chopped

1/4 small white onion, finely chopped

1/2 medium tomato, chopped into
  1/4-inch dice

Cutting an avocado in half for guacamole

Removing the pit from an avocado for guacamole

Scraping avocado flesh from skin for guacamole

Cut the avocados in half, running your knife around the pit from stem to blossom end and back up again. Twist the halves in opposite directions to free the pit, and pull the halves apart. Dislodge the pit, then scoop the avocado flesh into a medium bowl.

Mash the avocado with a large fork or potato masher. Stir in the garlic and about 1/2 teaspoon salt, plus any other sets of ingredients you've chosen. If your list includes white onion, rinse it first under cold water, then shake well to rid it of excess moisture before adding to the avocado. (This reduces the risk of having the onion flavor overwhelm the guacamole.) Taste and season with additional salt if appropriate. If not using immediately, cover with plastic wrap pressed directly on the surface of the guacamole and refrigerate—preferably for no more than a few hours.

A Riff on "Stage Two" Guacamole

Replace the lime juice with (or, for extra-tangy guacamole, add along with the lime juice) about 1/2 cup homemade (page 152) or bottled tomatillo salsa—perfect as a topping or a dip, especially when you need to make the guacamole ahead (the additional acid from the tomatillos helps keep the guacamole greener for longer).

◎ **AVOCADO SAUCE:** For a tangy sauce to drizzle over raw (or blanched) vegetables or on tacos, tostadas and the like, follow the above variation, increasing the tomatillo salsa to 1 cup; puree everything in a blender. If the sauce is too thick to drizzle, thin with additional tomatillo salsa. A little heavy cream, sour cream or crème fraîche can be added for wonderful richness.

◎ **MY TWENTY-FIFTH WEDDING ANNIVERSARY BREAKFAST:** I resurrected this forgotten recipe that I had created the year Deann and I got married. Shred 2 medium-large (10 to 12 ounces total) red-skin boiling or Yukon Gold potatoes; squeeze out excess moisture between your hands. Heat a very large (12-inch) skillet over medium and lightly coat with oil. Form 4 small potato pancakes, sprinkle with salt and press flat with a spatula. When browned on one side, flip and brown the other side. Smear with the simplest guacamole, top each with a poached egg and sprinkle with salt, black pepper and chopped cilantro.

THE GRILLER'S SKILLS:
TIPS FOR QUICK-GRILLING TEN GREAT FOODS

◎◎◎◎◎◎◎◎◎◎◎◎◎◎◎◎◎◎◎◎◎◎◎

Skirt or Flank Steak

These are two deliciously beefy-tasting cuts, flank being the leanest (and driest if cooked past medium). Outside skirt is smaller, thicker and more tender than inside skirt. Inner skirt is often butterflied by Mexican butchers for grilling or griddling to well done and chopping into little bits for street-stall–style soft tacos. Outer skirt is more worthy of the name "steak."

GRILL SETUP: *Direct grilling on a gas grill*—All burners on medium-high. *Direct grilling on a charcoal grill*—Medium-high fire about 6 inches below the grill grate.

GREAT FLAVOR COMBOS: For skirt steak, Yucatecan Garlic-Spice Marinade (page 142) with Guacamole (page 160); for flank steak, Adobo Marinade (page 140) with Toasty Guajillo Chile Salsa (page 156).

GRILLING SKILLS: Both of these very beefy-tasting cuts like to be cooked quickly directly over the coals to a medium doneness—too rare, and they will be chewy; too well done, and they can be tough and dry (especially flank steak). Letting the flank steak rest for several minutes after grilling promotes juiciness. Both must be sliced across the grain, or they will be stringy. For skirt steak, that means cutting the meat into 3- or 5-inch sections, then cutting each section across the grain into strips. For flank, working across its width, slice the meat into long thin strips; angling your cut (what chefs call a "bias cut") will give you the widest, nicest-looking strips. If you've seen street vendors cook skirt steak well-done in Mexico, you may have noticed also that they chop it into small pieces before making it into tacos (this mitigates the resulting toughness).

◎◎◎◎◎◎◎◎◎◎◎◎◎◎◎◎◎◎◎◎◎◎◎

Rib-eye, New York Strip or Chuck Steak

Rib-eye is my favorite steak: beefy-tasting and juicy. New York strip is leaner and a touch lighter in flavor. Chuck steak has wonderful flavor and is the least expensive by far, but it can be a little chewy. I didn't list sirloin because I'm not a fan—too fine-grained for me, too lean (meaning it can go dry with a moment's overcooking), too light in beef flavor.

GRILL SETUP: *Direct grilling on a gas grill*—All burners on medium-high. *Direct grilling on a charcoal grill*—Medium-high fire about 6 inches below the grill grate.

GREAT FLAVOR COMBOS: Ancho or Chipotle Rub (page 137 or 138) with Smoky Chipotle Salsa (page 149).

GRILLING SKILLS: These cuts cook well directly over the heat unless they are very thick or you're angling toward well-done—then you'll want to turn off half of the burners or bank the coals to one side, giving yourself a cooler spot for more extended cooking, or the exterior will burn before the meat is as done as you like. Like skirt and flank, chuck steak is most tender and tasty cooked to medium. All steaks benefit greatly from a 5-minute rest in a low oven before being served.

◎◎◎◎◎◎◎◎◎◎◎◎◎◎◎◎◎◎◎◎◎◎◎

Pork Loin, Tenderloin or Chops

Pork has been bred leaner and leaner in the United States, translating into a healthier meat, no doubt, but one with little character. When you add to that the worry about the safety of anything but ultra-well-done pork, there's no wonder pork holds little interest for the majority of us. *However, . . . if you taste naturally raised pork from a heritage breed, slow-cooked to just the right doneness, you'll be smitten. Pork might just become your favorite meat in the world.*

GRILL SETUP: *Direct and indirect grilling on a gas grill—Half of the burners on medium. Direct and indirect grilling on a charcoal grill—Medium fire about 6 inches below the grill grate, with the coals banked to one side.*

GREAT FLAVOR COMBOS: Adobo Marinade (page 140) with Toasty Guajillo Chile Salsa (page 156), made with orange juice rather than water.

GRILLING SKILLS: It's all about "mark and move": Sear the pork directly over the fire to brown it ("mark it," as chefs say), then move it away from the coals to coast slowly to about 150 degrees (check it with an instant-read thermometer). For the juiciest pork, let it rest in a low oven for 5 to 10 minutes before serving.

Boneless, Skinless Chicken Breasts

I know that these are the favorites of the "I want to eat healthy" clan, but they can be so boring—unless you give them a wonderful marinade and grill them with a sure hand.

GRILL SETUP: *Direct and indirect grilling on a gas grill—Half of the burners on medium-high. Direct and indirect grilling on a charcoal grill—Medium-high fire, with the coals banked to one side.*

GREAT FLAVOR COMBOS: Yucatecan Garlic-Spice Marinade (page 142) with Roasted Fresh Chile Salsa (page 158) and simple Guacamole (page 160).

GRILLING SKILLS: Though you can grill chicken breasts to doneness directly over the heat, I think they come out a little juicier when seared hot and finished slow. Sear the chicken breasts over medium-high heat until tantalizingly browned (I like the flavor dark grill marks add), then turn them and brown the other side. Move the grill-seared breasts away from the coals and let them cook slowly until they are as firm as the muscle under your thumb when you clench your fist somewhat tightly.

Chicken, Whole or Cut-Up

Chicken cooked with the skin and bone is the juiciest and most flavorful, especially if it's allowed to cook slowly.

GRILL SETUP: *Indirect grilling on a gas grill—Half of the burners on medium. If you have a grill with three burners, heat the outer two to*

medium; leave the center one off. *Indirect grilling on a charcoal grill—Medium fire, with half of the coals banked to one side and the rest banked to the other side.*

GREAT FLAVOR COMBOS: Smoky Chipotle Rub (page 138) with Roasted Tomatillo Salsa (page 154).

GRILLING SKILLS: Whole or cut-up chicken wants longer, slower cooking than boneless, skinless breasts. Lay the chicken on the cooler part of the grill, skin side up, and let it cook. That's it: no moving, no fuss. I check doneness by pressing firmly on a thigh to ensure that the meat is done enough to come easily free of the bone (you can also cut into the thigh to make certain that the juices run clear).

Lamb Chops or Racks

This tender, full-flavored cut is a favorite among those who, like me, love searching out new dimensions of taste. It's rich and satisfying, only hinting at the fullness of wild game if cooked well-done.

GRILL SETUP: *Direct and indirect grilling on a gas grill—Half of the burners on medium-high. Direct and indirect grilling on a charcoal grill—Medium-high fire about 6 inches below the grill grate; if cooking racks, bank the coals* to one side (there is no need to bank the coals for chops).

GREAT FLAVOR COMBOS: For chops, Yucatecan Garlic-Spice Marinade (page 142) with Fresh Tomatillo Salsa (page 152) or Roasted Fresh Chile Salsa (page 158). For racks, Adobo Marinade (page 140) with Smoky Chipotle Salsa (page 149).

GRILLING SKILLS: As with beef steaks, lamb chops have the best texture and liveliest flavor, in my opinion, when cooked directly (and briefly) over rather high heat until they're no more than medium. Treat lamb racks as you would thick pork chops: "Mark and move," meaning that you sear them directly over the heat until richly browned on both sides, then move them to a cooler spot to slowly come to a juicy doneness.

◎◎◎◎◎◎◎◎◎◎◎◎◎◎◎◎◎◎◎◎◎

Boneless, Skinless Duck Breasts

Think of duck breasts as the lamb of the poultry world, though less rich and finer-grained. Their full flavor is most attractive, I feel, when the meat is between medium and medium-rare. If you cook it more, slightly gamey flavors emerge, overwhelming the natural sweetness. If you cook it less, the meat is tough. If your duck breast still has its thick skin intact, simply pull it

off as you would chicken breast skin, using a paring knife to help free it where two breast halves are joined (or occasionally at the edges).

GRILL SETUP: *Direct and indirect grilling on a gas grill—* Half of the burners on medium. *Direct and indirect grilling on a charcoal grill—* Medium fire about 6 inches below the grill grate, with the coals banked to one side.

GREAT FLAVOR COMBOS: Adobo Marinade (page 140) and Smoky Chipotle Salsa (page 149) sweetened with a little honey.

GRILLING SKILLS: Grill duck breasts as you would chicken breasts, searing both sides over the hottest part of the grill, then moving them to a cooler spot to coast gently toward your perfect juicy doneness.

◎◎◎◎◎◎◎◎◎◎◎◎◎◎◎◎◎◎◎◎◎

Salmon, Halibut, Striped Bass or Catfish

While there are many other great large-flake fish to grill (snapper, mahimahi, cobia, grouper, cod), wild-caught salmon, halibut and striped bass are the most well-managed fisheries, ecologically speaking; and most of the catfish in our markets is farm-raised using sustainable practices.

GRILL SETUP: *Direct and indirect grilling on a gas grill—Half*

of the burners on medium-high. *Direct and indirect grilling on a charcoal grill—* Medium-high fire 6 inches below the grill grate, with the coals banked to one side.

GREAT FLAVOR COMBOS: Garlic-Lime Marinade (page 139) with Fresh or Roasted Tomatillo Salsa (page 152 or 154).

GRILLING SKILLS: Though fish can be grilled entirely over direct heat, it's delicate and can overcook quickly. I suggest that you lay the fish over direct heat and leave it until the grill marks are a rich brown and the fish is well over half-cooked—that's when it will have released from the grill grates and be easiest to turn. Flip it over onto the cooler side of the grill and let it coast slowly to perfect doneness. For these fish, that'll be when the fish flakes under *firm* pressure—if it flakes easily under gentle pressure, the fish is well-done; if only the outer layer flakes under firm pressure, the fish is medium-rare to rare inside, which many of us like, especially with salmon.

◎◎◎◎◎◎◎◎◎◎◎◎◎◎◎◎◎◎◎◎◎

Tuna and Swordfish Steaks

I grill tuna and swordfish steaks a little less done than other fish; because of their leanness (especially tuna's), fully cooked tuna and swordfish can taste dry. Just as important as the cooking technique should be your source: North Atlantic and Pacific swordfish are considered the least overfished populations, as are big-eye and albacore tuna (especially those caught by hand lines and trolling in Hawaiian waters); these offer not only the best-tasting delicacies, but also the ecologically healthiest.

GRILL SETUP: *Direct grilling on a gas grill*—All burners on medium-high. *Direct grilling on a charcoal grill*—Medium-high fire about 6 inches below the grill grate.

GREAT FLAVOR COMBOS: Adobo Marinade (page 140) with Smoky Chipotle Salsa (page 149), with a generous addition of chopped cilantro.

GRILLING SKILLS: Because these fish are firmer than those listed above and are typically enjoyed less well done, I cook them start-to-finish over direct heat. Under firm pressure, only the outer layer should flake. If you're worried about a cool center, let the fish warm to room temperature before grilling.

◉◉◉◉◉◉◉◉◉◉◉◉◉◉◉◉◉◉◉◉◉◉◉◉

Shrimp

With good reason, shrimp are among the world's favorite foods. There are wild and farm-raised varieties, the former typically having the best taste and texture (especially if you're eating them fresh from the water). I'm wild about shrimp, but I'm aware of how questionable they can be from an ecological perspective: shrimping can be destructive to natural habitats; shrimp farms have caused destruction of some coastal environments. So I eat shrimp in moderation and keep abreast of new shrimping and shrimp farming techniques.

GRILL SETUP: *Direct grilling on a gas grill*—All burners on medium. *Direct grilling on a charcoal grill*—Medium fire about 6 inches below the grill grate.

GREAT FLAVOR COMBOS: Garlic-Lime Marinade (page 139) with Chunky Fresh Tomato Salsa (page 144). Feel free to sear the salsa in a hot pan just before serving for another delicious approach.

GRILLING SKILLS: Grilling shrimp is a snap . . . except that there are lots of pieces, which can get caught (or fall through) the grill grates. Solve the problem by skewering 6 to 8 together or cooking them on a perforated grill pan. If you devein the shrimp (cut a 1/4-inch-deep incision down the back and pull out the, usually dark, intestinal tract), you'll also be able to see when the shrimp is cooked to juicy deliciousness—at the deepest part of the incision, the meat will just be turning from translucent to milky white.

JUDGING TEMPERATURE, JUDGING DONENESS

Without a doubt, the most difficult aspects of cooking to translate into words are the temperatures of a burner or grill (oven temperatures can be quite accurately set) and the doneness of meat, poultry and fish. All cookbook authors struggle to devise ways for describing just the right way to get their readers to the very best dish. Yet even those striving for the greatest precision can't really achieve it: the editors at the ultra-exact *Cook's Illustrated* magazine tell us that a medium-hot charcoal fire is one that you can hold your hand 5 inches above for only 3 to 4 seconds before you need to withdraw it, which never works for me—my hands (or my pain threshold) seem to be quite different from theirs.

So rather than pretend that you can get Rembrandt results following my paint-by-number directions, I'll just admit that there is a lot of craft to cooking, craft that can only be honed through repeated practice. Which isn't to say that I'm leaving you to fend for yourself by telling you to cook whatever's on the heat until it's done as you like. No, I'm offering a host of clues that I think will get you to a great result: cooking temperatures, appearances, approximate times and internal temperatures for thick cuts. But I'm offering those clues with the understanding that you'll put them to the test, experimenting to find out if your understanding of medium-high heat is the same as mine, if you like skirt steak done to medium (and how long that typically takes on your grill), or just what richly browned onions look like and whether or not you like that flavor. As I tell novice cooks in my restaurant: it's not until you've felt a hundred charcoal fires and seen how the chicken breast or pork loin responds to each of them—

and, more important, how you like the results—that you'll have developed the craftsman-cook's understanding of how to adjust time to temperature to create the perfect result you're striving for.

There *is* one more thing I can offer: a few words to describe what a steak or a chicken breast or a fish fillet feels like when done to different stages. To tell the truth, professional chefs rely on touch more than time and temperature to judge the doneness of most foods. Do this exercise: With your hand relaxed, open and facing you, press gently on the fleshy muscle that extends from the base of your thumb toward your wrist. That's what rare meat feels like. Now make a clenched fist, squeezing as hard as you can. Press on the muscle again: that's what well-done meat feels like. As you unclench your fist, you'll feel that muscle move from the feel of well-done to

medium-well to medium to medium-rare.

Of course, that muscle is only going to give a general approximation of degrees-of-doneness, especially since everyone's hand, like each cut of meat, is going to be slightly different. A rich rib-eye will feel softer at medium-rare than a lean chicken or duck breast. And the feel of cooking fish is a different matter altogether. But at least this exercise can start you down the road to feeling your way to doneness.

For many of us, it's mastering this craft of cooking that is exhilarating—occasionally challenging, hopefully never discouraging. It's certainly what keeps me eager to approach the stove after so many years of professional dedication.

A STICKY SUBJECT

Marinated or not, everything I grill gets a spray (or light brushing) of oil before it's laid on the grill. And with the exception of whole chicken, everything first goes over the hottest spot on the grill and is left, undisturbed, until the grill grates have seared in

their browned goodness— and, if all is going right, released the food from their grasp. Though grill-sticking can sometimes be caused by marinades, the usual culprit is grill grates that are not hot enough. Always work with a fire that's at least medium-hot

and with preheated grill grates, and don't try to move the food until the grill marks are a rich brown. The heavier the grill grates, the better— well-seasoned cast iron is my favorite.

GRILLING SPRINGBOARDS: CLASSIC TO CONTEMPORARY

Grilled Red-Chile Steak with Sweet Plantains, Red Onion and Chipotle Salsa

Carne Asada con Plátano Macho y Salsa de Chipotle

◎✿◎✿◎✿◎✿◎✿◎✿◎✿◎✿◎✿◎✿◎✿◎✿◎✿◎✿◎✿◎✿◎

Though most grilled steaks in Mexico get little more than a generous dusting of salt—maybe a little lime or garlic, too—my favorites are the steaks that combine the richness of ground ancho with the grill's seductive smokiness. Some may think that steak is too special for a weeknight dinner, but that doesn't have to be true if you grill a single beautifully seasoned steak, then carve off modest portions of thin slices that you "shingle" out for a nice (and generous) look. It's a technique almost every chef uses. Another chef's pointer: letting the grilled meat rest for 5 to 10 minutes on a cool part of the grill or in a low oven will give you the juiciest steak; the rest affords time for the meat juices to reabsorb, avoiding run-out on your cutting board.

Serves 4

For the Garlicky Ancho Chile Rub

4 cloves garlic, peeled and finely chopped or crushed through a garlic press

1/3 cup ground ancho chile powder (available from national companies such as McCormick, Mexican groceries and internet sites)

4 teaspoons brown sugar

1 teaspoon dried oregano, preferably Mexican

1/2 teaspoon ground cumin

4 teaspoons ground black pepper

Salt

◎✿◎

A 1 1/4-pound flank steak (or an equivalent weight of strip steak, rib-eye, chuck steak or whatever else may be your favorite)

2 black-ripe plantains

Vegetable oil

1 medium red onion, sliced into 1/4-inch-thick rounds

About 1 cup Smoky Chipotle Salsa (page 149), for serving

Heat one side of a gas grill to medium-high. Or light a charcoal fire and let it burn until the charcoal is covered with white ash but is still *quite* hot; bank the coals to one side.

Mix together the garlic, ancho powder, sugar, oregano, cumin, pepper and 5 teaspoons salt until thoroughly blended. Spread a heavy coating over the steak(s)—you'll need 1 to 2 tablespoons for a 1 1/4-pound flank steak. (Cover and refrigerate leftover rub for another steak.)

Cut the ends off both plantains, then split them lengthwise in half. Lightly oil both the cut surfaces of the plantain and the onion slices. Lay the plantain (cut side down) and the onion on the hot part of the grill and cook until well browned, 2 to 3 minutes; turn and brown the other side. Move the plantains and onion to the cooler part of the grill while you cook the steak(s).

Lay the steak(s) on the grill directly over the fire—I typically spray lean flank steak lightly with oil before grilling. When richly colored underneath (about 3 to 4 minutes), flip and cook on the other side until nearly as done as you like, about 2 or 3 minutes more for medium-rare steak. Move onto the cooler part of the grill and let coast to perfect doneness over the next several minutes.

Move the plantains, onions and steak to a cutting board. Slip the plantains from their skins, chop into 1/4-inch pieces and scoop into a bowl. Chop the onions to match and add to the plantains. Stir 3 tablespoons of the salsa into the plantain mixture. Taste and season with salt. Divide among four plates. Slice the steak and lay overlapping slices next to the plantain. Serve with the salsa.

Riffs on My *Carne Asada*

The ancho chile rub I've used here has a nice pungency; for something mellower, use the Adobo Marinade on page 140. The plantains are a wonderful touch, though they could be left out—something you might be forced to do if your grocery doesn't have ripe plantains. (Plantains can take a week or more to ripen from green, hard and starchy to blackened, soft and sweet.) Replace them with grilled potato or sweet potato wedges—lightly oiled and salted (even coated with a bit of the marinade), they will take 20 to 25 minutes to cook over medium to medium-high heat. Or replace the plantains with a scoop of Fried Beans (page 84). If time doesn't allow for making your own salsa, buy a good bottled chipotle salsa.

GRILLED CHICKEN BREASTS (OR THIGHS) WITH TANGY YUCATECAN SPICES,
SEASONAL VEGETABLES AND ROASTED FRESH CHILE SALSA

Grilled Chicken Breasts (or Thighs) with Tangy Yucatecan Spices, Seasonal Vegetables and Roasted Fresh Chile Salsa

Escabeche de Pollo Asado con Verduras de Temporada y Salsa de Chile Verde Asado

The attractively exotic blend of spices that Yucatecan cooks combine with vinegar's sparkle and roasted garlic's sweet savor is one of the human race's most satisfying creations. But there's another lesson here: the chicken's bones and skin impart wonderful flavor and texture. Sure, you can make your *escabeche* with boneless, skinless chicken breasts (or even thighs, for that matter), but there'll be a sacrifice. If that's your plan, though, reduce the cooking time by about half. In Mexico's Yucatán, the fresh chile in the salsa would be the floral-scented, tropical tasting, near-nuclear habanero.

Serves 4

For the Yucatecan Garlic-Spice Marinade

1 head garlic, broken into individual
  cloves (expect about 12 cloves)

1/3 cup vegetable or olive oil

6 tablespoons vinegar (apple cider
  vinegar is common in Mexico)

A pinch of ground cloves

1/2 teaspoon ground black pepper

1/2 teaspoon ground cinnamon, preferably Mexican *canela*

1 teaspoon dried oregano, preferably
  Mexican

1/2 teaspoon sugar

Salt

◎⌘◎

4 chicken breast halves or 8 thighs
  (about 2 pounds total), skin and bones
  intact

1 cup chicken broth

2 medium ripe tomatoes (**summer**),
  cored and sliced 1/4 inch thick
  OR 2 medium-large zucchini or other
  tender squash (**fall**), sliced 1/4 inch
  thick
  OR 4 medium red-skin boiling or Yukon
  Gold potatoes or 2 medium beets (**winter**), peeled and sliced 1/4 inch thick
  OR 1 pound asparagus (**spring**), thick
  lower stems trimmed and peeled (or
  cut off)

About 1/2 cup Roasted Fresh Chile Salsa
  (page 158), for serving

Cut a slit in the side of each garlic clove. Place them in a microwaveable bowl, cover
with plastic wrap and microwave on high (100%) for 30 seconds. Cool until handleable, then slip off the papery husks. One by one, drop the garlic cloves into a running
blender or food processor, letting each get thoroughly chopped before adding the
next. Stop the machine, remove the lid and add the remaining marinade ingredients
along with 1/2 teaspoon salt and process until smooth.

Scrape half of the marinade into a medium bowl. Add the chicken and stir (or toss
with your hands) to coat evenly. Scrape the remaining marinade into a small
saucepan. Add the broth and about 1/4 teaspoon salt (depending on the saltiness
of the broth). Set aside.

Heat one side of a gas grill to medium. Or light a charcoal fire and let it burn until
the charcoal is covered with white ash and about medium-hot; bank the coals to
one side.

Lay the chicken pieces skin side down on the grill over the medium-hot fire. When
richly browned, usually 5 or 6 minutes, use a pair of tongs to flip them over onto the

cooler side of the grill. Cook until completely tender at the bone (the juices will run clear when a fork pierces the thickest part)—expect about 10 minutes longer, maybe more if the breasts are large.

While the chicken is cooking, prepare the vegetables: In **summer**, arrange the sliced tomatoes slightly overlapping on four dinner plates and sprinkle with salt. In **fall**, scoop the sliced zucchini into a microwaveable bowl and toss with a good sprinkling of salt. Cover with plastic wrap, poke a couple of holes in the top and microwave until crisp-tender, about 3 minutes on high (100%). In **winter**, scoop the sliced potatoes or beets into a microwaveable bowl and toss with a good sprinkling of salt. Sprinkle with about a tablespoon of water, cover with plastic wrap, poke a couple of holes in the top and microwave until tender, about 6 minutes on high (100%). Pour off the water. In **spring**, scoop the asparagus into a microwaveable bowl and sprinkle with about a tablespoon of water. Cover with plastic wrap, poke a couple of holes in the top and microwave until crisp-tender, about 4 minutes on high (100%), then pour off all the water and toss with a good sprinkling of salt. Arrange a portion of the fall, winter or spring vegetables as a bed on each of four dinner plates.

Bring the broth mixture to a boil; taste and season with salt if necessary. Top the vegetables on each plate with a portion of chicken. Douse with a quarter of the broth mixture and carry to the table. Pass around the salsa for all who want to spice things up.

Riffs on Chicken *en Escabeche*

If there's no time to make the salsa, set out a bottle of green chile hot sauce, such as El Yucateco Habanero Salsa, Frontera Habanero Hot Sauce or Tabasco's Jalapeño Hot Sauce. If there's extra time, make some simple pickled red onions: slice a red onion, sprinkle it with salt, squeeze on some lime juice and let stand for at least half an hour. Don't hesitate to replace the chicken with fish (fillets or steaks) such as snapper or bass for another traditional dish.

GRILLED FISH IN TANGY YUCATECAN *ACHIOTE* WITH GREEN BEANS AND ROASTED TOMATO SALSA

Grilled Fish in Tangy Yucatecan *Achiote* with Green Beans and Roasted Tomato Salsa

Tikin Xik—Pescado Asado al Achiote con Ejotes y Salsa de Molcajete

◎✖◎✖◎✖◎✖◎✖◎✖◎✖◎✖◎✖◎✖◎✖◎✖◎✖◎✖◎✖◎✖◎✖◎✖◎

A*chiote* tinges Yucatán's most classic food with its uniquely earthy aroma and rusty-red color. It's not a spicy spice, or even a particularly pungent one, but a flavor that tastes as though it's been unchanged since pre-Columbian times. Since it's made from a very hard seed that requires long soaking or a powerful stone mill to soften into a paste, I use preground *achiote* for everyday cooking. All the *achiote* pastes I've seen in the United States are imported from Yucatán, which means that they're elaborated with garlic, spices and something tangy (usually vinegar).

The salsa that adorns *achiote*-seasoned food in Yucatán, called *chiltomate*, is infused with a faint hint of habanero chile but otherwise it has simple flavors—often simpler than the more central Mexican–flavored roasted tomato salsa I've called for in this recipe. I've added the grilled green beans (one of my favorite ways to prepare green beans), but fried black beans are always welcome.

Serves 4

For the Achiote *Marinade*

One 3 1/2-ounce package *achiote* paste (I've had good luck with El Yucateco brand, available from Mexican groceries or internet sites)

1/3 cup fresh lime juice

◎⌘◎

Four 5- or 6-ounce fish fillets or steaks (try ultrafresh full-flavored fish like bluefish, kingfish or mackerel or more readily available sturdy fish such as striped bass, halibut, mahimahi, tuna or salmon)

8 ounces (about 3 loosely packed cups) green beans, tops and tails broken off

A little vegetable or olive oil

Salt

1 or 2 limes, cut into wedges, for serving

About 1 cup Rustic Roasted Tomato Salsa (page 146), for serving

Heat one side of a gas grill to medium-high. Or light a charcoal fire and let it burn until the charcoal is covered with white ash but still *quite* hot; bank the coals to one side.

While the grill is heating, remove the *achiote* from its plastic bag and break it up into a food processor. Add the lime juice. Process until smooth.

Place the fish in a baking dish and drizzle with about 2 tablespoons of the marinade. Smear evenly over the fish with the back of a spoon, then flip and smear on another portion of marinade. (Cover and refrigerate the remaining marinade for another meal.)

Scoop the green beans into a microwaveable bowl and add a tablespoon of water. Cover with plastic wrap, poke a couple of holes in the top and microwave on high (100%) until crisp-tender, about 3 minutes. Uncover and drain off all the liquid. Drizzle lightly with oil, sprinkle with salt and toss to coat evenly.

When the grill is hot, brush or spray the top of each fish fillet with oil. Lay oil side down on the hottest part of the grill. Cook (without attempting to move or lift the fish from the grill grate) until well browned underneath, usually 3 to 4 minutes. Oil the now-top side, then use a spatula to flip the fillets over onto the slightly cooler part of the grill. Lay the green beans on the hottest part of the grill (to avoid major loss, make sure the beans are lined up across the grates or, easier, put them in a mesh or perforated grill basket). Use tongs to turn them over and over until hot and lightly browned, about 3 minutes.

When the fish gives slightly under the firm pressure of a finger, transfer each fillet or steak to a dinner plate. Top with the grilled green beans and serve. Pass the lime wedges and salsa separately for each hungry soul to drizzle on to his or her liking.

Riffs on *Achiote* Fish

Though I've given you many fish suggestions, I have to say that this dish is delicious made with boneless, skinless chicken breasts or pork tenderloin (cooking time will be longer for both, so don't have your fire too high). Skewered shrimp—marinated, grilled and laid on a bed of fried black beans, the salsa spooned over and around— makes for very good eating. The green beans can easily be replaced with asparagus, chayote spears or fennel wedges (microwave-blanch and grill them like the green beans—fennel takes longer than the others). The salsa can be replaced with the Yucatan's always-incendiary Roasted Fresh Chile Salsa made with habaneros (page 158) and thin-sliced red onion that has been lightly pickled with fresh lime juice and salt. Or, when time is of the essence, choose bottled salsa for a quick option.

GRILLED ROADSIDE WHOLE CHICKEN WITH KNOB ONIONS

Grilled Roadside Whole Chicken with Knob Onions

Pollo a las Brasas con Cebollitas

◎✿◎✿◎✿◎✿◎✿◎✿◎✿◎✿◎✿◎✿◎✿◎✿◎✿◎✿◎✿◎✿◎✿◎✿◎✿◎

Though folks in the north and west of Mexico think the most flavorful, most succulent, most compellingly seasoned roadside chicken comes from Sinaloa (confimed by the vast number of roadside stalls in other states advertising "Sinaloa" birds), truthfully, there is really great charcoaled chicken to be tasted all through Mexico. I think of the standard Sinaloa-style marinade as similar in flavor to chorizo sausage—ground dried red chile, vinegar, a host of spices. Straightforward Mexican. So is this cooking method of slow-grilling a split bird (for reasons I can't explain, most Mexican cooks split their chickens down the breast rather than the back—the back is more manageable for me). Slow-grilling in Mexico is done directly over a bed of hardwood charcoal that's quite a distance from the chicken; we can achieve a similar result by heating only part of a gas grill or by banking live coals to the sides. A good number of Mexican chicken grillers are rotisserie jockeys, so if you're an aficionado of the rotisserie attachment for your grill, you're in good company.

Serves 4

For the Marinade

1 1/2 tablespoons ground ancho chile powder (available from national companies such as McCormick, Mexican groceries and internet sites)

1 teaspoon dried oregano, preferably Mexican

A big pinch of ground cloves

1/4 teaspoon ground cinnamon, preferably Mexican *canela*

2 garlic cloves, peeled and finely chopped or crushed through a garlic press

3 tablespoons vinegar (apple cider vinegar gives a Mexican flavor)

1/4 cup orange juice

1 teaspoon salt, plus a little more for the onions

◎✿◎

1 large (3-pound) chicken (what some butchers call a large frying chicken, others call a small roasting chicken)

2 large bunches green onions, preferably the type with large (1-inch) white bulbs (these "knob" onions are available at Mexican markets and many farmers' markets), roots and wilted outer leaves removed

A little vegetable or olive oil for brushing the onions

About 1 cup Roasted Tomatillo Salsa (page 154), for serving

In a small bowl, mix together all the marinade ingredients.

Heat one side of a gas grill to medium. If you have a grill with three burners, heat the outer two to medium, leaving the center one off. Or light a charcoal fire and let it burn until the charcoal is covered with white ash and about medium-hot; bank half the coals to one side of the grill, half to the other.

While the grill is heating, remove the giblets (if there are any) from the cavity of the chicken. Flip the chicken onto its breast. Using poultry shears, cut down both sides of the backbone from tail to neck; discard backbone. Or, if you don't have shears, lay the bird on its back, insert a long heavy knife into the body cavity and press down hard with a rocking motion to cut down through both sides of the back-

Cutting chicken for
Grilled Roadside Chicken

bone. Open the bird out onto your work surface, breast side up. Make sure that the legs are turned inward. Using your fist or a mallet, wallop the bird on the breast, hard enough to dislodge the center bones and flatten out the breast. Twist the last joint of the wings up over the breast and then down behind the "shoulders," tucking them in firmly to keep them in place during grilling.

Flattening chicken for
Grilled Roadside Chicken

Smear both sides of the chicken with the marinade. Lay in the center of the grill (it will not be over direct heat). Cook, without turning, basting from time to time with any remaining marinade, until the juices run clear when a thigh is pierced deeply with a fork (an instant-read thermometer should register about 160 degrees when inserted at the thickest part of the thigh), about 45 minutes. If you're cooking over charcoal, you'll want to add more charcoal to the fire after half an hour or so—the internal temperature of the grill should stay at about 325 degrees.

About 10 minutes before the chicken is ready, brush or spray the green onions with oil and sprinkle with salt. Grill directly over the fire, turning frequently, until tender and browned.

Remove the chicken to a cutting board. It will lose less juice if you cover it loosely with foil and let it rest for 5 to 10 minutes.

Cut the chicken into quarters (or smaller pieces). Transfer a portion to each of four dinner plates. Top with the grilled onions, and you're ready to serve. Pass the salsa separately.

A Couple of Riffs

I love to grill zucchini and eggplant (thickly sliced, brushed with oil and sprinkled with salt) alongside or in place of the onions; a squeeze of lime juice and a sprinkling of chopped cilantro make them taste very Mexican. If cutting up a chicken isn't your thing, grill marinated chicken pieces. Using the Adobo Marinade (page 140) rather than the one called for here will give the bird a southern Mexican flavor.

GRILLED PORK ADOBADO WITH SMOKY ROASTED
SWEET POTATOES AND GUAJILLO SALSA

Grilled Pork Adobado with Smoky Roasted Sweet Potatoes and Guajillo Salsa

Puerco Adobado a la Parilla con Camote y Salsa de Chile Guajillo

◎✠◎✠◎✠◎✠◎✠◎✠◎✠◎✠◎✠◎✠◎✠◎✠◎✠◎✠◎✠◎✠◎✠◎✠◎✠◎

The complex tang of red chile adobo is classic in Oaxaca, where it's smeared on thin-sliced sheets of pork leg (*cecina*) and grilled over hot coals—rustic and thoroughly satisfying. You could call this recipe a dressed-up version of the marketplace standard, since the more tender pork loin replaces the chewier leg; and alongside I've grilled sweet potatoes, rather than the typical knob onions.

Serves 4

For the Adobo Marinade

1 tablespoon vegetable oil, plus a little more for the sweet potatoes

4 garlic cloves, peeled and finely chopped or crushed through a garlic press

1/3 cup ground ancho chile powder (available from national companies such as McCormick, Mexican groceries and internet sites)

2 tablespoons vinegar (apple cider vinegar works well here)

1 teaspoon dried oregano, preferably Mexican

1/2 teaspoon sugar

Salt

◎✠◎

1 to 1 1/4 pounds pork loin

2 medium sweet potatoes, peeled if you wish, each cut into 8 lengthwise wedges

About 1 cup Toasty Guajillo Chile Salsa (page 156), for serving

In a small saucepan, heat the oil over medium. Add the garlic and stir until fragrant but not browned, about 1 minute, then add the remaining marinade ingredients, 3/4 teaspoon salt and 3/4 cup water, whisking to combine thoroughly. Simmer over medium-low heat for about 10 minutes to blend the flavors. Allow to cool to room temperature.

Heat one side of a gas grill to medium. Or light a charcoal fire and let it burn until the charcoal is covered with white ash and about medium-hot; bank the coals to one side.

Scoop about half of the marinade into a small bowl. Brush a light coating of the marinade on all sides of the pork. Lay the pork on the hottest part of the grill. When it is well browned, 4 to 5 minutes, flip it over and brown the other side. Move it to the cooler side of the grill. Cook, basting lightly with the marinade and turning from time to time, until as done as you like (I like it still a little rosy inside—about 145 to 150 degrees on an instant-read thermometer, about 25 to 30 minutes more).

Meanwhile, once you move the pork to the cooler side, scoop the sweet potatoes into a bowl and toss with a little oil and salt. Lay them on the cooler side of the grill, next to the pork. Turn frequently, basting lightly with the marinade, until tender and nicely browned, 20 to 25 minutes.

When the pork and sweet potatoes are done, remove them to a warm platter. The pork will be at its juiciest if you let it rest, covered with foil, for about 10 minutes before slicing.

Slice the pork and lay the slices, slightly overlapping, on four dinner plates. Divide the sweet potatoes among the plates. Serve right away, with the salsa passed separately for everyone to spoon on *al gusto*.

A Couple of Riffs

Wedges of baking potato can easily stand in for the sweet potato, as can chayote. Pork chops and pork tenderloin can replace the pork loin; both cook more quickly. For the absolute best version, replace the powdered ancho chile with 1/3 cup whole ancho puree (page 141), decreasing the water to 1/3 cup and increasing the salt to a generous teaspoon. I've called for guajillo salsa, but a bottled salsa made from other dried red chiles (chipotle, árbol, etc.) could take its place.

5

Soft Tacos, Enchiladas, Tostadas and Tortas

Let's face it: when we say we're in the mood for Mexican, it's usually something involving a tortilla that we're craving. Soft or crispy tacos, tender enchiladas, piled-high tostadas—they're all so uniquely Mexican they've become icons of Mexican cuisine the world over, much as hamburgers and hot dogs, perhaps sadly, have come to represent our cooking. Even if there are more complex or sophisticated dishes to be savored, the elemental deliciousness of this informal, lighter Mexican fare is easy to love. You could say that these dishes are more pop than classical.

When you bite into a steak taco, especially a Chipotle Beef Taco with Caramelized Onions, you experience the same satisfaction as with a mouthful of your favorite hamburger, only spicier, I'd guess. Ditto a Green Chile Chicken Soft Taco, though perhaps more so for the grilled chicken set than those given to hamburgers.

But soft taco fillings aren't limited just to steak and chicken. Chorizo-potato tacos are classic; mine here mixes in sautéed mushrooms for added texture and flavor. All through central Mexico, a chipotle-spiked shredded meat *tinga*, usually made of pork (sometimes chicken or beef) with potatoes and tomatoes, is a homey favorite. And quick meals in practically every family involve spicy scrambled egg tacos—most often with a spoonful of beans and a bowl of salsa to complete the experience. But I love the homiest fillings of all: The tacos of greens like

Swiss chard (braised with onions and garlic), drizzled with red chile salsa. Or the zucchini tacos that come in all the classic flavors, from tomatoes and green chiles to the chorizo-and-mushroom version, with smoky chipotle and optional chorizo sausage, that I've offered here.

Few people—even in Mexico—know of Mexico's salad tacos. I'm a big fan, so I've included recipes in most of my books. Here I offer a simple version of the Yucatecan tacos filled with shrimp *a la vinagreta*, plus a contemporary take on cool shredded chicken tacos with avocado, romaine and chipotle dressing.

In Mexico, enchilada fillings are typically simpler than taco fillings—often it's chicken and fresh cheese, occasionally it's vegetables, sometimes it's nothing at all. That's because enchiladas are all about the sauce. I'm not one to pick favorites, but red chile enchiladas always draw my attention, especially when they're topped with melted cheese, like the ones I grew up on. Roasted tomato sauce, with a drizzle of sour cream and sprinkling of *queso añejo*, and creamy tomatillo sauce tie for second. I've included recipes here for all of them.

And I'm offering you my everyday, all-purpose tostada recipe, because once you understand the basic architecture, you can make a tostada out of practically any leftover in the refrigerator. And the classic submarine-like *torta* is another easily adaptable concept; let me go on record saying, however, that I think the initial spread of black beans and chorizo outlined in my recipe makes everything else you put on the *torta* taste better.

Chorizo, Potato and Mushroom Tacos

Tacos de Chorizo con Papas y Hongos

When I think of quick, savory satisfaction in Mexico, chorizo—like bacon in the States—usually comes to mind. Chorizo and eggs, chorizo and beans, chorizo and potatoes. The simple combinations are classic all over the Mexican Republic because they satisfy in a way that a simple fried egg or bowl of beans or plate of potatoes just won't. Practically every street-side vendor with a griddle offers soft tacos filled with the local chorizo hashed with potatoes (the mixture is also classic in fried quesadillas, even chiles rellenos), but rarely do they contain mushrooms, even in regions known for an abundance of wild mushrooms. It's inexplicable, from my perspective: chorizo and mushrooms are perfect consorts.

Serves 4

12 ounces fresh Mexican chorizo sausage, casing removed (about 1 1/2 cups)

About 1 tablespoon vegetable oil, if needed

1 medium white onion, sliced 1/4 inch thick

6 ounces mushrooms (shiitake or oyster mushrooms are good), stemmed and sliced about 1/2 inch thick (you'll have about 2 cups)

3 medium (12 ounces total) red-skin boiling or Yukon Gold potatoes, grated through your grater's largest holes

Salt

1/2 cup (loosely packed) chopped cilantro

12 warm corn tortillas, store-bought (see reheating instructions on page 214) or homemade (page 212)

About 3/4 cup Roasted Tomatillo Salsa (page 154) or Guacamole (page 160), or bottled salsa or hot sauce, for serving

Lay the chorizo in a very large (12-inch) skillet (preferably nonstick) and set over medium heat. Cook, stirring frequently and breaking up clumps, until some of the fat starts to render and the sausage looks about half-cooked, about 4 minutes.

Increase the heat to medium-high. If the chorizo hasn't rendered any fat, add about 1 tablespoon vegetable oil to the skillet. Add the onion and mushrooms and cook, stirring almost constantly, until they begin to soften, about 3 minutes.

Sprinkle the grated potatoes over the mixture. Cook, continuing to stir frequently, until the potatoes are soft, about 5 minutes. If the potatoes begin browning long before they're soft, reduce the temperature a little. Taste and season with salt if you think the mixture needs it—some chorizo is so highly seasoned little additional salt will be needed.

Scrape the mixture into a deep bowl and sprinkle with the cilantro. Serve with the warm tortillas and salsa, guacamole or hot sauce for making soft tacos.

◎ **A VEGETARIAN VERSION:** Roast, peel, seed and slice 2 large poblano chiles. In a very large skillet, sauté the onion (I'd make it a large onion for this version) and mushrooms in 3 tablespoons olive oil. When the onion and mushrooms begin to soften, add the grated potatoes and cook until tender, then stir in the roasted poblano, and you're done. I like to sprinkle a little Mexican oregano into this mixture. For a deluxe (nonvegetarian) version, use both chorizo *and* roasted poblano.

◎ **A CONTEMPORARY VERSION:** Thinly slice a small fennel bulb and sauté it with the onion and mushrooms—it needs to cook to softness, which may take longer than the onion, so be prepared to cover the skillet for a couple of minutes, trapping steam and speeding the cooking.

Smoky Pork *Tinga* Tacos with Avocado and Fresh Cheese

Tacos de Tinga Poblana con Aguacate y Queso Fresco

Twenty-five years ago, the first time I spent any appreciable time in Puebla, I fell in love with the crusty submarine-like *tortas* filled with spicy, chipotle-smoky shredded pork, local fresh cheese and intensely flavorful avocados. The same crowd-pleasing filling is welcome in soft tacos too, as you might imagine. Or just served on its own, as you would a bowl of chili. The flavor of *tinga* appeals to practically everyone everywhere.

I know this recipe may look long, but I've streamlined it so it's easy. I've marked the chorizo and onion as options because the dish is perfectly delicious without those typical ingredients.

Serves 8

4 medium (1 pound total) red-skin boiling or Yukon Gold potatoes, cut into 1/2-inch cubes

2 pounds boneless pork shoulder, cut into 1-inch pieces

One 28-ounce can diced tomatoes in juice (preferably fire-roasted)

3 to 4 canned chipotle chiles *en adobo*, seeded and sliced 1/4 inch thick

1 tablespoon chipotle canning sauce

1 tablespoon Worcestershire sauce

1 teaspoon dried oregano, preferably Mexican

3 garlic cloves, peeled and finely chopped or crushed through a garlic press

1 medium white onion, sliced 1/4 inch thick (optional)

Salt

4 ounces fresh Mexican chorizo sausage, casing removed (about 1/2 cup) (optional)

24 warm corn tortillas, store-bought (see reheating instructions on page 214) or homemade (page 212)

1 cup crumbled Mexican *queso fresco* or other fresh cheese, such as feta or goat cheese, for serving

2 large avocados, pitted, flesh scooped from the skin and cut into 1/2-inch pieces, for serving

Spread the potatoes over the bottom of a slow-cooker and top with the pork. In a large bowl, mix the (undrained) tomatoes with the chipotles, chipotle canning sauce, Worcestershire, oregano, garlic, optional onion and 1 1/2 teaspoons salt. Pour the mixture evenly over the meat and potatoes. Cover and slow-cook on high for 6 hours (the dish can hold on the slow-cooker's "keep warm" function for 4 more hours or so).

When you are ready to eat, fry the optional chorizo in a medium (8-inch) skillet until thoroughly done, about 4 minutes. Uncover the pork *tinga* and spoon off the fat that has accumulated on top. Sprinkle on the chorizo, then stir everything together, breaking the pork into smaller pieces—right for wrapping in tortillas. (If there is a lot of liquid, tip it off and boil it rapidly until reduced and syrupy, then stir it back into the meat mixture.) Taste and season with additional salt if you think the *tinga* needs it. Serve with the warm tortillas, crumbled fresh cheese and avocados for making soft tacos.

No Slow-Cooker?

Lay the pork in a medium-large (4- to 6-quart; 10- to 12-inch-diameter) heavy pot (preferably a Dutch oven), and top with the potatoes. Cover with the tomato mixture, set the lid in place and braise in a 300-degree oven for 2 to 2 1/2 hours, until the pork is completely tender. Complete the dish as described.

Riffs on *Tinga*

Both chicken and beef *tinga* are common in snack shops (*antojiterías*), market stalls and street stalls all over central and southern Mexico. To vary this recipe, replace the pork with 2 pounds boneless, skinless chicken thighs or an equivalent amount of cubed boneless beef chuck (I'd skip the optional chorizo with the beef). If the dish is still going to be recognizable as *tinga*, the meat and potatoes are about the only ingredients you can vary. It's a little exotic, but cubes of peeled malanga, yuca or Mexican white sweet potato—*camote morado*—are delicious in *tinga*.

Chipotle Beef Tacos with Caramelized Onions

Tacos de Carne Asada Enchipotlada

◎✳◎

C hamois-soft, warm corn tortillas wrapped around slices of seared beef—spicy, smoky, chipotle-smeared seared beef—and caramelized onions: even without the chipotle, it's Mexico's *taquería* crowd pleaser, persistently captivating crowds of tourists and nationals alike (long before the advent of sizzling fajitas). I occasionally find myself disappointed that the whole world doesn't clamor in the same way for a plate of classic *mole poblano* or fish *a la veracruzana*, but then I'm off to look for that next great steak taco. There's just something so charismatic, so agreeable about that first bite.

I like to round out a steak taco meal with some *Frijoles Charros* (page 86) and a salad. For the greatest tenderness, make sure to choose thicker outer skirt steak and cook it to medium. (The thin inner skirt that most *taquerías* and street vendors use is best cooked well-done and chopped into small pieces.) Flank steak is most tender when cooked medium-rare and thinly sliced.

CHIPOTLE BEEF TACOS WITH CARAMELIZED ONIONS

Serves 4

One 7-ounce can chipotle chiles *en adobo*

1 pound skirt or flank steak (skirt steak should be trimmed of fat and white silverskin)

3 tablespoons vegetable or olive oil (divided use)

2 medium white onions, sliced 1/4 inch thick

Salt

12 warm corn tortillas, store-bought (see reheating instructions on page 214) or homemade (page 212)

About 3/4 cup Smoky Chipotle Salsa (page 149), or bottled salsa or hot sauce, for serving

Turn the oven onto its lowest setting. Open the can of chipotles and scrape them into a food processor or blender along with the canning sauce. Process until smooth. Use a brush to smear a light chipotle patina on the steak (go a little heavier on flank than skirt steak). You'll have chipotle marinade left over; cover and refrigerate for up to several weeks.

In a very large (12-inch) skillet, the heavier the better, heat *2 tablespoons* of the oil over medium-high. Add the onions and cook, stirring frequently, until golden but still crunchy, about 4 to 5 minutes. Scoop into a heatproof serving bowl, leaving as much oil as possible in the skillet, and slide into the oven.

Return the skillet to medium-high heat (or a little lower for flank steak). Add the remaining *1 tablespoon* oil. When it is hot, lay in the steak. Brown on both sides, cooking until as done as you like: about 3 minutes per side for medium skirt steak, about 5 minutes per side for medium-rare 1 1/2-inch-thick flank steak. The meat will be juiciest if you let it rest in the oven for 5 to 10 minutes on a wire rack over a plate, but you can cut and serve it right away.

Cut the skirt steak into roughly 3-inch lengths, then cut each piece across the grain into 1/4-inch strips. Or cut the flank steak across the grain straight down into 1/4-inch slices; on the thick end, you may want to cut the slices lengthwise in half into thinner strips.

Toss the meat with the onions. Taste and season with salt, usually about 1 teaspoon. Serve with the warm tortillas and salsa or hot sauce for making soft tacos.

Steak Taco Riffs

I'll bet you're already thinking about firing up the grill for cooking the beef and onion, which will, of course, make this fabulous dish Elysian. Feel free to substitute the Garlicky Ancho Chile Rub (page 137) or the Adobo Marinade (page 140) if the superfast chipotle marinade called for here is too spicy. Red onions cook up sweeter than the white ones, which many people prefer—but not me. Boneless, skinless chicken breasts make tasty chipotle-and-caramelized-onion tacos; and don't overlook catfish.

Green Chile Chicken Soft Tacos

Tacos de Pollo al Chile Poblano

◎❉◎❉◎❉◎❉◎❉◎❉◎❉◎❉◎❉◎❉◎❉◎❉◎❉◎❉◎❉◎❉◎❉◎❉◎

It may surprise you that until recently, delicious little soft tacos of seared chicken and roasted peppers didn't play much of a role in Mexico's *taquerías*. Boneless breasts from the good-size free-range chickens that country is known for just don't benefit from quick griddle-searing or grilling. But now that a good number of the toothsome barnyard chickens have been replaced by smaller, tenderer birds, chicken tacos are giving the classic beef ones a run for their money. It doesn't hurt that folks see them as a healthy alternative—without any sacrifice of flavor. For a super-aromatic dish, use the Yucatecan Garlic-Spice Marinade (page 142) in place of the black pepper–lime seasoning I've called for here.

Serves 4

2 large fresh poblano chiles

2 tablespoons vegetable or olive oil (divided use)

1 large white onion, sliced 1/4 inch thick

Salt

1 pound (3 medium-large halves) boneless, skinless chicken breast halves

Ground black pepper

3 tablespoons fresh lime juice

2 garlic cloves, peeled and finely chopped or crushed through a garlic press

12 warm corn tortillas, store-bought (see reheating instructions on page 214) or homemade (page 212)

About 3/4 cup Roasted Tomatillo Salsa (page 154) or Guacamole (page 160), or bottled salsa or hot sauce, for serving

Roast the poblanos over an open flame or 4 inches below a broiler, turning regularly until blistered and blackened all over, about 5 minutes for an open flame, 10 minutes for the broiler. Place in a bowl, cover with a kitchen towel and let cool until handleable.

Turn on (or adjust) the oven to its lowest setting. Heat *1 tablespoon* of the oil in a very large (12-inch) skillet over medium-high. Add the onion and cook, stirring frequently, until golden but still crunchy, 4 to 5 minutes. Scoop into a heatproof serving bowl, leaving as much oil as possible in the skillet, and slide it into the oven. Set the skillet aside.

Rub the blackened skin off the chiles and pull out the stems and seed pods. Rinse the chiles to remove bits of skin and seeds. Cut into 1/4-inch strips and stir into the onions. Taste and season with salt, usually a generous 1 teaspoon. Return the bowl to the oven.

Sprinkle both sides of the chicken breasts generously with salt and pepper.

Return the skillet to medium heat. Add the remaining *1 tablespoon* oil. When the oil is hot, lay in the chicken breasts. Brown on one side, about 5 minutes, then flip and finish cooking on the other side, about 4 minutes more. When the meat is done, add the lime juice and garlic to the skillet. Turn the chicken in the lime mixture for a minute or so, until the juice has reduced to a glaze and coats the chicken.

Cut the chicken breasts into 1/4-inch strips and toss with the onion-poblano mixture. Taste and season with additional salt if you think necessary. Serve with the warm tortillas and salsa, guacamole or hot sauce for making soft tacos.

A Couple of Riffs on Chicken Tacos

Grilling the chicken breasts is a delicious alternative to pan-searing them, but you'll miss the lime-garlic glaze. To solve that problem, I suggest you add the lime juice and garlic to the onions when they're browned, cooking until the liquid has reduced to a glaze. (You may want to have a little extra lime and garlic for marinating the chicken breasts before grilling.) If chicken tenders are more easily available than the breasts, use them; cooking time will be shorter. Beef skirt or flank steak works well here too; cooking times and temperatures can be found on page 196. And, of course, any of the large fleshy chiles (from Anaheims to red bell peppers) can stand in for the poblanos.

Chipotle Chicken Salad Tacos with Avocado, Red-Skin Potatoes and Romaine

Tacos de Ensalada de Pollo Enchipotlado con Aguacate, Papas y Lechuga Orejona

◎✖◎✖◎✖◎✖◎✖◎✖◎✖◎✖◎✖◎✖◎✖◎✖◎✖◎✖◎✖◎✖◎✖◎✖◎✖◎

From Mexico's tradition of "you can turn just about any leftover into a taco filling," I've done a simple version of a favorite Bayless-home salad taco. Mix together some coarse shreds of chicken (leftover grilled chicken is pretty hard to beat) with potatoes, avocado, sliced romaine and a smoky, tingly chipotle *vinagreta*, and you've got a cool filling for warm tortillas that you'll think about long after the meal's done. Or forget the tortillas and just eat it as a satisfying salad.

Serves 4

1 large red-skin boiling or Yukon Gold potato, sliced 1/4 inch thick

Salt

3 tablespoons vinegar (cider vinegar is good here, or use balsamic if you like more sweetness)

1 teaspoon dried oregano, preferably Mexican

2 canned chipotle chiles *en adobo*, seeded and chopped

1/4 small white onion, finely chopped

6 ounces (about 1 1/2 cups) coarsely shredded cooked chicken (I use either the meat I've pulled from a rotisserie chicken, or leftover roast or grilled chicken, or a large boneless, skinless chicken breast half that I've gently simmered in salted water for a few minutes until tender)

2 cups sliced romaine leaves—slice them about 1/4 inch across

1 ripe avocado, pitted, flesh scooped from the skin and cut into 1/4-inch cubes

2 tablespoons vegetable or olive oil

12 warm corn tortillas, store-bought (see reheating instructions on page 214) or homemade (page 212)

Scoop the sliced potato into a large microwaveable bowl, drizzle with 1/4 cup water and sprinkle generously with salt. Cover with plastic wrap, poke a couple of holes in the top and microwave on high (100%) for about 4 minutes, until tender but not mushy. Scoop the potatoes onto a cutting board, leaving the liquid behind, and let cool.

Add the vinegar, oregano, chipotle chiles and onion to the bowl with the potato-cooking water to make a dressing. Mix well, then taste and season with salt, usually about 1 teaspoon.

Use a fork to break the cooled potatoes into 1/2-inch pieces, then scoop them into a large bowl. Add the chicken, then drizzle on the dressing and toss everything together. (If there is time, refrigerate the mixture for about half an hour to blend flavors.)

Just before serving, add the lettuce and avocado to the bowl. Drizzle with the oil and toss to combine everything. Serve with the warm tortillas for making soft tacos.

Riffs on Salad Tacos

The idea of a substantial salad becoming a taco filling is flexible enough to embrace just about anything you can dream up—though I personally don't think mayonnaise-dressed salads work as well as those with a vinaigrette. Think beyond chicken salad to tuna (or other seafood), steak and grilled vegetables. Or go all vegetarian: crumbled fresh goat cheese, blue cheese or Mexican *queso fresco* are wonderful featured in a salady taco like this. The potato can be replaced by other vegetables—broccoli, for instance, or chayote, zucchini or asparagus, all cut into small pieces and microwave-steamed the same way as the potatoes. Though I love romaine's sweet crunch, the filling will also welcome the more substantial Napa cabbage, the slightly bitter, toothsome frisée or the more tender (but not too delicate) Bibb lettuce.

SEAFOOD SALAD TACOS WITH TOMATO, RADISH AND HABANERO

Seafood Salad Tacos with Tomato, Radish and Habanero

Tacos de Mariscos a la Vinagreta

◎✠◎✠◎✠◎✠◎✠◎✠◎✠◎✠◎✠◎✠◎✠◎✠◎✠◎✠◎✠◎✠◎✠◎✠◎✠◎

After many years away from the twisting, jumbled market complex in downtown Mérida, Yucatán, I returned with one thing on my mind: seafood salad tacos. In the stifling heat that envelops the whole peninsula, a cool filling in a warm, just-made tortilla offers the refreshment of an oasis. Though practically any fish or shellfish can be given this *a la vinagreta* treatment, shrimp (purchased already cooked and peeled) is the easiest. In Mérida, they often leave out the chile and serve the tacos with bottled habanero hot sauce or the habanero version of our Roasted Fresh Chile Salsa (page 158). I think it's pretty good with Roasted Tomatillo Salsa (page 154), even though tomatillos don't really play a role in Yucatecan cuisine.

Serves 4

1 to 1 1/4 pounds medium-small (40 to 60 per pound) shrimp, cooked, peeled and (if you wish) deveined
    OR 1 to 1 1/4 pounds mahimahi, halibut, bass, snapper or catfish fillets

1/4 cup fresh lime juice

1 small white onion, finely chopped

6 radishes, thinly sliced

1 fresh habanero (or jalapeño) chile, stemmed and finely chopped

2 large ripe tomatoes, cored and chopped into 1/4-inch pieces

1/2 cup (loosely packed) chopped cilantro

Salt

12 warm corn tortillas, store-bought (see reheating instructions on page 214) or homemade (page 212)

If using shrimp, scoop them into a medium bowl. Or, for fish, bring about a quart of water to a boil in a medium (3- to 4-quart) saucepan and add 1 tablespoon salt. (If I have a small lime, I'll squeeze the juice into the water, even throw in the squeezed lime for more flavor.) Add the fish (it's easiest to manage if the fish is in 2 or 3 pieces). Let the water return to the boil, then turn down the heat to medium to medium-low and simmer gently 3 to 4 minutes. Remove the pan from the heat and let the fish cool in the liquid while you prepare the remaining ingredients. When the fish is handleable, drain and coarsely shred it into a medium bowl.

Add the lime juice, onion, radishes, chile, tomatoes and cilantro to the bowl with the shrimp or fish. Stir, taste and season with salt, usually about 1 teaspoon.

Serve with the warm tortillas for making soft tacos.

Riffs on Seafood Salad Tacos

Vinagreta makes a wide variety of ingredients taste delicious: instead of shrimp, try shredded slow-simmered pork shoulder or beef chuck or brisket (in Yucatán, they use venison); gently poached, grilled or roasted chicken; roasted or grilled asparagus (cut into 2-inch lengths) or mushrooms (shiitakes, oysters and portobellos are good choices). Though it's not traditional, when tomatoes aren't in season, I replace them with tomatillos—raw, chopped in small pieces. For the vegetarian versions, I usually serve crumbled Mexican *queso fresco* or fresh goat cheese. In any of these variations, 1 or 2 roasted poblanos, peeled, seeded and chopped, can replace the habanero, shifting the focus from brilliant heat and fruity aromas to rich roasted green chile unctuousness.

Swiss Chard (or Spinach) Tacos with Caramelized Onion, Fresh Cheese and Red Chile

Tacos de Acelgas (o Espinacas) con Cebolla Caramelizada, Queso Fresco y Chile Rojo

◎✳◎✳◎✳◎✳◎✳◎✳◎✳◎✳◎✳◎✳◎✳◎✳◎✳◎✳◎✳◎✳◎✳◎

As a kid, I would never have expected to someday be taking an enthusiastic bite of braised greens and caramelized onions wrapped in a warm tortilla and topped with spicy red chile sauce and crumbled fresh cheese. Braised greens alone were beyond my world. In a soft taco, they were unthinkable—my understanding of tacos being those crisp-shell repositories for ground beef, iceberg lettuce, yellow cheese and mild, mild salsa. But in my twenties, when I got to Toluca in the highlands of central Mexico, I discovered a fresh-baked blue corn tortilla rolled around the almost meaty texture of the local greens (*quelites*), crunchy caramelized onions, bitey salsa and salty cheese. Now I can't seem to live without these utterly captivating and delicious portraits of healthy food.

SWISS CHARD (OR SPINACH) TACOS WITH CARAMELIZED ONION, FRESH CHEESE AND RED CHILE

Serves 4

A 12-ounce bunch Swiss chard (or collard, mustard or beet greens), thick lower stems cut off
OR 10 ounces cleaned spinach, lamb's-quarters or amaranth greens (about 10 cups)

1 1/2 tablespoons vegetable oil, olive oil, fresh pork lard or bacon drippings

1 large white or red onion, sliced 1/4 inch thick

3 garlic cloves, peeled and finely chopped or crushed through a garlic press

About 1 teaspoon red pepper flakes

1/2 cup chicken broth, vegetable broth or water

Salt

12 warm corn tortillas, store-bought (see reheating instructions on page 214) or homemade (page 212)

1 cup (4 ounces) crumbled Mexican *queso fresco* or other fresh cheese such as feta or goat cheese, for serving

About 3/4 cup Smoky Chipotle Salsa (page 149) or Toasty Guajillo Chile Salsa (page 156), or bottled salsa or hot sauce, for serving

Cut the chard crosswise into 1/2-inch slices (small spinach leaves, lamb's-quarters and amaranth greens can be left whole). In a very large (12-inch) skillet, heat the oil (or its stand-in) over medium-high. Add the onion and cook, stirring frequently, until golden brown but still crunchy, about 4 to 5 minutes. Add the garlic and red pepper flakes and stir for a few seconds, until aromatic, then add the broth or water, 1/2 teaspoon salt and the greens. Reduce the heat to medium-low, cover the pan (if you don't have a lid, a cookie sheet works well) and cook until the greens are *almost* tender, anywhere from 2 minutes for tender spinach and amaranth greens to 7 or 8 minutes for thick collard greens; Swiss chard needs about 5 minutes.

Uncover the pan, raise the heat to medium-high and cook, stirring continually, until the mixture is nearly dry. Taste and season with additional salt if you think necessary.

Serve with the warm tortillas, crumbled cheese and salsa or hot sauce for making soft tacos.

A Couple of Riffs on Braised Greens Tacos

To make a heartier meal, I add some shredded leftover grilled, roasted or poached chicken or steak to the greens during the final few minutes of cooking. Flaked tuna or hot-smoked salmon is a nice add-in, and I have to admit I'm also partial to cubes of the smoked firm tofu they sell at our natural foods grocery store.

Zucchini-Mushroom Tacos with (or without) Chorizo

Tacos de Calabacitas y Hongos con (o sin) Chorizo

Zucchini tacos are a tradition in the homey taco stands that specialize in *tacos de guisados*—*guisados*, in this instance, being old-fashioned economical stews made from ingredients cut small enough to fit in a soft tortilla. The version I've seen most starts with pork and tomatoes stewed until succulent with the pungent perfume of *epazote* before the zucchini is added. A quick sauté, starting with the rousing flavor of Mexican chorizo and dolled up with smoky chipotle chile, shows off the sexier side of zucchini.

Serves 4

4 ounces fresh Mexican chorizo sausage, casing removed (about 1/2 cup) (optional)
1 1/2 tablespoons vegetable or olive oil, if needed
1 medium white onion, sliced 1/4 inch thick
3 ounces mushrooms (shiitake, oyster, portobello or the like), stemmed and sliced about 1/2 inch thick (you'll have a scant cup)
One 15-ounce can diced tomatoes in juice (preferably fire-roasted), drained
1 canned chipotle chile *en adobo,* seeded
1 1/2 teaspoons chipotle canning sauce
2 medium (about 12 ounces) zucchini, cut into 1/2-inch cubes
Salt
1/2 to 3/4 cup (2 to 3 ounces) crumbled Mexican *queso fresco* or other fresh cheese such as feta or goat cheese
12 warm corn tortillas, store-bought (see reheating instructions on page 214) or homemade (page 212)
Hot sauce (Mexican Búfalo or Frontera Chipotle is great here), for serving

If using chorizo, lay it in a very large (12-inch) skillet and set over medium heat. Cook, stirring regularly and breaking up clumps, until cooked through, about 4 minutes.

If the chorizo has rendered considerable fat, tip off and discard all but enough to lightly coat the pan; if it has rendered very little—*or if you're not using the chorizo*—add the oil to the skillet and raise the heat to medium-high. Add the onion and cook, stirring regularly, until beginning to soften, about 2 minutes. Add the mushrooms and cook about 2 minutes more, stirring regularly, until their liquid has evaporated and the mushrooms are beginning to brown.

While the mushrooms are cooking, pour the tomatoes into a food processor or blender. Add the chipotle chile and its canning sauce and process until smooth.

When the mushrooms are ready, add the tomato mixture and cook, stirring regularly, until the mixture has thickened to the consistency of canned tomato sauce, about 3 to 4 minutes. Add the zucchini and continue to cook, stirring every once in a while, until the zucchini is cooked through but still a little crisp, 8 to 10 minutes. Taste and season with salt, usually about 1/2 teaspoon (more if not using chorizo).

Scoop into a bowl and garnish with the crumbled cheese. Serve with the warm tortillas and hot sauce for everyone to make soft tacos.

Riffs on Zucchini Tacos (Some without Zucchini)

Any summer squash, from crooknecks to pattypans, can stand in for the zucchini here. Tomatillos (pan-roast 12 ounces halved tomatillos as described in the recipe on page 154) make a bright-tasting replacement for the tomatoes, though the color of the finished dish isn't as rich. During our local morel mushroom season, I use the wild mushrooms in place of the cultivated ones. If there is no chorizo in the house and I want a little meat in my tacos, I cook 4 slices of chopped bacon in the chorizo's place. Because the zucchini simply gets simmered to tenderness in the finished dish, you can easily replace it with practically any other vegetable that can be cut into small pieces, from broccoli and chayote to asparagus, parsnips, green beans, even peas and winter squash (if you have the stamina to peel and cube the last).

Mexican Scrambled Egg Tacos

Tacos de Huevos Revueltos a la Mexicana

◎✕◎

If this is a book of simple "foundation" recipes from the Mexican kitchen, this preparation is part of the bedrock on which that foundation is laid. No doubt all of you, at one time or another, have enjoyed a big forkful of scrambled eggs shot through with Mexican spirit—that is, with tomatoes, chiles, onions and cilantro. If those eggs were rolled into warm corn tortillas, I'll bet the experience seared itself into your brain. You can find eggs like this everywhere in Mexico, from simple market stalls to the trendy dining room at the W Hotel in Mexico City's chic Polanco section (where the chef adds roasted cactus to the mix). They are always served with warm tortillas for making tacos or simply eating alongside; I always want a spoonful of black Fried Beans (page 84) to make the meal complete.

Serves 4

3 garlic cloves, peeled

Fresh hot green chiles to taste (I like 2 serranos or 1 jalapeño), stemmed, seeded, if you wish, and each cut into 3 or 4 pieces

1 medium white onion, roughly chopped

2 tablespoons vegetable or olive oil, fresh pork lard or bacon or chorizo drippings

1 pound (2 medium-large round or 5 to 7 plum) ripe tomatoes, cored and cut into 1/4-inch cubes

8 eggs

Salt

1/2 to 2/3 cup (loosely packed) chopped cilantro

1 ripe avocado, pitted, flesh scooped from the skin and cut into 1/4-inch pieces (optional)

12 warm corn tortillas, store-bought (see reheating instructions on page 214) or homemade (page 212)

About 3/4 cup Roasted Tomatillo Salsa (page 154), or bottled salsa or hot sauce, for serving

With a food processor or blender running, drop in the garlic and chiles one piece at a time, letting each piece get finely chopped before adding the next. Stop the food processor (or blender) and add the onion, then pulse until most of the onion pieces are no larger than 1/4 inch.

Heat the oil (or its alternative) in a very large (12-inch) skillet, preferably nonstick, over medium. Add the onion mixture and cook, stirring regularly, until starting to brown, about 4 to 5 minutes. Raise the heat to medium-high and add the tomatoes. Cook, stirring frequently, until all of the tomato liquid evaporates and the oil separates out again, about 4 minutes.

While the tomatoes are cooking, crack the eggs into a bowl and add 1 teaspoon salt. With a fork, beat the eggs just enough to roughly blend the whites and yolks.

Pour the eggs into the skillet and cook—slowly stirring and scraping up the cooked eggs from the bottom of the skillet—until the eggs are as done as you like. Scoop into a serving bowl and sprinkle with the cilantro and optional avocado. Serve with the warm tortillas and salsa or hot sauce for making soft tacos.

Riffs on *Huevos a la Mexicana*

You probably know that the classic preparation for these eggs starts with browning hand-chopped onions and tomatoes with minced chiles and garlic, but that requires both time (or very proficient knife skills) and really great summer tomatoes. I devised this simpler, year-round version for quick home suppers. Sometimes I add crisp-cooked bacon or chopped cooked shrimp to the skillet with the eggs. Or I'll fry chorizo in the skillet, then scoop it out with a slotted spoon and make the dish using the renderings; I add the chorizo back to the skillet with the eggs.

◎ **ANOTHER TORTILLA-AND-EGG DISH—*HUEVOS RANCHEROS*:** Make the sauce on page 215, adding a little less broth to ensure that the sauce doesn't run off the eggs. Heat 8 corn tortillas, store-bought (see reheating instructions on page 214) or homemade (page 212). Cook 8 sunny-side up eggs. Lay 2 tortillas slightly overlapping on each of four dinner plates. Top each pair with 2 eggs, then spoon the sauce over everything (leaving the yolks exposed looks attractive). Sprinkle with cilantro and Mexican *queso fresco* or *queso añejo*.

Corn Tortillas

Tortillas de Maíz

Now, I don't expect you (or me) to make fresh-baked corn tortillas for everyday dinners. But I *do* want to arm you with the know-how for that special moment when the full, fresh-baked Mexican experience is all that will satisfy. After all, fresh-baked corn tortillas are, like fresh-baked bread, one of life's greatest pleasures. And, like an authentic French baguette, corn tortillas go stale just hours after being griddle-baked (neither French bread nor Mexican tortillas contain any moisture-preserving fat). So, at least once, have the full experience when you've got time to track down the fresh-ground corn *masa* (or powdered *masa harina*) and have laid your hands on a tortilla press.

The rest of the time, I have these suggestions: Buy corn tortillas that are made by a local *tortillería* if at all possible—they're typically fresher, made in an authentic fashion and often have no preservatives. Store the tortillas in the refrigerator for no more than a few days—freezing can often lead to brittle, dried-out tortillas or ones that have gotten mushy around the edges because of moisture condensation. If the tortillas have been made that day, you can quickly reheat them one at a time on a dry griddle or skillet (or even over a low direct flame, as many of my Mexican friends do); otherwise, steam-heat them in a microwave or vegetable steamer as described on page 214.

Makes 15 tortillas

1 3/4 cups *masa harina* (Mexican corn
  "flour" for making tortillas—Maseca
  brand is available in well-stocked
  groceries and Mexican markets)
  OR 1 pound fresh smooth-ground corn

masa for tortillas (available almost
  exclusively from tortilla factories—
  make sure they're grinding it from
  whole corn rather than reconstituting
  the powdered *masa*, which you could
  do yourself)

If using powdered *masa harina*, measure it into a bowl and add 1 cup plus 2 table-spoons hot tap water. Knead with your hand until thoroughly combined. Cover and let it stand 15 minutes. Or, if using fresh *masa*, scoop it into a bowl. Break it up and knead it a few times until smooth.

Set a large griddle (one that stretches over two burners) or two skillets on your stovetop. Heat one end of the griddle (or one skillet) to medium, the other end (or other skillet) to medium-high.

Gently squeeze the dough. If it is stiff (it probably will be), knead in water 1 or 2 teaspoons at a time until the dough feels like soft cookie dough—not stiff, but not sticky. Divide into 15 pieces, rolling each into a ball. Cover with plastic.

Cut 2 squares of plastic bag 1 inch larger all around than your tortilla press. Open the press and lay in one piece of plastic. Lay a dough ball in the center and gently mash it. Top with the second piece of plastic and close the press. Using the press's lever, gently flatten the dough into a 1/8-inch-thick disk. Open the press and peel off the top piece of plastic.

Flip the tortilla onto your right hand (if right-handed); the top of the tortilla should line up with the side of your index finger. Gently roll it onto the side of the griddle (or into the skillet) heated to medium: let the bottom of the tortilla touch the griddle, then lower your hand slightly and move it away from you—the tortilla will stick to the hot surface so you can roll your hand out from under it as it rolls down flat.

After about 30 seconds, the edges of the tortilla will have dried slightly and the tortilla will release from the griddle—up to this moment, the tortilla will be stuck. With a metal spatula (or calloused fingers), flip the tortilla onto the hotter side of the griddle (or into the hotter skillet). After about 30 seconds, the tortilla should be lightly browned underneath. Flip it over. Cook 30 seconds more: the tortilla should puff in places (or all over—a gentle press with metal spatula or fingers encourages puffing). Transfer to a basket lined with a napkin or towel.

Press and bake the remaining tortillas, stacking the baked tortillas in the basket. Keep them well wrapped so they stay warm.

REHEATING CORN TORTILLAS

With a microwave oven: Dribble 3 tablespoons water over a clean kitchen towel, then wrap your cold tortillas in it. Slide the package into a microwaveable plastic bag and fold the top over—don't seal it. Microwave at 50% power for 4 minutes to create a steamy environment around the tortillas. Let stand for 2 or 3 minutes before serving.

With a vegetable steamer: Set up a vegetable steamer (one without that little post sticking up). Pour about 1/2 inch of water into the bottom. Wrap the cold tortillas—no more than 12 at a time—in a clean kitchen towel. Lay the package in the steamer, set the lid in place and set the pot over high heat. When steam comes puffing out, set the timer for 1 minute. Then turn off the heat and let the tortillas sit in their steamy world for 10 minutes. They're ready.

Tomatillo-Sauced Enchiladas with Spinach and Mushrooms

Enchiladas Verdes de Espinacas y Hongos

◎❀◎❀◎❀◎❀◎❀◎❀◎❀◎❀◎❀◎❀◎❀◎❀◎❀◎❀◎❀◎❀◎❀◎❀◎

Enchiladas have a casual reputation—fun family food, a good way to use leftovers, not a big deal. But by the time you've made the filling and sauce, put together the tortilla-wrapped rolls and sprinkled on the garnishes, the clock's been ticking for more than a few minutes. Yet it seems we're all inexplicably drawn to the texture of a soft, sauce-soaked tortilla—I particularly like it if the sauce is made from tomatillos jazzed with green chile and cilantro—around a toothsome filling with something cheesy or fresh on top. So, I've simplified the steps to this pleasure, using a light hand where heavy has often been the norm. Fried tortillas have been replaced with baked ones, meat has been swapped for (or augmented with) spinach and mushrooms and the typically Mexican-American melted cheese blanket has become the more typically Mexican light sprinkling of flavorful fresh cheese. Your only challenge will be temperature: In Mexico, most enchiladas are put together from warm ingredients and served right away—no baking. (But, then again, in Mexico, folks don't like their food as hot as we do in the States.) My suggestions: When the tortillas come out of the oven, turn the oven off and slide your (ovenproof) dinner plates in to warm. And make sure the sauce, filling and tortillas stay as warm as possible.

TOMATILLO-SAUCED ENCHILADAS WITH SPINACH AND MUSHROOMS

Serves 4

3 garlic cloves, peeled

Fresh hot green chiles to taste (I like 2 serranos or 1 jalapeño), stemmed and quartered

1 1/2 pounds (10 to 12 medium) tomatillos, husked, rinsed and cut into quarters

3/4 cup (loosely packed) roughly chopped cilantro, plus a few extra sprigs for garnish

3 tablespoons vegetable oil, olive oil or bacon drippings (divided use), plus some for the tortillas

2 cups chicken broth

8 ounces mushrooms (button, oyster or shiitake are good), stemmed and sliced

1 large red onion, thinly sliced

10 ounces (about 10 cups) spinach, stems removed

1 cup (about 4 ounces) shredded cooked chicken (about one-quarter of a large rotisserie chicken) or cubed ham (optional)

Salt

12 corn tortillas, preferably store-bought

3 tablespoons Mexican *crema*, sour cream, heavy cream or *crème fraîche*

1/2 teaspoon sugar (optional)

1 cup (4 ounces) crumbled Mexican *queso fresco* or other fresh cheese such as feta or goat cheese

Turn on the oven to 350 degrees. With a food processor or blender running, drop in the garlic and chiles one piece at a time, letting each piece get finely chopped before adding the next. Add the tomatillos and cilantro; process until smooth.

Heat *1 1/2 tablespoons* of the oil or bacon drippings in a medium (3-quart) saucepan over medium-high. Add the puree and cook, stirring nearly constantly, until the mixture has reduced to the consistency of thick tomato sauce, about 7 minutes. (The more you cook down this base, the richer and sweeter the tomatillo sauce will be.) Add the chicken broth and simmer over medium heat for about 10 minutes to blend the flavors.

While the sauce is simmering, heat the remaining *1 1/2 tablespoons* oil or bacon drippings in a very large (12-inch) skillet over medium-high. Add the mushrooms and cook, stirring nearly constantly, for a cou-

Making filling for Tomatillo-Sauced Enchiladas

Dipping tortilla in sauce for Tomatillo-Sauced Enchiladas

Filling enchiladas for Tomatillo-Sauced Enchiladas

Saucing enchiladas for Tomatillo-Sauced Enchiladas

ple of minutes, until they begin to brown. Add about *three-quarters* of the onion (reserve the rest for garnish) and continue cooking, stirring frequently, for another minute or two, until the onion looks translucent. Add the spinach and optional chicken or ham and cook, stirring constantly, for a minute or so, until the spinach is wilted. Season with salt, usually a scant teaspoon. Cover to keep warm.

Lay out the tortillas on a baking sheet and spray or brush lightly on both sides with oil or bacon drippings, then stack them in twos. Slide the tortillas into the oven and bake just long enough to make them soft and pliable, about 3 minutes. Remove from the oven and stack them in a single pile; cover with a kitchen towel to keep warm.

Stir the *crema* (or its stand-in) into the sauce. Taste and season with salt, usually about 1 teaspoon (add the sugar if the sauce seems quite tart to you). Holding a tortilla by one edge, dip most of it into the sauce, then lay it on a plate. Spoon a heaping 2 tablespoons filling down the center, roll up and lay seam side down on a dinner plate. Repeat with 2 more tortillas, arranging them on the same dinner plate. Douse the enchiladas with about 1/4 cup of the warm sauce, sprinkle with a quarter of the crumbled cheese and garnish with some of the reserved onion and cilantro sprigs. Assemble the rest of the servings, and carry to the table without hesitation.

A Few Riffs on *Enchiladas Verdes*

You can simplify this recipe in two ways. First, you can skip the vegetable filling and use only shredded cooked chicken (you'll need about 2 cups, or 8 ounces: about half of a large rotisserie chicken). And second, you can use store-bought tomatillo salsa (you'll need about 4 cups): Blend it until smooth, then transfer to a saucepan and bring it to a boil. Add the *crema* and check the seasonings (it will likely be quite spicy and tangy, so you may want to add extra *crema* and/or sugar). At our restaurant, we make these vegetarian enchiladas with roasted root vegetables in the fall, put each portion in an individual heatproof dish, top with a sprinkling of Chihuahua-style melting cheese and run them under a broiler. Coarse shreds of smoked ham hock (or several rashers of crisp bacon) are really delicious in the (then nonvegetarian) filling.

Tomato-and-Jalapeño–Sauced Enchiladas with Sour Cream and Aged Cheese

Enjitomatadas con Crema y Queso Añejo

◎✖◎✖◎✖◎✖◎✖◎✖◎✖◎✖◎✖◎✖◎✖◎✖◎✖◎✖◎✖◎✖◎✖◎

This is a version of the original Mexican enchilada as it was before that concept grew into an overstuffed tortilla smothered in melted cheese. This market-stall favorite is a plain-Jane (unfilled) tortilla awash in Mexico's iconic roasted tomato sauce (jalapeño and cilantro make it far from humdrum) with a little drizzle of rich *crema*, a sprinkling of aged cheese and a few slivers of bitey white onion—just right for small meals or when you're looking for the perfect accompaniment to simple grilled chicken, fish, shrimp or scallops.

Serves 4

2 garlic cloves, peeled

1 to 2 jalapeño chiles (or 2 to 3 serranos), stemmed and cut into quarters

One 28-ounce can diced tomatoes in juice (preferably fire-roasted)

1 1/2 tablespoons vegetable or olive oil, plus some for the tortillas

2 cups chicken or vegetable broth

12 corn tortillas, preferably store-bought

Salt

Toppings

1 1/2 cups (about 8 ounces) coarsely shredded cooked chicken, beef or pork (optional)

1/4 cup Mexican *crema*, sour cream or *crème fraîche*, thinned with about 1 tablespoon milk

1/2 medium white onion, thinly sliced

1/2 cup (loosely packed) chopped cilantro (or flat-leaf parsley—common in Oaxaca)

1/4 cup grated Mexican *queso añejo* or other garnishing cheese such as Romano or Parmesan

Turn on the oven to 350 degrees. With a food processor or blender running, drop in the garlic and chiles one piece at a time, letting each piece get finely chopped before adding the next. Drain the tomatoes, reserving their juice. Add the tomatoes and process until smooth.

Heat the oil in a medium (3-quart) saucepan over medium-high. Add the puree and cook, stirring nearly constantly, until the mixture has reduced to the consistency of thick tomato sauce, about 7 minutes. Add the broth and reserved tomato juice and simmer over medium-low for 10 minutes to blend the flavors.

While the sauce is simmering, lay out the tortillas on a baking sheet and spray or brush lightly on both sides with oil, then stack them in twos. Slide the tortillas into the oven and bake just long enough to make them soft and pliable, about 3 minutes. Remove from the oven and stack them in a single pile; cover with a kitchen towel to keep warm.

Taste and season the sauce with salt, usually about 1 teaspoon. Holding a warm tortilla by one edge, dip most of it into the hot sauce, then lay it on a deep dinner plate and fold it in quarters. (Having the plates warm will ensure a warm dinner.) Do the same with 2 more tortillas, slightly overlapping them on the plate. Ladle a generous 1/4 cup of hot sauce (bring it back to a boil if it has cooled down) over the tortillas, letting it pool over and around them. Strew with the optional meat, then drizzle with cream and sprinkle with onion, cilantro (or parsley) and cheese. Prepare the remaining servings in the same way, and serve without hesitation.

Riffs on *Enjitomatadas*

Adding a large branch of herby fresh *epazote* to the sauce as it simmers will give it the flavor of central and southern Mexico. A handful of chopped cilantro is a nice add-in too. You can use this approach for tomatillo-sauced enchiladas, simply replacing the canned tomatoes with 1 1/2 pounds husked, roasted tomatillos (run them under a broiler until they are soft and splotchy black in places, about 6 minutes per side). One of my favorite variations on *enjitomatadas* is to spoon a heaping tablespoon of Mexican-style ricotta (it's drier than ours) or goat cheese onto each dipped tortilla before folding it into quarters; don't omit the *queso añejo*.

Red Chile Enchiladas with Chicken and Melted Cheese

Enchiladas Rojas de Pollo con Queso Derretido

◎✖◎✖◎✖◎✖◎✖◎✖◎✖◎✖◎✖◎✖◎✖◎✖◎✖◎✖◎✖◎✖◎✖◎✖◎✖◎

When most Americans say enchilada, this preparation is—more or less—what their mouths are watering for. That's fine by me, since I've eaten enchiladas like these since I was a kid in Oklahoma City, and I still get a hankering for the chicken-filled, red-sauced, cheese-burnished Tex-Mex standard. Rather than animating the sauce with chile powder, as is common throughout Texas, I'm taking you down the Mexican road with real dried guajillo chile pods. They give the sauce a rich complexity that I love (see the **Shortcuts** below if guajillo pods are unavailable to you).

Serves 4 to 6

4 medium (about 1 ounce total) dried guajillo chiles, stemmed, seeded and torn into flat pieces

2 garlic cloves, peeled and quartered

One 28-ounce can diced tomatoes in juice (preferably fire-roasted)

1/4 teaspoon ground cumin

1/4 teaspoon ground black pepper

1 tablespoon vegetable or olive oil, plus a little extra for the tortillas

2 cups chicken broth, plus a little extra if necessary

12 corn tortillas, preferably store-bought

Salt

1/2 teaspoon sugar

2 generous cups (about 8 ounces) coarsely shredded cooked chicken (about half of a large rotisserie chicken)

1 cup (about 4 ounces) shredded Mexican melting cheese (such as Chihuahua, quesadilla or asadero) or Monterey Jack, brick or mild cheddar

1 small white onion, cut into rings, for garnish

Cilantro sprigs, for garnish

Turn on the oven to 350 degrees. Set a medium (8- to 9-inch) skillet over medium heat. When it is hot, toast the chile pieces a few at a time, pressing them against the hot surface with a spatula until aromatic and lightened in color underneath—about 10 seconds per side. (If you see more than a whiff of smoke, they're burning.) Transfer the toasted chiles to a blender jar. Add the garlic, tomatoes with their juice, cumin and black pepper. Blend to as smooth a consistency as possible. (A food processor will work, but it won't completely puree the chile.)

Heat the oil in a large (4-quart) saucepan over medium-high. Set a medium-mesh strainer over the pan and pour in the sauce. Press through the strainer to remove bits of chile skin. Then cook, stirring until the sauce is reduced to the consistency of tomato paste, 5 to 7 minutes. Pour in the broth, reduce the heat to medium-low and let simmer for 10 minutes while you prepare the tortillas, filling and toppings.

Lay out the tortillas on a baking sheet and spray or brush lightly on both sides with oil, then stack them in twos. Slide the tortillas into the oven and bake just long enough to make them soft and pliable, about 3 minutes. Remove from the oven and stack them in a single pile; cover with a kitchen towel to keep warm.

Taste the sauce and season with salt, usually about 1 1/2 teaspoons, and the sugar. Stir in additional broth if the sauce has thickened beyond the consistency of light cream soup.

Spread about 1/2 cup sauce over the bottom of a 13 × 9-inch baking dish. Stir another 1/2 cup sauce into the chicken. Lay out a warm tortilla, top with a portion of chicken and roll up. Lay seam side down in the baking dish. Continue filling and rolling the rest of the tortillas, then ladle the remaining sauce over the enchiladas and sprinkle with the cheese.

Bake for 10 to 15 minutes, until the cheese is starting to brown (the chicken should be warm by then). Sprinkle with the onion rings and cilantro sprigs, and you're ready for dinner.

Shortcuts

Skip the straining—though if you do, you'll need either a super-duper blender (like a VitaMix) that will render tough chile skins unperceivable or greater mental powers than I possess to ignore the "contrasting texture" those little bits of skin add. Lacking guajillo pods (or time to procure or work with them), you can substitute 2 to 3 tablespoons chile powder—pure guajillo powder, pure ancho powder, pure hot or mild New Mexico powder, even regular grocery-store chili powder (skip the cumin and black pepper in that case, since grocery-store chili powder contains spices). To create a sauce with as homogeneous a consistency as the guajillo pod sauce, add 1 teaspoon flour to the blender.

Red Chile Enchilada Riffs

A quick but spicy variation on the sauce replaces the guajillo chiles with 2 to 3 canned chipotle chiles; bolster the smokiness by adding a tablespoon of the canning sauce. For a bright-tasting *Enchilada Suiza*, use the tomatillo sauce on page 215. For a darker, slightly sweeter sauce, substitute 1 ounce (2 large) anchos for the guajillos; for a lighter flavor, substitute 1 ounce (3 medium) New Mexico chiles. Beef is really good in these enchiladas: leftover pot roast and brisket are my favorites, barbecued beef brisket is out of this world. And though it may seem like gilding an already-rich-enough lily, a sprinkling of Mexican *queso añejo* is really delicious over the finished enchiladas.

Crusty Black Bean–Chorizo Subs

Tortas de Chorizo y Frijoles Negros

◎✖◎✖◎✖◎✖◎✖◎✖◎✖◎✖◎✖◎✖◎✖◎✖◎✖◎✖◎✖◎✖◎✖◎✖◎

There are many regional variations on the crusty Mexican "submarines" called *tortas*, each of which will represent the perfect *torta* for some reader. So I'll give you the basic architecture: they're built on the bottom half of a split crusty oval roll (some of the soft center bread pulled out), which is spread with mashed beans, topped with meat if you like (here, for expedience, I've mixed the chorizo in with the beans) and finished with cheese, avocado, something spicy and the golden brown tops. There are two buns commonly used in Mexico for *tortas*: the oval split-top, crusty "French" roll called a *bolillo* and the softer, flatter, three-hump roll called a *telera*. *Teleras* are best for *tortas* that are crisped between the hot plates of a sandwich (panini) grill.

Serves 4

8 ounces fresh Mexican chorizo sausage, casing removed (about 1 cup)

3 to 4 tablespoons vegetable or olive oil (divided use)

Two 15-ounce cans black (or other) beans
OR 3 1/2 cups home-cooked black (or other) beans (see page 82), with just enough liquid to cover them

Salt

4 *telera* or *bolillo* rolls, crusty French rolls or submarine sandwich rolls (6 to 7 inches long, 3 inches wide)

About 6 ounces Mexican *queso fresco* or other fresh cheese such as feta or goat cheese, sliced 1/4 inch thick

1 ripe avocado, pitted, flesh scooped from the skin and cut into 1/4-inch slices

About 3/4 cup Roasted Tomatillo Salsa (page 154), or bottled hot sauce, such as Mexican Tamazula or Búfalo

Set a very large (12-inch) skillet over medium heat and add the chorizo. Cook, breaking up the clumps, until browned and thoroughly cooked, about 8 to 9 minutes. Add *1 to 2 tablespoons* of the oil (depending on how much fat the chorizo has rendered) and the beans. As the beans come to a simmer, mash them to a smooth paste with a Mexican bean masher, old-fashioned potato masher or the back of a large cooking spoon. Cook, stirring nearly constantly, until the consistency of very soft mashed potatoes—expect about 10 minutes after adding the beans. Taste and season with salt if you think necessary. Keep warm over the lowest heat, covered to keep the beans soft and moist.

Heat a large griddle or skillet over medium. Slice the rolls open. Use fingers or a spoon to scrape out some of the soft bread in the center of each half, making a small hollow. Brush the insides with the remaining *2 tablespoons* oil, then lay them cut side down on the griddle or skillet to crisp to a rich golden brown, about 2 minutes. (You may have to do this in batches if your rolls are large or your griddle/skillet small.)

Smear about 1/2 cup of the chorizo-bean mixture over the bottom half of each roll. (You'll have about 1 cup of the mixture left over; cover and refrigerate for a midnight snack.) Top with slices of the cheese and the avocado. Spoon on the salsa or dash on the hot sauce. Set the top of each roll in place, and you're ready to serve.

Freewheeling Riffs on *Tortas*

Feel free to evolve this recipe as you like. Layer in sliced rotisserie or smoked or grilled chicken. Use leftover roast pork or beef. Choose your favorite cheese (I love goat cheese on a *torta*). Grill some onions or add a final, full-flavored layer of pungent herbs such as cilantro (or Pueblan *pápalo*) or pickled chiles (jalapeños or smoky chipotles). For most Mexican cooks to consider this a *torta*, you'll need to keep that smear of beans. For me, you'll need to keep the avocado and salsa too.

The All-Purpose Quick Tostada

Tostadas Rápidas "Mil Usos"

◎✠◎✠◎✠◎✠◎✠◎✠◎✠◎✠◎✠◎✠◎✠◎✠◎✠◎✠◎✠◎✠◎✠◎✠◎

In every Mexican market (and many American groceries), you can buy a package of fried tortillas (tostadas) to smear with beans and top with whatever you've pieced together from the cupboard or refrigerator: a quick satisfying meal that can become a tradition if you come up with unique toppings or combinations that family and friends can't get out of their minds. All the kids I know love tostadas, especially when they get to construct their own. I love mine with grilled chicken and a lot of hot sauce.

In Oaxaca, in southern Mexico, they make huge tortillas called *tlayudas* that come out wonderfully crisp when toasted directly on a griddle or grill—no frying. I'd love to emulate this style with U.S. tortillas in my home kitchen, but every time I try, they come out tooth-shatteringly hard. It's because our corn is different, experts tell me. I haven't called for the traditional tomato slices here because I want to keep this a twelve-month, "all-purpose" recipe, and tomatoes have such a short season. When you find good tomatoes, layer them with other fillings (or feature them solo), or serve your tostadas with Tomato Salad (page 67).

Serves 4

3 tablespoons vegetable oil, olive oil, fresh pork lard or bacon drippings

2 garlic cloves, peeled and finely chopped or crushed through a garlic press

Two 15-ounce cans black (or other) beans OR 3 1/2 cups home-cooked black (or other) beans (see page 82), with just enough liquid to cover them

Salt

Toppings

The following are easy suggestions, but by no means exhaustive; you'll need about 2 cups—choose one, or a combination:

Coarsely shredded chicken (you'll need about half of a rotisserie bird)

Cooked Mexican chorizo sausage (start with about 8 ounces)

Small cooked shrimp (8 to 12 ounces)

Sliced ham (8 to 12 ounces), cut into strips

Flaked tuna (two 7-ounce cans or pouches is a generous amount)

Cubed tofu—flavored and smoked firm tofu are my favorites (about 12 ounces)

◎✿◎

1 large romaine heart (about 10 ounces), sliced into 1/4-inch-wide ribbons (you need about 6 cups)

1/3 cup sour cream (you can get away with plain yogurt, but then the dressing won't be as creamy-clingy)

3 tablespoons Tamazula, Cholula, Búfalo or other Mexican hot sauce, plus more for serving

12 tostadas (crisp-fried corn tortillas), store-bought or homemade (see page 230)

1 ripe avocado, pitted, flesh scooped from the skin and cut into 1/4-inch pieces (optional)

About 3/4 cup grated Mexican *queso añejo* or other garnishing cheese such as Romano or Parmesan

1/2 to 3/4 cup (loosely packed) chopped cilantro

Heat the oil, lard or bacon drippings in a medium (8- to 9-inch) skillet over medium. Add the garlic and stir for about a minute, then add the (undrained) beans. Mash with a Mexican bean masher, old-fashioned potato masher or back of a spoon until you have a coarse puree, then cook, stirring regularly, until the beans are thickened just enough to hold their shape in a spoon, about 10 minutes. Taste and season with salt if needed. Turn the heat to the lowest setting.

Set out your topping(s). Place the romaine in a large bowl. Mix together the sour cream and hot sauce. Drizzle over the romaine and toss to combine.

Spread each tostada with a portion of beans. Top with your chosen topping(s) and lettuce. Dot with the optional avocado. Sprinkle generously with the cheese and cilantro, and serve right away with more hot sauce for doctoring.

Another Thought on Tomatoes

During the winter in our restaurant, we slice soft sun-dried tomatoes and marinate them in lime juice, olive oil, crushed garlic and Mexican oregano. They make a wonderful topping (especially with grilled chicken) for tostadas.

HOMEMADE TOSTADAS

Tostadas

Makes 12 tostadas
12 tortillas
Vegetable oil for frying

Lay the tortillas out in a single layer for a few minutes to dry to a leathery feel.

In a medium (8-inch) skillet, heat 1/2 inch of oil over medium-high until it is hot enough to make an edge of a tortilla sizzle. Fry the tortillas one at a time: Lay a tortilla in the oil and after about 15 seconds, use tongs to flip it over. Push it down into the oil every few seconds, keeping it as flat as possible. When the bubbling begins to subside (usually less than a minute), remove it to paper towels to drain. Repeat with the remaining tortillas. If they have been fried long enough, the tortillas should be completely crisp when cooled.

QUESO FRESCO/QUESO AÑEJO

6

Seafood, Poultry and Meat Main Dishes

At its heart, this is a book of easy, full-flavored everyday main dishes, with a few delicious salads and a handful of fruit desserts to round it out. So, for many, this will be the chapter that's turned to most. It's where the indisputable icons of Mexican flavor are too.

This chapter contains profoundly delicious dishes that weave together tomatoes and green chiles: pan-seared Pork Tenderloin *a la Mexicana*, slow-cooked Chicken *a la Veracruzana* with capers and olives, and Jalapeño-Baked Fish with Roasted Tomatoes and Potatoes.

Roasted poblanos, the most widely loved large green chiles in the Mexican kitchen, star in dishes like Quick-Seared Poblano Beef Tips and Seared Salmon with Spinach and Creamy Roasted Peppers.

Tangy tomatillos define browned Chicken with Roasted Peppers and Salsa Verde and Tomatillo Pork Braise with Pickled Chiles. And though they play a smaller role, tomatillos bring character to the slow-cooked *Pollo Pulquero*.

Rustic red chiles resonate symphoniously through slowly simmered dishes like Guajillo-Spiced Pork and Potatoes and Lamb *Birria*, as well as a skillet-full of seared Red Chile Steak with Beans. And they play a little more subtle role in Red Chile Chicken and Rice with Black Beans and Mexican Beans with Chorizo and Greens.

Tomatoes and smoky chipotle chiles work their magic on a quick shrimp sauté (*Camarones Enchipotlados*) and the homey, time-honored Chipotle Meatballs jazzed with bacon and mint.

The earthy, rusty-red spice called *achiote*, one of Yucatán's defining flavors, infuses its quintessential aroma into one of Mexico's greatest contributions to world cuisine: the banana-leaf–wrapped, slow-cooked pork called *Cochinita Pibil*. I like *achiote* sautéed with shrimp too, so I've included Shrimp in *Achiote*, a riff on Chipotle Shrimp.

Yucatán is also famous for its escabeches, the garlicky, vinegar-sparked, spice-perfumed dishes like Chicken in Tangy Escabeche of Caramelized Onions, Carrots and Jalapeños. Garlic defines any Mexican classic christened *mojo de ajo*; I've included two different seafood takes, Snapper with Zucchini and Toasty Garlic *Mojo* and the slightly less rambunctious Trout with Macadamias, Serrano and Green Beans.

Though typically associated with special-occasion cooking, there are a couple of simple *moles* and *pipianes*, with their remarkably traditional complexity of flavor, that have a place in streamlined everyday cooking: Salmon in Luxurious Green Sesame *Pipián* and Chicken in Oaxacan Yellow *Mole*.

Connect the dots between all those traditional flavor combinations, and you've sketched out the foundation of a Mexican kitchen. Ten or so classic tastes that can offer endless pleasure, endless variety to your everyday eating.

Salmon in Luxurious Green Sesame *Pipián*

Salmón en Pipián Verde de Ajonjolí

◎❉◎❉◎❉◎❉◎❉◎❉◎❉◎❉◎❉◎❉◎❉◎❉◎❉◎❉◎❉◎❉◎❉◎❉◎

In Mexico, *pipián* is a simple *mole* that emphasizes the nuts or seeds that are blended in to thicken the sauce. Where *mole* is an exuberant symphony orchestra, *pipián* is a lively string quartet. The seed that has traditionally thickened a sauce like this since pre-Columbian times is Mexico's native pumpkin seed. After centuries of trade between Acapulco and Southeast Asia (for three centuries, most goods destined for Europe from Asia traveled from the Philippines to Acapulco, then overland to Veracruz and overseas to European ports), the Asian sesame seed found a home in Mexico's *pipián*—making it super-creamy, wonderfully aromatic and deliciously toasty-nutty (although a little hard to pull off, since sesame seeds are hard to blend to a smooth puree). But with a good-quality bottled tomatillo salsa and a jar of tahini, dinner's only moments away.

Serves 4

2 cups store-bought tomatillo salsa
  OR 2 cups Roasted Tomatillo Salsa
  (page 154)
1 1/2 tablespoons vegetable or olive oil
1 cup chicken broth
3 tablespoons tahini (sesame paste)
Salt
1/4 to 1/2 teaspoon sugar

1 heaping cup peas (fresh or frozen)
Four 4- to 5-ounce (1 to 1 1/4 pounds
  total) skinless fish fillets (such as
  salmon, halibut, walleye, snapper or
  striped bass)—buy about 1 1/2 pounds
  if using fish steaks
1 tablespoon sesame seeds, for garnish
About 1/4 cup (loosely packed) chopped
  cilantro, for garnish

In a blender or food processor, process the salsa to a smooth puree. Heat the oil in a very large (12-inch) skillet over medium-high. When it is quite hot, add the salsa all at

SALMON IN LUXURIOUS GREEN SESAME *PIPIÁN*

once. Stir as the salsa reduces to the consistency of tomato paste, about 5 minutes. Stir in the broth and tahini. Return to a boil, then reduce the heat to medium-low and let simmer 10 minutes. Taste and season with salt, usually about 1/2 teaspoon, and a little sugar. (The sugar will help balance the natural tartness of the salsa.)

While the sauce is simmering, pour the peas into a microwaveable bowl, sprinkle on a tablespoon of water, cover with plastic wrap and poke a couple of holes in the top. Microwave on high (100%) until the peas are hot and tender, anywhere from 1 minute for frozen peas to 4 or 5 minutes for fresh peas; discard water.

When the sauce has simmered for 10 minutes, nestle the fish fillets in it, completely submerging them. Continue simmering gently until the fish flakes when pressed firmly, usually 5 to 6 minutes for 1/2-inch-thick fillets. (Check it by lifting up a fillet on a metal spatula and pressing it with your finger or the back of a spoon.)

Transfer a fish fillet to each dinner plate. Spoon a portion of the sauce over the top. Strew with the peas, sesame seeds and cilantro, and you're ready for dinner.

Riffs on Green *Pipián*

You can replace the peas with a couple of medium-large red-skin boiling or Yukon Gold potatoes cut into eighths (microwave them until tender, about 8 minutes). I like to mix the potatoes into the sauce after transferring the fillets to the dinner plates. A can of white beans makes a great replacement for the peas; drain and rinse them before adding them to the sauce, as I describe for the potatoes. This dish is also wonderful made with boneless, skinless chicken breasts or semi-boneless quail: poach the birds in the sauce as described or, for added flavor, brown them in oil in the large skillet, then remove them and, without washing the skillet, cook down the pureed salsa. Tahini is an easy addition because it's smoothly ground, but you can use the very traditional pumpkin seeds or almonds or peanuts: Puree them with the salsa, but stir carefully as you cook the mixture down to a paste (it will stick more easily than the salsa alone). After the sauce has simmered 10 minutes, it will likely be quite coarse looking; reblend the hot sauce in a *loosely covered* blender to smooth it out.

◎ **VEGETARIAN GREEN PIPIÁN:** Prepare the sauce with vegetable broth, and serve with 4 to 6 cups roasted, steamed or grilled vegetables for a really delicious meal. Grilled vegetables—along with grilled tofu—are my favorite with this green *pipián*. Mexican white rice is my accompaniment of choice.

JALAPEÑO-BAKED FISH WITH ROASTED TOMATOES AND POTATOES

Jalapeño-Baked Fish with Roasted Tomatoes and Potatoes

Pescado Horneado al Jalapeño

◎✶◎✶◎✶◎✶◎✶◎✶◎✶◎✶◎✶◎✶◎✶◎✶◎✶◎✶◎✶◎✶◎✶◎

This is one of the simplest, tastiest, come-back-to-it-often dishes I know. It can be made even simpler if you replace the tomato mixture with 2 cups of bottled tomato salsa. I'd be hard-pressed to say where they make a dish like this in Mexico, especially since baked dishes aren't a part of the traditional, mostly stovetop cuisine. But the idea of fish cooked in roasted tomato sauce sparked with jalapeño chiles and cilantro is about as traditional as you can get. Even the potatoes make a regular showing in dishes like this. If, like me, you weave lots of vegetables into your everyday eating, feel free to sprinkle the dish with steamed peas before spooning on the sauce.

Serves 4

4 medium (1 pound total) red-skin boiling or Yukon Gold potatoes, sliced 1/4 inch thick

1 tablespoon vegetable or olive oil

Salt

One 15-ounce can diced tomatoes in juice (preferably fire-roasted)

1 large garlic clove, peeled and cut in half

1/3 cup (loosely packed) coarsely chopped cilantro, plus extra for garnish

About 1/4 cup sliced canned pickled jalapeños (you can seed and slice whole pickled jalapeños or buy "nacho slices")

1 tablespoon jalapeño pickling juice

Four 4- to 5-ounce (1 to 1 1/4 pounds total) skinless fish fillets (mahimahi, halibut, black cod and striped bass are all good here), preferably 3/4 to 1 inch thick

Turn on the oven to 400 degrees. Scoop the sliced potatoes into a microwaveable 8 × 8-inch baking dish. Drizzle on the oil and sprinkle with 1/2 teaspoon salt. Toss to coat, then spread the potatoes in an even layer. Cover with plastic wrap and poke a couple of holes in the top. Microwave on high (100%) until the potatoes are nearly tender, about 4 to 5 minutes.

Meanwhile, in a food processor or blender, combine the tomatoes with their juice, garlic, cilantro, jalapeños and pickling juice. Process to a puree, leaving just a little texture.

Lay the fish fillets in a single layer over the potatoes. Pour the tomato mixture evenly over the fish and potatoes.

Slide the baking dish into the oven. Bake for 15 to 20 minutes, until the fish flakes when pressed firmly.

Scoop a portion of fish-potatoes-sauce onto each dinner plate, sprinkle with cilantro and serve right away.

Riffs on Jalapeño-Baked Fish

This is a wonderful place to feature the Mexican white-fleshed sweet potato (*camote morado*), yuca or other roots from Caribbean groceries. All of them have pretty fibrous exteriors, so trim them, slice them and microwave them with a good sprinkling of water (they are naturally drier than potatoes) and salt. Be prepared for them to take a little longer than potatoes to cook.

Herbs like Mexican oregano, thyme and marjoram make a delicious addition to the sauce, as do a handful of golden (or regular) raisins. You can go all the way to the classic Veracruzana flavors by adding some chopped olives and capers. A delicious alternative to the basic recipe replaces the tomato mixture with 2 cups tomatillo salsa (store-bought or the Roasted Tomatillo Salsa on page 154). That version is wonderful too when you substitute sliced baby artichokes (peel off the tough outer leaves first, trim the fibrous exterior off the base and slice 1/4 inch thick) for half the potatoes—microwave the artichokes with the potatoes.

Seared Salmon with Spinach and Creamy Roasted Peppers

Salmón con Espinacas en Crema Verde

◎✕◎

Though salmon isn't a traditional Mexican fish (salmon, like cold water, isn't part of Mexican geography), there's nothing more wonderful than a creamy roasted poblano sauce with the full-flavored pink flesh of a seared salmon fillet. Pair those flavors with a small pile of roasted potatoes, and I'm in heaven. Now, though most of us find using a food processor second nature, this creamy roasted pepper sauce comes out much smoother, much more beautifully green when everything is pureed in a blender. (Besides, the food processor won't hold all the milk.) No *masa harina*? You can make the sauce with an equivalent amount of all-purpose flour—it just won't be quite as rich in flavor.

Serves 4

2 fresh poblano chiles

10 ounces cleaned spinach (about 10 cups)

3 tablespoons vegetable or olive oil

3 garlic cloves, peeled and halved

1 to 2 tablespoons *masa harina* (Mexican corn "flour" for making tortillas—look for it in well-stocked groceries)

1 1/2 cups milk, plus a little more if needed

Four 4- to 5-ounce (1 to 1 1/4 pounds total) skinless salmon fillets (snapper, halibut and catfish are also good here)

Salt and ground black pepper

Roast the poblanos over an open flame or 4 inches below a broiler, turning regularly until blistered and blackened all over, about 5 minutes for an open flame, 10 minutes for the broiler. Place in a bowl, cover with a kitchen towel and let cool until handleable.

SEARED SALMON WITH SPINACH AND CREAMY ROASTED PEPPERS

Place the spinach in a microwaveable bowl, cover it with plastic wrap, poke a few holes in the top and microwave on high (100%) until completely wilted, usually about 2 minutes. (If your spinach comes in a microwaveable bag, simply microwave it in the bag.) Uncover (or open the bag) and set aside.

Turn the oven on to its lowest setting. Heat the oil in a very large (12-inch) skillet, preferably nonstick, over medium. Add the garlic and cook, stirring regularly, until soft and lightly browned, about 4 minutes. Using a slotted spoon, scoop the garlic into a blender. Set the skillet aside.

Rub the blackened skin off the chiles and pull out the stems and seed pods. Rinse the chiles to remove bits of skin and seeds. Roughly chop and add to the blender, along with the *masa harina* and milk. Blend until smooth.

Return the skillet to medium-high heat. Sprinkle both sides of the fish liberally with salt and pepper. Lay the fillets in the hot oil and cook until richly browned, about 2 to 3 minutes. Use a spatula to flip the fillets, and cook until the fish barely flakes when pressed firmly with a finger or the back of a spoon (you want it slightly underdone), usually a couple of minutes longer for fish that's about 1 inch thick. Using the spatula, transfer the fish to an ovenproof plate and set in the oven.

With the skillet still over medium-high, pour in the poblano mixture and whisk until it comes to a boil and thickens, about 1 minute. Reduce the heat to medium-low and simmer, stirring frequently, for 5 minutes to blend the flavors. If the sauce has thickened past the consistency of a cream soup, whisk in a little more milk. Taste and season with salt, usually a generous 1/2 teaspoon. Add the spinach to the sauce and stir until it is warm and well coated with sauce.

Divide the creamy spinach among four plates. Top each portion with a piece of seared fish. (Or, if it seems more appealing to you, spoon the sauce over the fillets.) Serve without delay.

Riffs on Fish in Creamy Roasted Pepper Sauce

I'm sure your mind has already wandered to other chiles that would be good in this sauce: roasted red bells, fresh pimientos, roasted Anaheims or yellow Hungarian wax/bananas, Cubanelles, practically any large, fleshy chile—though in my opinion, none of them holds a candle to the classic poblano. One twist I do recommend, however, is to roast a red bell along with the poblanos, make the sauce with the poblanos and then add the peeled, seeded and diced red pepper to the finished sauce.

During grilling season, grill the fish rather than sauté it; replace the spinach with sliced grilled asparagus or quartered bok choy (toss with oil and sprinkle with salt before grilling), or with grilled zucchini or other summer squash (grill thick slices, then cut the slices crosswise into short strips before adding them to the finished sauce). Scallops, shrimp and boneless, skinless chicken breasts are natural stand-ins for the fish, but don't overlook pork chops or roasted pork loin; they're wonderful too. If you like the flavor of cilantro, blend a handful in with the poblanos. Or add a little fresh thyme, marjoram or oregano. Replacing 1/2 cup of the milk with white wine will give the sauce a decidedly European profile.

◎ **THINK VEGETARIAN:** Forget the fish. Replace the spinach with Swiss chard (cut a large bunch crosswise into 1/2-inch slices and microwave-steam it in a covered bowl for a little longer than the spinach) and mix the chard with the sauce (here's where I'd want to add another roasted poblano or two, cleaned and cut into strips). Divide it among small shallow bowls and sprinkle liberally with Mexican *queso fresco* or goat cheese. A great soft taco filling.

Snapper with Zucchini and Toasty Garlic *Mojo*

Huachinango al Mojo de Ajo con Calabacitas

◎✠◎

Seared fresh fish, bathed luxuriously with toasty garlic slow-cooked in a pool of rich olive oil, is a dish I always look forward to at Mexico's seaside restaurants. It's such a treat for this landlocked Midwesterner to be there that I always celebrate the richness of it all. For everyday eating, I make this simpler, less rich version—which I have to say is incredibly satisfying. Zucchini is a perfect messenger for all these thrilling flavors, and the soft sautéed garlic binds the oil with the broth, creating a wonderfully silky sauce.

Serves 4

1/3 cup olive oil

8 garlic cloves, peeled and halved

2/3 cup chicken broth

Salt

1/2 teaspoon ground black pepper (I like it coarsely ground here), plus more for seasoning the fish

Four 4- to 5-ounce (1 to 1 1/4 pounds total) skinless fish fillets (choose snapper, halibut, mahimahi, catfish or bass fillets), preferably about 3/4 inch thick

2 large (about 1 pound total) zucchini, cut into 1/2-inch cubes

1/2 cup (loosely packed) chopped cilantro

1 large lime, cut into wedges, for serving

Turn the oven on its lowest setting. In a very large (12-inch) skillet, warm the olive oil over medium heat. Add the garlic and cook until soft, lightly browned and very aromatic, about 4 minutes. With a slotted spoon, scoop the garlic into a food processor or blender jar, leaving as much oil as possible in the skillet. Set the skillet aside.

Add the broth to the processor or blender, along with 1/2 teaspoon salt and the pepper. Blend until smooth.

Return the skillet to medium-high heat. Generously season the fish with salt and pepper. When the oil is hot, lay in the fish. When richly browned underneath, about 2 to 3 minutes, flip and cook until the fish gives slightly under firm pressure from your finger, about 2 minutes. Use a spatula to transfer each piece of fish to an oven-proof dinner plate. Keep warm in the oven.

With the skillet still over medium-high heat, add the zucchini and cook, stirring regularly, until lightly browned but still a little crunchy inside, about 6 minutes. Add the garlic mixture and cilantro. Stir until the sauce comes to a boil and becomes homogeneous. Taste and season with more salt if it needs it.

Spoon the zucchini and sauce over and around the fish and serve right away, with lime wedges for each person to squeeze on.

A Couple of Riffs on *Mojo de Ajo*

If I put my mind to it, I believe I could manage to make anything *al mojo de ajo*, with a bath of garlic. Chicken (yes, the ubiquitous boneless and skinless breast) is a natural, and all you have to do is put it in where the fish is called for—just cook it a few minutes longer. To replace the zucchini, asparagus is the first vegetable that comes to mind (probably because it's one of our favorite local spring vegetables in Chicago—if yours is artichokes or fiddlehead ferns or leeks, all of those can be worked in). A handful of raisins or chopped prunes or dried apricots is captivating in the sauce (I like to soak them in a little white wine before adding them). And if chile's your game, add chopped canned chipotle to the skillet along with the zucchini. Or crumble toasted guajillo over the dish just before serving.

Trout with Macadamias, Serrano and Green Beans

Trucha con Macadamias, Chile Serrano y Ejotes

◎✵◎✵◎✵◎✵◎✵◎✵◎✵◎✵◎✵◎✵◎✵◎✵◎✵◎✵◎✵◎

A dish of pan-seared trout with garlicky toasted macadamia nuts doesn't sound very Mexican, but it has become a new tradition around Uruapan, Michoacán, where avocado ranchers have diversified to raise large crops of the captivating nut and farmed trout. Think of the preparation as a nutty version of the classic *mojo de ajo* (toasted garlic bath) with a good shot of green chile, cilantro and fresh lime juice, which add beautiful balance to the nut's richness. If you have access to the slender French beans (*haricots verts*), their tenderness and sweet flavor shine here.

Serves 4

3 tablespoons olive or vegetable oil

4 pan-dressed (head and tail off) boneless trout (they generally weigh about
6 ounces each)

Salt

3 garlic cloves, peeled and finely
chopped or crushed through a garlic
press

2/3 cup chicken broth

12 ounces green beans, tops and tails
broken off (you'll have about 4 cups)

Fresh hot green chiles (I like 2 serranos
or 1 jalapeño), stemmed

1/2 cup coarsely chopped roasted
macadamia nuts (you'll need about
2 ounces)

2/3 cup (loosely packed) chopped
cilantro

3 tablespoons fresh lime juice

Turn the oven on to its lowest setting. Measure the oil into a very large (12-inch) skillet and set over medium-high heat. If the skin of the two halves of each trout is still connected, cut the fillets apart. Generously sprinkle the fish all over with salt and lay skin side up in the hot oil. Cook until golden underneath, 2 to 3 minutes. (If all the fillets don't fit comfortably in the pan, cook them in 2 batches.) Use a spatula to turn the fish and cook for a minute longer, until the flesh separates from the skin (use a corner of your spatula to check at one edge). With the spatula, transfer a pair of fillets to each of four ovenproof dinner plates, flipping them skin side down. Keep warm in the oven.

Reduce the heat under the skillet to medium. Add the garlic and cook a few seconds, stirring constantly, until fragrant. Pour the broth into the skillet and add 1/2 teaspoon salt and the green beans. Cover the skillet (a cookie sheet works if you don't have a lid large enough) and cook until the green beans are barely tender, 6 to 7 minutes.

While the green beans are cooking, cut the chiles in half lengthwise and scrape out the seeds. Finely chop.

When the beans are ready, uncover the skillet and add the chiles. Increase the heat to high and cook for a minute or so to concentrate the broth. Then add the macadamias, cilantro and lime juice and mix well. Taste and season with salt, usually another 1/2 teaspoon if you are using unsalted macadamia nuts.

Spoon a portion of sauce over each fillet, and dinner's ready.

Riffs on This "New" Mexican Classic

The trout can be replaced by other fine-textured thin fillets; think flounder, tilapia or skate. Of course, nuts beside macadamias can be featured: roughly chopped whole toasted almonds and pine nuts are particular favorites of mine. Feel free to use half butter, half olive oil, if that appeals. Baby artichokes (pull off the tough outer leaves, trim the fibrous base, then quarter), broccoli florets, asparagus (cut peeled thick stalks on a sharp bias into 1/2-inch-thick slices) and diced chayote (peeled and pitted) are just a few of the vegetables that work well in this dish. Using lemon juice and basil (about 1/2 cup) instead of lime juice and cilantro will yield a delicious dish that tastes Mediterranean rather than Mexican.

◎ **DELICIOUSLY SMOKY TROUT WITH MACADAMIAS:** If smoky whets your appetite, cut 2 or 3 slices of bacon crosswise into 1/2-inch pieces and fry until crisp in the large skillet, then use the drippings (adding a little olive oil if necessary) to prepare the dish. Replace the green chile with 1 or 2 seeded, finely chopped canned chipotle chiles *en adobo*.

◎ **GOING VEGETARIAN:** Brown 1/2-inch-thick slices of firm tofu, flavored or not, in place of the fish (or choose a softer variety and simply warm in the microwave before spooning the macadamia mixture over the top). You can do the same with 1/2-inch-thick slices of eggplant or pattypan squash; they will take longer to cook than the trout.

Chipotle Shrimp

Camarones Enchipotlados

◎✠◎✠◎✠◎✠◎✠◎✠◎✠◎✠◎✠◎✠◎✠◎✠◎✠◎✠◎✠◎✠◎✠◎✠◎✠◎

Along the Veracruz coast, some variation of this beguiling preparation of smoky, spicy shrimp is on practically every restaurant menu—from punchy glazed crustaceans to soupy, saucy concoctions that taste of ketchup and fire. The most complex versions rely on the local *salsa negra* ("black salsa"—it's really more of a paste) made from dried chipotle chiles, roasted garlic and unrefined sugar. My quick-but-satisfying, saucy everyday version relies on canned roasted tomatoes and canned chipotles.

To turn the dish into a one-skillet meal, you can sauté some chopped peeled chayote or zucchini in the oil (you'll need to add an extra tablespoon) before adding the garlic; serve this version with lots of warm corn tortillas. My favorite accompaniment for chipotle shrimp, however, is white rice—either simply steamed or the Mexican-style one on page 88. To devein shrimp (that is, to remove their tiny intestinal tracts), simply make a shallow incision down the back of each one and pull out the (usually) dark vein that's exposed. Many specialty groceries now carry peeled, deveined shrimp with the tail left on.

Serves 4

One 15-ounce can diced tomatoes in
   juice (preferably fire-roasted), drained

2 to 3 canned chipotle chiles *en adobo*

1 tablespoon chipotle canning sauce

2 tablespoons vegetable or olive oil

3 garlic cloves, peeled and finely chopped
   or crushed through a garlic press

About 1 1/2 cups fish or chicken broth
   or water

Salt

1 to 1 1/4 pounds medium-large shrimp
   (21 to 25 shrimp per pound), peeled
   and deveined, tail left on if you wish

About 1/4 cup (loosely packed) roughly
   chopped cilantro, for garnish

Pour the drained tomatoes into a blender or food processor. Add the chipotle chiles and chipotle canning sauce. Process until smooth.

In a very large (12-inch skillet), heat the oil over medium. Add the garlic and stir until fragrant and golden, about 1 minute. Pour in the tomato mixture. Cook, stirring frequently, for 5 minutes to allow the flavors to meld. Add enough broth or water to achieve a light tomato sauce consistency. Taste and season highly with salt, usually about 1 teaspoon.

Add the shrimp to the pan. Cook, stirring nearly constantly, until the shrimp are cooked through, about 4 minutes. Stir in a little more broth or water if the sauce has thickened too much.

Scoop onto dinner plates and sprinkle with the cilantro.

A Couple of Simple Riffs

Replace the shrimp with scallops—the large sea scallops are meaty and delicious, but more expensive (for full scallop flavor, ask for "dry pack" ones); bay scallops are smaller but can be unbelievably sweet, especially Nantucket bays at the height of their season. A tangier but equally delicious dish can be made using the Smoky Chipotle Salsa (page 149) or bottled chipotle salsa: simply sauté the shrimp in the oil for a minute, then add 3/4 cup salsa and the broth and stir until the shrimp are done (I like the texture best with a smoothly pureed salsa).

◎ **GOING VEGETARIAN:** In a very large (12-inch) nonstick skillet, heat 2 table-spoons olive oil over high heat. Add 1 pound firm tofu, cut into 3/4-inch cubes, and stir until it starts to brown, about 5 minutes; remove to a plate. Add another table-spoon of oil to the pan, with 1 small eggplant, peeled and cubed; lower the heat to medium-high and stir-fry until the eggplant is soft but not mushy. Add the recipe's garlic and stir for a minute, then add the tomato mixture, 3/4 cup vegetable broth and 2 teaspoons soy sauce (I like this mixture to be a little less saucy than the shrimp version). Add the tofu back to the pan, season and serve.

◎ **NOW FOR SOMETHING COMPLETELY DIFFERENT—YUCATÁN-STYLE SHRIMP IN *ACHIOTE*:** A similar preparation with a completely different flavor comes from substituting 1 1/2 tablespoons prepared *achiote* paste (see pages 35–36) for the chipotles and their canning liquid. I like to add a couple tablespoons of fresh lime juice as part of the broth or water.

CHICKEN IN OAXACAN YELLOW *MOLE* WITH GREEN BEANS
AND CHAYOTE (OR POTATOES)

Chicken in Oaxacan Yellow *Mole* with Green Beans and Chayote (or Potatoes)

Mole Amarillo con Pollo con Ejotes y Chayote (o Papas)

◎✖◎✖◎✖◎✖◎✖◎✖◎✖◎✖◎✖◎✖◎✖◎✖◎✖◎✖◎✖◎✖◎✖◎

Don't let the word *mole* scare you away from this recipe—*moles* being the famous, time-consuming, special-occasion dishes that Mexicans make from a huge grocery list of ingredients. Typically, that's what they are. But this *mole*—one of the classic seven *moles* of Oaxaca—is an everyday *mole*, put together in a matter of minutes rather than hours or days. It offers a satisfying spice-and-herb-tinged yellow-orange sauce (actually, it's more like thick broth) buoying pieces of tender chicken and fresh vegetables.

Because the dried chile plays a lesser role in yellow *mole* than it does in, say, the famous *mole poblano*, I have found it possible to skip its toasting and soaking, saving twenty or thirty minutes. Plus, the traditional thickening of this *mole* with corn tortilla dough (I use the dehydrated powder *masa harina* in this version) offers a mellowness that rounds out any rough edges the chile may have.

About the *hoja santa*: No one in Oaxaca would think that a pot of yellow *mole* was complete without a handful of torn *hoja santa* leaves added just before serving, but then most cooks have an *hoja santa* bush near the kitchen window. Though it's very easy to grow in moderate climates (during the winter in Chicago, I bring mine inside), many of us can't easily lay our hands on this sarsaparilla-flavored herb. So I say, use cilantro. It's not the same as *hoja santa*, but it's good.

Serves 4

4 (1 ounce total) dried guajillo chiles, stemmed and torn into several pieces each

Half a 15-ounce can diced tomatoes in juice (preferably fire-roasted), drained

1/2 small white onion, cut into 4 pieces

2 garlic cloves, peeled and halved

1/4 teaspoon *each* ground cumin, allspice and cinnamon, preferably Mexican *canela*

1 teaspoon dried oregano, preferably Mexican

4 cups chicken broth (divided use)

2 tablespoons vegetable or olive oil

1 tablespoon powdered *masa harina* (Mexican corn "flour" for making tortillas—look for it in well-stocked groceries)

4 (1 pound total) boneless, skinless chicken thighs, cut into 1-inch cubes

6 ounces green beans, tops and tails broken off and cut into 2-inch pieces (you need about 2 cups)

2 large (1 pound total) chayotes, peeled (if you wish), pitted and cut into 1-inch cubes

OR 4 medium (1 pound total) red-skin boiling or Yukon Gold potatoes, peeled (if you wish) and cut into 1-inch cubes

Salt

1 to 2 fresh *hoja santa* leaves, torn into 1-inch pieces

OR 1/2 cup (or more) roughly chopped cilantro

In a blender jar, combine the torn guajillo chiles, tomatoes, onion, garlic, spices, oregano and *1 cup* of the chicken broth. Blend until as smooth as possible. (A food processor will work, but it won't completely puree the chile.)

In a medium-large (4- to 6-quart) heavy pot, heat the oil over medium-high. Set a medium-mesh strainer over the top and pour in the chile mixture; press the mixture through the strainer into the hot oil. Cook, stirring, until the mixure is reduced to the consistency of tomato paste, about 5 minutes.

Whisk the *masa harina* into the remaining *3 cups* broth, then pour into the cooked chile mixture. Whisk until the sauce comes to a boil and thickens to the consistency of a light cream soup. Reduce the heat to medium-low. Add the chicken, green beans, chayote or potatoes and 1 teaspoon salt. Simmer gently, stirring regularly, for about 20 minutes, until all the chicken and vegetables are tender.

Straining blended ingredients for
Chicken in Yellow *Mole*

Cooking the sauce to a paste for
Chicken in Yellow *Mole*

Finishing the sauce for
Chicken in Yellow *Mole*

Add the *hoja santa* or cilantro, then taste and season with salt, usually between 1/2 and 1 teaspoon, depending on the saltiness of your chicken broth, and serve.

Riffs on Yellow *Mole*

Because I have such respect for kitchen tradition (and because of the fact that I've already taken a few liberties here with this revered classic), I'm hesitant to go much further. I will say, however, that a seafood version of yellow *mole* is one of my favorite things in the world. When the vegetables have cooked for 10 minutes, in place of the chicken add a dozen or so scrubbed clams or (debearded) mussels and about 12 ounces firm-fleshed fish fillets (like halibut, bass or grouper) cut into about 3/4-inch pieces. In Oaxaca, they also make a much thicker version of this sauce (they would add the equivalent of about 6 tablespoons of *masa harina* versus the 2 I've called for here) to use as a filling for what they call empanadas: They press out a corn tortilla from the prepared corn *masa* and lay it on a griddle to brown lightly, then flip it and top it with a spoonful of the thick sauce, a few shreds of cooked chicken and a big piece of *hoja santa* leaf. After folding it in half, they cook the empanada on the griddle until toasty and aromatic.

CHICKEN IN TANGY ESCABECHE OF CARAMELIZED
ONIONS, CARROTS AND JALAPEÑOS

Chicken in Tangy Escabeche of Caramelized Onions, Carrots and Jalapeños

Pollo en Escabeche de Cebollas Caramelizadas, Zanahorias y Jalapeños

◎❊◎❊◎❊◎❊◎❊◎❊◎❊◎❊◎❊◎❊◎❊◎❊◎❊◎❊◎❊◎❊◎

This dish is seductive—exotic aromas are woven together with the browned onion sweetness, vinegar dazzle and jalapeño fireworks. It's a Mexican classic that strikes an immediate chord with folks everywhere. Plus, it has the added benefit of being completely delicious whether served warm or cool. Serve warm when you want to huddle close to the fire. Serve cool, and you'll be looking for a place to picnic.

Serves 4

1 teaspoon ground black pepper

1/2 teaspoon ground allspice

2 teaspoons dried oregano, preferably Mexican

Salt

4 (2 pounds total) chicken breast halves, bones and skin intact

2 tablespoons vegetable or olive oil

1 large white onion, cut into 1/4-inch slices

2 large carrots, peeled if you wish and sliced 1/4 inch thick on a diagonal

4 garlic cloves, peeled and halved

1/4 cup vinegar (apple cider vinegar is traditional)

2 to 4 canned pickled jalapeños, stemmed, seeded and thinly sliced

1 cup chicken broth

In a small bowl, combine the black pepper, allspice, oregano and 1 teaspoon salt. Sprinkle half of this mixture over the chicken breasts.

Heat the oil in a very large (12-inch) skillet over medium. Lay in the chicken, skin side down, and cook, turning once, until richly browned, 3 to 4 minutes on each side. Remove the chicken to a plate, leaving behind as much oil as possible.

Add the sliced onion and carrots to the skillet and cook, stirring regularly, until the onion is browned, about 7 minutes. Add the garlic and stir for about 1 minute, then add the remaining seasoning mixture, the vinegar, jalapeños and broth. Nestle the chicken pieces skin side up in the onion mixture, cover the skillet (a cookie sheet works if your skillet doesn't have a lid) and simmer gently over medium-low heat until the chicken is just cooked through, about 15 minutes.

Taste the broth, and season with additional salt if you think it's appropriate. Transfer a piece of chicken to each dinner plate, spooning a generous portion of the juicy vegetable mixture over the top. Dinner's ready.

Serving Ideas and Riffs

Though I love to serve escabeche chicken with classic Mexican white rice, it's great with fried black beans and simple roasted potatoes too. White wine can replace part of the chicken broth. And roasted green chiles (such as poblanos or Anaheims) can easily take the place of the jalapeños. Though this dish is all about the spices, you can omit the allspice from the spice sprinkle and add sprigs of thyme and marjoram, plus a couple of bay leaves, along with the broth. An unconventional though totally delicious variation is to add fresh fennel: slice a fennel bulb (cut out the root end first) and brown it along with the onion.

◎ **GRILLED DUCK BREASTS (OR QUAIL) IN ESCABECHE:** Grill (instead of sauté) 4 spice-seasoned boneless, skinless duck breasts (or 4 large semi-boneless quail) until they are just done—8 to 10 minutes for both duck and quail over a medium fire. Make the escabeche in a skillet and serve it over the duck (or quail); or, for a more elegant presentation, let the duck rest in a very low oven for 5 minutes, then slice it on the bias, fan out the slices, and spoon the vegetable escabeche over the top.

Slow-Cooked Chicken with Tomatillos, Potatoes, Jalapeños and Fresh Herbs

Pollo Pulquero

◎✻◎✻◎✻◎✻◎✻◎✻◎✻◎✻◎✻◎✻◎✻◎✻◎✻◎✻◎✻◎✻◎✻◎✻◎

It was the perfect marriage of people, place and piquancy. No, actually "piquancy" is too narrow a distinction for the package of bold flavor on my fork at Guillermo Ramírez's Tlaxcala ranch, where he produces *pulque*, the ancient libation made from the fermented milky juice (*aguamiel*) of huge agave plants. The spiky leaves (*pencas*) of the agaves, larger than those of the blue agaves used to make tequila, have an outer membrane (*mixiote*) that can be stripped off. And the *pulqueros*, as the ranch hands are called, used it to wrap a chicken-potato-tomatillo-herb construct. The chicken was a muscley one from their barn yard. *Epazote* grew in a huge patch by the back door. Potatoes and tomatillos, which keep for a long time between infrequent market visits, were plentiful. Pickled jalapeños added gusto to their solitary existence. And their "oven" for cooking was a blazing pile of the driftwood-looking "bones" from long-deceased agave leaves—ready for nestling their *mixiote*-wrapped packages of goodness, ready to blast heat from all sides to concentrate and fuse flavors.

Though not exactly the dish of that magical moment, this slow-cooked version of the *pulqueros'* feast is really worth making. *Epazote* makes it taste authentic, and, in my opinion, really delicious. Some of the *pulqueros* squeezed lime over theirs as they ate. You may want to, too.

Serves 4

1 medium white onion, cut into 1/4-inch-thick rounds

Salt

4 medium (about 1 pound total) red-skin boiling or Yukon Gold potatoes, sliced 1/4 inch thick

8 skinless chicken thighs (bone in or out, 1 1/2 or 2 pounds respectively)

1 cup (loosely packed) cilantro leaves OR 1/3 cup (loosely packed) fresh *epazote* leaves

1 1/4 pounds (8 to 12 medium) tomatillos, husked, rinsed and sliced 1/4 inch thick

1/4 cup sliced canned pickled jalapeños (you can seed and slice whole pickled jalapeños or buy "nacho slices")

2 tablespoons jalapeño pickling juice

Spread the onion over the bottom of a slow-cooker. Sprinkle with salt. Continue with layers of the potato slices, chicken thighs, cilantro or *epazote* and then tomatillos, sprinkling salt evenly over each layer before moving on to the next. (This is the only salt in the dish, so make sure to add enough.) Scatter the jalapeño slices over everything, then drizzle on the pickling juice. Cover and slow-cook on high for 6 hours (the dish can hold on the slow-cooker's "keep warm" function for 4 more hours or so).

Carefully transfer a portion of your *pollo pulquero* onto each dinner plate. If there is a large amount of juice in the cooker, tip or ladle it into a saucepan, set it over high heat and boil quickly to reduce to a rich consistency. Taste and season with more salt if it needs it, then drizzle over each serving. If you have any extra cilantro in the refrigerator, chop some to sprinkle over each portion.

Riffs on Slow-Cooked Chicken

Practically any sliced root vegetables (from sweet potatoes to malanga) could be layered in this dish—beets are tasty, but they will turn the whole assemblage red. Pork shoulder and beef chuck, cut into 1-inch cubes, are fine substitutes for the chicken thighs; just stay away from leaner cuts (they'll turn out dry). If banana leaves are available, make a super-aromatic version of *pollo pulquero* by lining the slow-cooker or Dutch oven in the following variation with leaves before assembling all the parts.

◎ **A QUICKER OVEN VERSION OF *POLLO PULQUERO*:** Heat the oven to 400 degrees. Layer the dish as described in a medium-large (4- to 6-quart; 10- to 12-inch-diameter) heavy pot, preferably a Dutch oven. Set the lid in place and bake for 45 minutes. Remove the lid and bake 15 to 20 minutes longer to reduce the juices. Spoon directly from the pot onto plates.

Chicken a *la* Veracruzana

Pollo a la Veracruzana

◎✠◎✠◎✠◎✠◎✠◎✠◎✠◎✠◎✠◎✠◎✠◎✠◎✠◎✠◎✠◎✠◎✠◎✠◎

This sauce is the classic fusion of the flavors all of Mexico (and beyond) associates with the Gulf town of Veracruz: Mexican red ripe tomatoes and pickly green chiles in perfect choreography with the briny gusto of Mediterranean capers and olives. Throw a few herbs and spices into the pot, spoon it over fish and you've got the classic *pescado a la Veracruzana*, Veracruz-style fish, that every fish restaurant in the Mexican Republic has on its menu. Slow-cook the sauce with chicken, as I do here, and you'll fill the house with comforting aromas that, in that welcome Mexican way, weave in hints of the exotic.

Serves 6

4 medium (about 1 pound total) red-skin boiling or Yukon Gold potatoes, each cut into 6 wedges

6 (about 3 pounds total) chicken leg-and-thigh quarters, skin pulled off

One 28-ounce can diced tomatoes in juice (preferably fire-roasted), drained

4 to 6 canned pickled jalapeños, stemmed, seeded and cut into strips

3 garlic cloves, peeled and finely chopped or crushed through a garlic press

2 tablespoons Worcestershire sauce

1/8 teaspoon dried thyme

1/8 teaspoon ground cloves

1/4 teaspoon ground cinnamon, preferably Mexican *canela*

Salt

1/4 to 1/2 cup coarsely chopped green olives (Manzanilla olives are traditional)

1/4 cup (loosely packed) roughly chopped flat-leaf parsley

Spread the potatoes over the bottom of a slow-cooker and top with the chicken. In a medium bowl, mix together the tomatoes, jalapeños, garlic, Worcestershire, thyme, cloves, cinnamon and a scant 2 teaspoons salt. Pour evenly over the chicken. Set the lid in place and slow-cook on high for 6 hours (the dish can hold on the slow-cooker's "keep warm" function for 4 more hours or so).

Carefully transfer a portion of chicken and potatoes to each of six dinner plates, leaving as much sauce behind as possible. Mix the olives and parsley into the sauce, then taste and season with more salt if it needs it. Spoon the sauce over the chicken.

No Slow-Cooker?

Lay the chicken in a medium-large (4- to 6-quart; 10- to 12-inch-diameter) heavy pot, preferably a Dutch oven, and top with the potatoes. Cover with the sauce, set the lid in place and braise in a 300-degree oven for 2 to 2 1/2 hours, until the chicken is completely tender. Complete the dish as described.

A Couple of Simple Riffs

Pork shoulder and beef chuck, cut into 1-inch cubes, are natural stand-ins for the chicken quarters; buy about 2 pounds. For the pork, I like to replace the potatoes with sweet potatoes cut into 1/2-inch cubes; for the beef, quartered little sweet turnips, cubed carrots or peeled, cubed yuca is good.

◎ **CHICKEN *VERACRUZANA* AS A SOFT TACO FILLING:** A favorite in the soft-taco stalls in Veracruz's downtown market. Cook the dish as directed. Pull the meat off the chicken in large shreds and stir it into the sauce with the olives and parsley; smash the potatoes into smaller pieces. Serve with a dozen warm tortillas.

◎ **SLOW-COOKED PUEBLAN CHICKEN *TINGA*:** Sprinkle the chicken with 4 ounces fresh Mexican chorizo sausage (casing removed, sausage broken up) and 1 sliced large white onion. Mix the tomatoes with 2 or 3 sliced seeded canned chipotle chiles instead of the pickled jalapeños, 1 tablespoon of their canning liquid, the garlic, Worcestershire, thyme and 2 scant teaspoons salt (leave out the spices). Cook as described, skipping the olives and parsley. With a slotted spoon, remove the meat and other solids; pull out the chicken bones. Tip or ladle the juice into a saucepan; boil over high heat until reduced to 1 cup. Pour over the meat mixture and serve with warm tortillas.

RED CHILE CHICKEN AND RICE WITH BLACK BEANS

Red Chile Chicken and Rice with Black Beans

Arroz Rojo con Pollo y Frijoles Negros

Arroz con pollo, the chicken-and-rice dish that practically every Latin American associates with *mama*'s or *abuelita*'s kitchen, has provided easy, tasty sustenance for centuries of folks from Taos to Tierra del Fuego—each prepared, of course, with those inimitable qualities unique to one's own mother. Well, none of those versions has ever tasted like this version, my version, a red chile–infused version that's studded with black beans and cubes of lean chicken breast. But believe me: it's an easy, smile-conjuring answer to, "What's for dinner?"

A note about ancho chile powder: look for chile powder that is cranberry red rather than dark brown, so the rice will turn out a pretty color; a very flavorful paprika works well too.

Serves 4

2 tablespoons vegetable or olive oil

4 (1 1/4 to 1 1/2 pounds total) boneless, skinless chicken breast halves

Salt

2 1/2 tablespoons ground ancho chile powder (available from national companies such as McCormick, Mexican groceries and internet sites), divided use

1 medium white onion, cut into 1/4-inch pieces

1 cup rice

4 garlic cloves, peeled and finely chopped or crushed through a garlic press

1 1/2 cups chicken broth

One 15-ounce can black beans, drained and rinsed (rinsing will keep them from making the rice sticky) OR 1 3/4 cups home-cooked black beans (see page 82), drained and rinsed

1/4 cup chopped green onions (roots and wilted outer leaves removed before chopping) OR 1/3 cup (loosely packed) chopped cilantro OR 2 to 3 tablespoons chopped fresh *epazote* or *hoja santa*

1/2 to 1 cup salsa (such as the Smoky Chipotle Salsa on page 149), or chipotle hot sauce, for serving

Heat the oil in a medium-large (4- to 6-quart) heavy pot over medium-high. Sprinkle both sides of the chicken breasts first with salt, then with *1 tablespoon* of the ground ancho chile. Lay them in the hot oil in a single layer. When browned on one side, 2 to 3 minutes, flip them over and brown the other side, another 2 to 3 minutes. Remove to a plate to cool, leaving behind as much oil as possible.

Add the onion and rice to the pot. Stir for several minutes, until the rice turns from translucent to opaque. Add the garlic and the remaining *1 1/2 tablespoons* ground ancho chile and cook 1 minute, then add the broth and 1 teaspoon salt (a little less if using salty broth). Stir well. When the mixture comes to a boil, reduce the heat to medium-low and cover the pot. Cook for 10 minutes.

Cut the chicken breasts into 1-inch cubes. Uncover the pot and add the chicken and beans. Re-cover and cook 12 minutes longer.

Uncover, sprinkle on the green onions (or herbs) and test a kernel of rice: it should have no more than a hint of chalkiness in the center; if it does, cook for another 5 minutes or so. Otherwise, simply re-cover the pot and let stand off the heat for 5 to 10 minutes to finish cooking the rice in its own trapped steam.

Fluff the rice mixture and serve with the salsa for each person to spoon on *al gusto*.

Riffs on Chicken and Rice

I'm currently wild about smoked paprika (look for it in specialty groceries or from internet sites like zingermans.com), and I like replacing the ancho in this dish with it; a similar (but spicier) version is to replace the final 1 1/2 tablespoons of ancho with chipotle powder. I also love a big handful of spinach added to the pot along with the green onions or herbs—it should wilt perfectly in the 5 to 10 minutes of final steam-cooking. Same goes for broccoli, but cut it into small florets and add it after the chicken has been cooking for about 5 minutes.

Turkey breast or thigh can take the place of chicken, though the breast is so lean it may taste dry. And, of course, if chicken breast isn't moist enough for you in this preparation, use 8 boneless, skinless chicken thighs. Throwing a dozen mussels into the pot with the chicken makes a quick *Nuevo Latino* paella.

◎ **CHICKEN AND RICE WITH YUCATECAN FLAVORS:** Omit the chile powder. Season the chicken with 1 teaspoon *achiote* paste (see pages 35–36) mixed with 1 tablespoon fresh lime juice, then brown the chicken as described. Add 1 tablespoon *achiote* paste to the pot when you're frying the rice and onions—break it up with the edge of a spoon or spatula so that it will mix in thoroughly. Finish the rice as described, but serve it with habanero salsa or hot sauce.

◎ **DOUBLING THE RECIPE:** This recipe is great for a large group. Make the double batch in a 10- to 12-inch-wide Dutch oven, doubling everything but the broth—use only 2 1/2 cups. Bake it, covered, in a 350-degree oven for about 20 to 25 minutes rather than cooking it on top of the stove (baking affords the larger quantity of rice more even, gentle heat from all sides).

Chicken with Roasted Peppers and *Salsa Verde*

Pollo con Rajas y Salsa Verde

The classic Mexican flavors on a forkful of chicken in *salsa verde* bounce from the bright, citrus tang of tomatillos to the caramely sweetness of well-browned onions and chicken. Usually, I like to roast the tomatillos, to underscore that tart-sweet balance, but for everyday cooking, I simply puree them raw, cook the puree into a rich-textured sauce base and then mellow it out with a touch of cream and sweet browned onions. You can add microwave-steamed potatoes to the sauce (cut 4 medium red-skin boiling or Yukon Gold potatoes into wedges, sprinkle with salt and microwave, covered, on high [100%] for about 8 minutes, until tender). But truth be told, I like this better served with classic Mexican white rice. The recipe may look a little long, but the steps are streamlined to go by very quickly.

Serves 4

2 fresh poblano chiles

2 tablespoons vegetable or olive oil

4 (1 1/4 to 1 1/2 pounds total) boneless, skinless chicken breast halves

Salt

1 large white onion, sliced 1/4 inch thick

1 1/2 pounds (about 12 medium) tomatillos, husked and rinsed

1 cup (loosely packed) roughly chopped cilantro
OR 1 small fresh *hoja santa* leaf
OR the leaves from 1 large sprig fresh *epazote*

1 cup chicken broth or water

2 to 3 tablespoons Mexican *crema*, heavy cream or *crème fraîche*

Sugar (optional)

Roast the poblanos over an open flame or 4 inches below a broiler, turning regularly until blistered and blackened all over, about 5 minutes for an open flame, 10 minutes for the broiler. Place in a bowl, cover with a kitchen towel and let cool until handleable.

Heat the oil in a very large (12-inch) skillet over medium-high. Sprinkle both sides of the chicken breasts with salt, then lay them in the hot pan. Brown well, usually about 2 minutes per side. Remove the chicken to a plate, then add the onion to the skillet and cook, stirring frequently, until golden but still crunchy, 4 to 5 minutes.

While the onion is cooking, puree the tomatillos and cilantro or other herb in a blender (unless you have a large super-duper blender, you'll want to do this in 2 batches).

Add the pureed tomatillos to the onions and cook, stirring frequently, until as thick as tomato paste, about 8 minutes.

While the tomatillo mixture is cooking, rub the blackened skin off the chiles and pull out the stems and seed pods. Rinse the chiles to remove bits of skin and seeds. Cut into 1/4-inch strips.

Stir the broth or water into the tomatillo mixture, along with the poblano strips and cream. Taste and season with salt, usually a generous teaspoon. (If the sauce is too tart for you, balance the tartness with a little sugar.)

Nestle the chicken breasts into the sauce, cover the pan (a cookie sheet works fine if you don't have a large lid) and simmer over medium-low heat until the chicken is done, usually 8 to 10 minutes.

Serve the chicken breasts bathed with the sauce and roasted pepper *rajas*.

Riffs on Chicken in *Salsa Verde*

Besides changing from breasts to boneless, skinless chicken thighs (which I do when preparing the dish ahead and reheating it), you can make a great dish with fish (salmon is spectacular) or pork tenderloin; fish will cook more quickly than chicken breast, pork tenderloin more slowly. Any large fleshy pepper can stand in for the poblanos. Though it would be a major change, tomatoes can replace the tomatillos— I'd use a drained 28-ounce can of diced fire-roasted tomatoes, and I wouldn't puree them (just chop the herbs and stir them in). And then I'd rename the delicious dish *Pollo a la Mexicana*.

◎ **GOING VEGETARIAN:** Switch the preparation to a wok. Stir-fry about 1 pound of vegetables cut into 1- to 2-inch pieces (think broccoli, asparagus, zucchini, quartered baby bok choy), then scoop them out and continue with the preparation as described, replacing the chicken broth with vegetable broth. The final simmering will only be long enough to heat the vegetables through. I love tofu (about 7 to 8 ounces) in this preparation too, but I stir-fry it separately, before I add it to the vegetables.

Tomatillo Pork Braise with Pickled Chiles

Puerco en Salsa Verde con Jalapeños Encurtidos

◎✖◎✖◎✖◎✖◎✖◎✖◎✖◎✖◎✖◎✖◎✖◎✖◎✖◎✖◎✖◎✖◎✖◎✖◎

I know that the idea of rich, meaty pork braised with tangy tomatillos, garlic and herbs may ring a bell for many of you, since a related (but more involved, more special-occasion) dish from my *Mexico One Plate at a Time* has become a favorite at dinner tables all across our country. It demands a sequel, because this version illustrates how a slow-cooker (plus a dash of Worcestershire) can be invaluable in the creation of deep, roasty flavors that would otherwise require the time-consuming roasting of individual sauce ingredients. This homier version of the dressier classic is perfect enjoyed in big bowls around the fireplace in the winter, or, without the beans, as a filling for soft tacos. It's a good buffet dish, too. FYI: I've borrowed the (perhaps unexpected) white beans from the traditional tomatillo-and-herb–infused Oaxacan green *mole* because I love how their earthy sweetness plays against the bright tomatillos.

Serves 6

1 1/2 pounds (10 to 12 medium) tomatillos, husked, rinsed and cut into 1-inch pieces

3 garlic cloves, peeled and halved

3 to 4 canned pickled jalapeños, stemmed, halved and seeds scraped out

1/2 cup (loosely packed) roughly chopped cilantro (divided use)

Salt

1 1/2 to 2 pounds boneless pork shoulder, cut into 1-inch cubes

1 tablespoon Worcestershire sauce

Two 15-ounce cans large white (great Northern or cannellini) beans, drained OR 3 1/2 cups home-cooked beans (see page 82), drained

About 1/2 teaspoon sugar, if needed

Scoop the tomatillos into a slow-cooker and spread them in an even layer. Scatter on the garlic, jalapeños and *half* of the cilantro. Sprinkle evenly with 1 1/2 teaspoons salt.

In a large bowl, combine the pork and Worcestershire, mixing until the cubes are well coated. Distribute the meat over the tomatillo mixture. Cover and slow-cook on high for 6 hours (the dish can hold on the slow-cooker's "keep warm" function for 4 more hours or so).

With a pair of tongs, remove the pork to a bowl. Tip or ladle the sauce mixture into a blender and add the remaining cilantro. *Cover loosely* and blend until smooth; return the mixture to the slow-cooker. (Alternatively, you can puree the sauce in the slow-cooker using an immersion blender.) Stir in the drained beans. Taste and season with salt if necessary; stir in a little water if the sauce has thickened beyond the consistency of a light cream soup. Add a little sugar if the sauce is too tart for you. Return the meat to the pot, let everything warm through and you're ready to serve.

No Slow-Cooker?

In a medium-large (4- to 6-quart; 10- to 12-inch-diameter) heavy pot, preferably a Dutch oven, layer the tomatillos, flavorings and meat as described. Cover with the sauce, set the lid in place and braise in a 300-degree oven for 2 1/2 to 3 hours, until the pork is completely tender. Complete the dish as described.

Riffs on Pork in Tomatillo Sauce

If beans don't appeal to you, replace them with potatoes or small sweet turnips (cut into wedges) or carrots (2-inch lengths cut into sticks). Toss them with a little salt and place them on top of the sauce ingredients (tomatillos, garlic and chile) before layering in the pork. Take them out with the meat while you finish the sauce. I also like to add a big handful of spinach to the blender when pureeing the sauce; a few tablespoons of Mexican *crema*, *crème fraîche* or heavy cream work magic on this spinach-enhanced sauce. *Epazote* is a favorite replacement for cilantro in many parts of Mexico; *hoja santa* is a personal favorite, but I don't add it until I'm blending the sauce. The pickled jalapeños take the sauce in a delicious direction, but you could use poblanos: roast, peel and seed 2 poblanos and add them to the blender when pureeing the sauce.

As you might expect, this dish is perfectly delicious made with 2 pounds boneless, skinless chicken thighs. If you're a lamb or beef lover, replace the pork shoulder with 1-inch pieces of boneless lamb shoulder or beef chuck; double the cilantro (the lamb and beef need the extra punch) and use 2 poblanos, as described just above. Both lamb and beef benefit greatly from browning before slow-cooking.

◎ **FOR MORE "BROWNED" FLAVOR:** Either brown the cubed pork in a little oil in a single layer in a large skillet, or spread it out on an oiled baking sheet (with sides) and slide it close up under a broiler. Slide the browned meat into the slow-cooker.

Guajillo-Spiced Pork and Potatoes

Puerco y Papas al Guajillo

◎✾◎✾◎✾◎✾◎✾◎✾◎✾◎✾◎✾◎✾◎✾◎✾◎✾◎✾◎✾◎✾◎✾◎

T his classic Mexican red chile pork braise is one of the reasons I'm so in love with Mexican food. It's a classic combination of flavors that I am revisiting here because the recipe illustrates how long, gentle slow-cooker simmering can develop the chiles' deep, rich flavor—a flavor that in other versions comes from cooking down the soaked-pureed-strained chiles in a little oil over high heat, a step that seems foreign to many American cooks. Still, for the best-tasting guajillo sauce, no matter which version you're making, dry-toasting the chiles is necessary to add complexity and bring out sweetness.

Serves 6

6 medium (1 1/2 pounds total) red-skin boiling or Yukon Gold potatoes, each cut into 6 wedges

1 1/2 to 2 pounds boneless pork shoulder roast, cut into 1-inch cubes

8 medium (2 ounces total) dried guajillo chiles, stemmed, seeded and torn into flat pieces

One 15-ounce can diced tomatoes in juice (preferably fire-roasted)

4 garlic cloves, peeled and halved

2 teaspoons dried oregano, preferably Mexican

2 tablespoons Worcestershire sauce

Salt

1/2 cup (loosely packed) coarsely chopped cilantro, for garnish

1/2 cup chopped white onion, for garnish

Spread the potatoes over the bottom of a slow-cooker and top with the pork.

Set a medium (8-inch) skillet over medium heat. When it is hot, toast the chile pieces a few at a time, pressing them against the hot surface with a spatula until they are aromatic and lightened in color underneath—about 10 seconds per side. (If you see more than a whiff of smoke, they are burning.) Transfer the toasted chiles to a blender jar.

Add the tomatoes with their juice, garlic, oregano, Worcestershire, a generous 1 1/2 teaspoons salt and 1 1/2 cups water. Blend until as smooth as possible. Strain the mixture through a medium-mesh strainer directly into the slow-cooker, over the meat and potatoes. Stir to mix thoroughly.

Set the lid in place and slow-cook on high for 6 hours (the dish can hold on the slow-cooker's "keep warm" function for 4 more hours or so).

Gently stir the stew—the sauce may look slightly broken, but it will come together with gentle stirring. If the sauce seems thick to you, stir in a little water. Taste, and season with salt if you think the dish needs it.

Serve in bowls, sprinkled with the cilantro and onion. A stack of warm corn tortillas is the perfect accompaniment.

No Slow-Cooker?

In a medium-large (4- to 6-quart; 10- to 12-inch-diameter) heavy pot, preferably a Dutch oven, assemble the dish as directed, layering the pork under the potatoes. Set the lid in place and braise in a 300-degree oven for 2 1/2 to 3 hours, until the pork is completely tender. Complete the dish as described.

Riffs on a Classic

Mexican cooks get creative with the chiles: using 1 ounce *each* guajillo and ancho chiles produces a darker, slightly sweeter-tasting sauce; combining guajillo and cascabel chiles produces a sauce with a toasty nuttiness; adding 1 or 2 chipotles to the dish contributes spice and smoke; and throwing in a small handful of árbol or pequín chiles is for the stalwart lovers of bright, bitey spice. The pork can be replaced with boneless, skinless chicken thighs. And the potatoes can be swapped out with peeled, cubed sweet potato, Mexican purple-skinned sweet potato (*camote morado*), yuca or malanga, depending on how adventurous you are.

◎ **PORK AND POTATOES *AL GUAJILLO* AS A SOFT TACO FILLING:** Cook the dish as I've directed, but cube the potatoes rather than leaving them in larger wedges. Coarsely shred the pork with two forks. Leave the sauce quite thick. Serve with a dozen warm tortillas for everyone to make soft tacos. Feel free to double the recipe for a larger group.

RED CHILE STEAK WITH BEANS

Red Chile Steak with Beans

Puntas en Chile Colorado con Frijoles

◎✿◎✿◎✿◎✿◎✿◎✿◎✿◎✿◎✿◎✿◎✿◎✿◎✿◎✿◎✿◎✿◎✿◎✿◎✿◎

I n northern Mexico (and spilling over into the American Southwest), earthy, rich-tasting red chile meat stews represent a cornerstone of cuisine—satisfying lunches at market stalls and kitchen tables; fillings for tacos, burritos and tamales; fiesta dishes in rural villages. They are as common as red curries in Thailand or teriyaki beef in Japan. Though traditionally made with whole chile pods in Mexico, the version I'm giving you here uses pure chile powder, as is common throughout the American Southwest, to give the dish its distinction. Though it's easier, you do have to know what you're doing: I've used a little flour to bind the sauce, added tomatoes to mellow the chile (chile pods are typically silkier, sweeter and more complex in flavor than powder) and finished it with beans, which not only round out the flavors, but turn a simple meat sauté into a complete, if rustic and homey, meal. For the more adventurous or enthusiastic, I give directions below for using whole chile pods.

Serves 4

2 tablespoons olive oil, vegetable oil or bacon drippings (divided use)

Two 10-ounce rib-eye, New York (strip loin) or tenderloin steaks (1 1/4 pounds total), trimmed of excess fat and cut into 1-inch cubes

Salt

1 medium white onion, sliced 1/4 inch thick

1 tablespoon all-purpose flour

2 garlic cloves, peeled and finely chopped or crushed through a garlic press

2 tablespoons ground ancho chile powder (available from national companies such as McCormick, Mexican groceries and internet sites)

1 1/2 teaspoons chipotle chile powder (or use 1/2 tablespoon more ancho powder)

1 1/2 cups beef broth, plus a little more if necessary

One 15-ounce can diced tomatoes in juice (preferably fire-roasted)

1/2 teaspoon dried oregano, preferably Mexican

1/4 teaspoon ground cumin

1/2 teaspoon sugar, if necessary

One 15-ounce can pinto—or practically any—beans, drained OR 1 3/4 cups home-cooked pinto beans (see page 82), drained

Heat *1 tablespoon* of the oil or bacon drippings in a very large (12-inch) skillet over medium-high. Sprinkle the meat all over with salt. When the oil is very hot, add the meat in an uncrowded single layer and cook, stirring and turning regularly, until browned but still rare inside, 3 to 4 minutes. With a slotted spoon, scoop the meat onto a plate, leaving behind as much oil as possible. Add the onion to the skillet and cook, stirring regularly, until richly golden but still crunchy, 4 to 5 minutes. Scoop onto the plate with the meat.

Reduce the heat under the skillet to medium. Add the remaining *1 tablespoon* oil or drippings, along with the flour, garlic and two chile powders. Cook for 1 minute, stirring constantly to prevent burning. Add the broth and whisk until a smooth, thick sauce is formed.

Add the tomatoes, with their juice, the oregano and cumin. Bring to a boil, then reduce the heat to medium-low and simmer gently for 10 minutes. Taste and season with salt, usually about 1 teaspoon. Add the sugar if the sauce has a bitter edge.

Thin with a little more broth if the sauce has thickened beyond the consistency of a light cream soup.

Add the meat and onions to the pan, along with the beans. Simmer for a couple of minutes, until everything is heated through and the meat is as done as you like. The dish is ready.

Making Red Chile Steak with Chile Pods, Not Powders

After browning the meat and onions, return the skillet to medium-high heat and add the remaining oil or drippings as directed—but no flour or powdered chiles. When the oil is hot, add 2 1/2 tablespoons ancho chile puree (see page 141) and the garlic. (You can add 1 to 2 chipotle chiles *en adobo* to the blender when making the puree or finely chop and add to skillet with the puree.) Stir for 4 or 5 minutes as it cooks down a little, then add the broth, tomatoes, oregano and cumin. Reduce the heat to medium and simmer 10 minutes. Finish as directed.

A Few Riffs on Red Chile Steak

I also love this dish with the bold flavor of lamb or venison loin, but the sweeter flavor of pork tenderloin is also good. Or replace the steak with cubed beef chuck, but then you'll want to simmer everything together, covered, for about 45 minutes, until the beef is tender. Of course the beans can be left out—many cooks would serve fried beans on the side. Or, for the broadminded, the beans can be replaced by 2 cups sliced shiitake mushrooms (add them with the tomatoes)—their earthy flavor is wonderful with red chile. For the more conservative, replace the beans with microwave-steamed potatoes (4 medium red-skin boiling or Yukon Gold potatoes, cut in wedges, sprinkled with salt and microwaved, covered, on high [100%] for about 8 minutes). As for the chiles, guajillo (powder or pod) is a brighter-tasting, slightly spicier substitute for the sweeter, richer-tasting ancho, while New Mexico chiles offer a lighter, less complex flavor. Use the same volume or weight of whichever you choose. Hotter chile powders (like árbol, pequín or chipotle) should be added in small amounts along with your primary chile; add enough to match your particular penchant for piquancy.

Pork Tenderloin *a la Mexicana*

Puerco a la Mexicana

◎❋◎❋◎❋◎❋◎❋◎❋◎❋◎❋◎❋◎❋◎❋◎❋◎❋◎❋◎❋◎❋◎❋◎

I can say little more about this flexible, reliable, eponymous Mexican dish than, "Make it a staple in your kitchen." Roasted chiles, ripe tomatoes, tender seared pork and aromatic herbs. A perfect balance of spicy, tangy, sweet and meaty, with enough fragrance to fill the house. I love to eat it with fried black beans, though white rice (either simply steamed or the classic version on page 88) is good, too.

Serves 4

2 large fresh poblano chiles

1 to 1 1/4 pounds pork tenderloin, cut into 1-inch cubes

Salt

2 tablespoons vegetable or olive oil

1 medium white onion, sliced 1/4 inch thick

3 garlic cloves, peeled and finely chopped or crushed through a garlic press

One 28-ounce can diced tomatoes in juice (preferably fire-roasted), drained

3/4 cup beef broth

OR 2/3 cup water plus 2 tablespoons Worcestershire sauce

1 large branch fresh *epazote*

OR 1/2 cup (loosely packed) coarsely chopped cilantro

Roast the peppers over an open flame or 4 inches below a broiler, turning regularly until blistered and blackened all over, about 5 minutes for an open flame, 10 minutes for the broiler. Place in a bowl, cover with a kitchen towel and let cool until handleable.

While the chiles are cooling, pat the meat dry on paper towels. Sprinkle liberally all over with salt. Heat the oil in a very large (12-inch) skillet over medium-high. When the oil is hot, add the pork in an uncrowded single layer and cook, stirring and turning regularly, until browned all over, about 4 minutes. With a slotted spoon, remove to a plate, leaving behind as much oil as possible. Set the skillet aside.

Rub the blackened skin off the chiles and pull out the stems and seed pods. Rinse the chiles to remove bits of skin and seeds. Cut into 1/4-inch strips.

Return the skillet to medium-high heat. Add the onion and cook, stirring frequently, until richly golden but still crunchy, 4 to 5 minutes. Add the garlic and chile strips and stir until fragrant, then pour in the drained tomatoes, broth (or water-Worcestershire combo) and *epazote* (save the cilantro to add later). Bring to a boil and let cook until slightly thickened, about 5 minutes. Add the meat to the pan (and cilantro, if that's what you're using). Reduce the heat to medium and simmer briskly until the pork is cooked through—I like it still a touch rosy inside, which usually takes just about 5 minutes of simmering.

Taste and season with salt, usually about 1 teaspoon. Remove the *epazote* from the pan, if necessary, and you're ready to serve.

A Few of the Many Possible Riffs

I'm not exaggerating when I say that this preparation works as well with boneless, skinless chicken breasts, cubed beef steak (especially rib-eye), lamb loin and shrimp or scallops as it does with pork tenderloin. Just go with a light broth (chicken or vegetable) for the poultry or fish. You can also substitute white wine (good with poultry and fish) or dark beer (good with beef, lamb and pork) for part of the broth. During tomato season, I roast 1 1/2 pounds ripe tomatoes (I like the heirloom plum tomatoes I can buy at the farmers' market) under a broiler until soft and splotchy black on both sides; I use them, peeled and diced, in place of the canned. Feel free to use any fleshy large peppers, keeping in mind that the poblanos are classic and flavor-rich without being too hot.

Mexican Beans with Chorizo and Greens

Frijoles con Chorizo y Espinacas o Acelgas

◎�◎�◎�◎�◎�◎�◎�◎�◎�◎�◎�◎�◎�◎�◎�◎�◎�◎

When asked what I crave most when traveling in countries other than Mexico, my response is immediate: beans. I know that the lowly bean may sound to some like an unlikely candidate to inspire cravings, but it's been a staple in my diet since childhood. The happy news is beans are a good thing to count on as a gastronomic bedrock. First, they taste delicious (earthy and slightly sweet), they easily absorb a multitude of other flavors (making them a cook's dream) and top-quality ones come in a can, ready to use. Second (though decidedly less important to most of us when we're hungry and need to get dinner on the table), beans are low in calories and fat, high in cholesterol-lowering fiber, high in complex carbohydrates and high in protein. But, of course, no nutrition data would make any impact if beans couldn't be easily prepared in ways that draw you back time and again. Chiles add the seduction for me—especially smoky chipotles or deep, rich anchos. Add greens and fresh cheese, and I've got a meal that's thoroughly captivating. Add chorizo and, well, I'm in fantasyland.

Serves 4

8 to 12 ounces fresh Mexican chorizo sausage, casing removed

10 ounces cleaned young spinach (about 10 cups)

OR one 12-ounce bunch Swiss chard, thick lower stems cut off, leaves sliced crosswise into 1/2-inch strips (about 8 cups)

Two 15-ounce cans black beans, drained

OR 3 1/2 cups home-cooked black beans (see page 82), drained

1 to 2 canned chipotle chiles *en adobo*, stemmed, seeded and finely chopped

Salt

1/2 cup crumbled Mexican *queso fresco* or other fresh cheese such as feta or goat cheese

1/2 cup chopped green onions or thin-sliced red onion, for garnish

In a medium-large (4- to 6-quart; 10- to 12-inch-diameter) heavy pot, preferably a Dutch oven, cook the chorizo over medium heat, stirring regularly and breaking up clumps, until lightly browned and thoroughly done, about 8 to 10 minutes.

While the chorizo is cooking, place the spinach or Swiss chard in a microwaveable bowl, cover with plastic wrap, poke a few holes in the top and microwave on high (100%) until completely wilted, usually about 2 minutes for spinach, 3 minutes or so for the Swiss chard. (If your spinach comes in a microwaveable bag, simply microwave it in the bag.) Uncover the bowl (or open the bag) and set aside.

When the chorizo is ready, add the beans, chopped chipotles and 1 1/2 cups water. Simmer for 5 to 10 minutes to blend the flavors. Taste and season with salt, usually about 1/2 teaspoon, depending on the saltiness of the chorizo and beans. Add the wilted greens and let the mixture return to a boil.

Ladle into bowls and serve, passing the cheese and onion for each person to add *al gusto*.

Riffs on Mexican Beans and Greens

Black beans aren't the only magic (though I think their earthiness goes particularly well with greens), so feel free to use any bean you want. As for the chipotle chile, it can be replaced with pickled jalapeños if you prefer, or with 2 large poblano chiles; rather than adding the poblanos chopped and still raw—which would give the dish flecks of their tough skin and grassy-green flavor—roast, peel, seed and then chop them. And, of course, the variety of greens you can use in this dish is only limited by your resources. If you're a gardener, be sure to save beet or turnip tops, or harvest the wild lamb's-quarters that sprout as "weeds" in everybody's garden. Don't overlook arugula—but don't microwave-wilt it; add it to the pot just before serving.

◎ **VEGETARIAN BEANS AND GREENS:** This dish is perfectly delicious made without the chorizo: Sauté 1 large sliced onion in a little olive oil over medium heat until very richly browned. Add 2 or 3 garlic cloves, peeled and finely chopped or crushed through a garlic press. Stir 1 minute, then add the beans, chiles and 1 1/2 cups water. Simmer 10 minutes. Add the microwave-wilted greens, heat through and serve with the garnishes.

CHIPOTLE MEATBALLS

Chipotle Meatballs

Albondigas al Chipotle

◎✄◎✄◎✄◎✄◎✄◎✄◎✄◎✄◎✄◎✄◎✄◎✄◎✄◎✄◎✄◎✄◎✄◎✄◎✄◎

While living in Mexico City, I ate chipotle meatballs all the time in the bare-bones *cocinas económicas* that dotted my neighborhood, those simple little holes-in-the-wall where grandma cooks three- or four-course meals of basic, everyday food from scratch, all for just a few bucks. When I bought a cookbook there—it was called *Marichu en la Cocina Mexicana*—nearly thirty years ago, I learned how to make this version. I've reworked the process to simplify it, but kept intact the savory punch of roasted tomatoes, smoky chipotle, bacon and mint.

Serves 4

3 slices bacon, cut into 1-inch pieces

3 garlic cloves, peeled (divided use)

2 large eggs

1/2 cup dried bread crumbs (3/4 cup if they're the coarse-textured panko)

Salt

1 1/4 pounds ground pork

1/2 cup (loosely packed) coarsely chopped mint leaves, plus extra leaves for garnish, if you wish

One 28-ounce can diced tomatoes in juice (preferably fire-roasted)

1 to 2 canned chipotle chiles *en adobo*, stemmed and seeded

1 to 2 tablespoons chipotle canning sauce

1 teaspoon dried oregano, preferably Mexican

About 1 1/2 cups beef or chicken broth

Turn on the oven to 450 degrees. In a food processor, combine the bacon and *1 garlic clove*. Process until finely chopped. Add the eggs, bread crumbs and 1 teaspoon salt. Pulse several times to combine thoroughly, then add the pork and mint. Pulse the machine a few more times until everything is well combined—but not at all processed into a paste. Remove the blade.

With wet hands, form the meat into 16 plum-size spheres, spacing them out in a 13 × 9-inch baking dish. Bake until lightly browned (they'll be browned more underneath than on top), about 15 minutes.

While the meatballs are baking, combine the tomatoes, with their juice, chipotles, canning sauce, oregano, the remaining *2 garlic cloves* (cut in half) and 1/2 teaspoon salt in a blender or food processor. Process to a smooth puree.

When the meatballs are ready, spoon off any rendered fat from the baking dish, then pour on the tomato mixture, covering the meatballs evenly. Bake until the sauce looks like tomato paste, 15 to 20 minutes.

Microwave the broth for about a minute to heat it (or heat in a small saucepan). Divide the meatballs among four dinner plates, leaving most of the sauce behind. Stir enough broth into the sauce to give it an easily spoonable consistency. Taste and season with additional salt if you think the sauce needs it. Spoon the sauce over the meatballs, decorate with extra mint leaves, if you wish, and carry to the table.

Riffs on Chipotle Meatballs

Though pork is most common in Mexico, you can make these from beef or a combination of beef and pork. Lamb can be worked into the mix too. Turkey is what will appeal to most people looking for the leanest dish. The bacon adds just the right touch of succulence and savor, so I'd fight to keep it in, even though the meatballs will turn out fine without it. Mint adds the traditional touch, but parsley, thyme (not too much), sage and basil are all delicious in meatballs.

Slow-Braised Lamb (or Goat) Jalisco-Style

Birria Jalisciense

◎✠◎✠◎✠◎✠◎✠◎✠◎✠◎✠◎✠◎✠◎✠◎✠◎✠◎✠◎✠◎✠◎✠◎✠◎✠◎

Having visited Guadalajara many times over the past three decades, I still say that one of the best places to eat there is the huge downtown Libertad market. Besides the beyond-spicy *tortas ahogadas*, the corn *masa* pockets called *gorditas*, the Chinese food and sushi (honestly), folks flock to the collection of stalls that sell slow-cooked goat *birria*, set under spotlights to highlight its rusty-red glaze. The cooks in the market, justly famous for their *birria*, braise the meat in a specially constructed oven and add a final chile-glazing step (which I've omitted from this simpler everyday recipe). With a simple red chile marinade and a slow-cooker, you can come remarkably close to the Guadalajara market version. Just add strolling *mariachis* for the full experience.

Serves 6

8 garlic cloves, unpeeled

1/4 to 1/3 cup ground guajillo or ancho chile powder (available from national companies such as McCormick, Mexican groceries or internet sites)

1/2 teaspoon ground cumin

1 teaspoon ground black pepper

3 tablespoons vinegar (cider vinegar is common in Mexico)

Salt

6 medium (about 1 1/2 pounds) red-skin boiling or Yukon Gold potatoes, each cut into 6 wedges

A 3-pound bone-in lamb (or goat) shoulder roast

One 15-ounce can diced tomatoes in juice (preferably fire-roasted)

1 teaspoon dried oregano, preferably Mexican

About 1/2 cup finely chopped white onion, for garnish

1/2 cup chopped cilantro, for garnish

1 lime, cut into 6 wedges, for serving

Cut a slit in the side of each garlic clove. Place them in a microwaveable bowl, cover with plastic wrap, poke holes in the top and microwave for 30 seconds on high (100%). Cool until handleable, then slip off the papery husks.

One by one, drop the garlic cloves into a running food processor, letting each get thoroughly chopped before adding the next. Add the chile powder, cumin, black pepper, vinegar, 1 teaspoon salt and 1/2 cup water and pulse to blend.

Spread the potatoes over the bottom of a slow-cooker. Sprinkle generously with salt. Lay the meat on top. Scrape the marinade onto the meat, then spread it sloppily over the top and sides, letting some fall onto the potatoes. Pour enough water into the slow-cooker to cover the potatoes and the lower 1/4 inch of the roast. Cover and slow-cook on high for 6 hours, until the lamb is fall-off-the-bone tender (the dish can hold on the slow-cooker's "keep warm" function for 4 more hours or so).

Carefully remove the tender meat to a large plate, pulling out the bone; cut away any visible gristle or fat. Use a slotted spoon to scoop the potatoes onto the plate with the meat. Keep warm in a low oven. Spoon off the fat that has risen to the top of the broth.

Set a medium (3-quart) saucepan over medium-high heat and pour in the tomatoes, with their juice. Cook, stirring frequently, until the juice has reduced to the consistency of tomato paste. Tip or ladle the broth from the slow-cooker into the pan. Add the oregano and bring to a boil. Taste and season with salt, usually about 1 1/2 teaspoons.

Divide the potatoes among six deep dinner plates (or wide bowls). Coarsely shred the lamb and distribute among the plates. Ladle a portion of broth over each one, then sprinkle generously with the chopped onion (rinsed after chopping for freshest flavor) and cilantro. Pass the lime wedges separately for each person to squeeze on to his or her own liking—an essential part of great *birria*.

No Slow-Cooker?

In a large (6- to 8-quart; at least 12-inch-diameter) heavy pot, preferably a Dutch oven, assemble the dish as directed, layering the lamb under the potatoes. Set the lid in place and braise in a 300-degree oven for 2 1/2 to 3 hours, until the lamb (or goat) is completely tender. Complete the dish as described.

◎ **NORTHERN MEXICAN *BARBACOA*:** If your slow-cooker is large enough, you can make *barbacoa* from the traditional northern Mexican cow's head . . . or use a 3-pound bone-in chuck roast. Make the marinade with ancho chile powder and skip the tomato and oregano at the end; instead, boil down the degreased broth to concentrate flavors, then ladle it over the meat and potatoes and garnish with the onions and cilantro. Brisket is happily adaptable to this preparation too, but I'd let it cook all day in a little more liquid than you'd use for the lamb.

Quick-Seared Poblano Beef Tips

Puntas de Filete al Chile Poblano

◎✿◎✿◎✿◎✿◎✿◎✿◎✿◎✿◎✿◎✿◎✿◎✿◎✿◎✿◎✿◎✿◎✿◎✿◎

It's been fifteen years since I tasted one particular plate of beef tips in Mexico City, but my mouth still waters every time I think of them. Cubes of beef tenderloin seared on a hot griddle, then tossed with the crunchy, deep-golden onions cooking next to them, plus a few pungent roasted green chiles. The cook ladled on a darkish liquid—the savory-smelling stuff crackled and spattered as it hit the griddle—and quickly scooped my beef tips onto a plate. His roasted green chiles were serranos split lengthwise; mine here are poblanos—a little fuller in flavor, a little less spicy, a little more crowd-pleasing—depending on your crowd, of course. I've added potatoes to round out the dish.

Serves 4

3 fresh poblano chiles

2 tablespoons vegetable or olive oil

1 to 1 1/4 pounds boneless beef steak (the *filete* of the title specifies tenderloin, but I also like rib-eye and New York strip; cheaper cuts like sirloin are fine, but not as juicy or tender), cut into 1-inch cubes

Salt

1 medium white onion, sliced 1/4 inch thick

4 medium (about 1 pound total) red-skin boiling or Yukon Gold potatoes, cut into 1/2-inch pieces

4 garlic cloves, peeled and finely chopped or crushed through a garlic press

1/2 cup dark beer, white wine or beef broth (even water will work, since we're using Worcestershire)

2 tablespoons Worcestershire sauce

1/3 cup (loosely packed) chopped cilantro

Roast the poblanos over an open flame or close under a hot broiler, turning regularly until blistered and blackened all over, about 5 minutes for an open flame, 10 minutes for the broiler. Place in a bowl, cover with a kitchen towel and let cool until handleable.

Heat the oil in a very large (12-inch) skillet over medium-high. When it is hot, sprinkle the beef generously with salt, then scoop it into the hot pan, spreading it into an uncrowded single layer. Cook, stirring frequently, until the meat is *almost* to the doneness you like—it should take about 4 minutes for medium-rare. Remove to a plate.

Return the skillet to medium-high heat. Scoop in the onion and potatoes and cook, stirring regularly, until the onion is richly browned, about 8 to 9 minutes. Add the garlic and stir for about a minute, until richly aromatic. Pour in the beer, wine or broth and Worcestershire, sprinkle in a scant 1/2 teaspoon salt, reduce the heat to medium and let cook, stirring regularly and scraping up any sticky bits on the bottom of the skillet, until most of the liquid has reduced to a syrupy sauce and the potatoes are tender, 8 to 10 minutes.

While the mixture is simmering, rub the blackened skin off the chiles and pull out the stems and seed pods. Rinse the chiles to remove bits of skin and seeds. Cut into 1/4-inch strips and add them to the skillet.

When the potatoes are tender, return the meat to the pan and sprinkle on the cilantro. When the meat has heated through, taste and season with additional salt if necessary. Scoop onto dinner plates, and you're ready to eat.

Freewheeling Riffs on Poblano Beef

I'm not being indiscriminate when I say that Poblano Beef can become a very delicious Poblano Chicken Breast or Poblano Pork Tenderloin or Poblano Lamb Loin. Or that it can become Anaheim Pepper Beef or Red Pepper Beef or Practically Any Large Chile Pepper Beef. It's just a very flexible recipe that welcomes pretty much whatever you throw its way—including a variety of herbs from cilantro and basil (I love the sharpness of Thai basil) to flat-leaf parsley and thyme (use much less of these). For green vegetables, feel free to add broccoli florets, quartered bok choy or cubed chayote to the skillet when you're cooking the potatoes and onions. With all those added vegetables, you might want to skip the poblano and make Spicy Chipotle Beef by adding 2 or 3 seeded, chopped canned chipotle chiles to the skillet just before serving.

Slow-Cooked *Achiote* Pork

Cochinita Pibil

◎✖◎✖◎✖◎✖◎✖◎✖◎✖◎✖◎✖◎✖◎✖◎✖◎✖◎✖◎✖◎✖◎✖◎✖◎

Just say *cochinita pibil* in the Yucatán (or practically anywhere in Mexico nowadays), and thoughts of celebration come to mind. After all, in all its glory, we're talking a whole pit-cooked pig, smeared generously with the uniquely savory rusty-colored *achiote* seasoning and served with the meaty cooking juices, a drizzle of habanero fireworks and the citrus-sour of pickled red onion. Truth is, though, you can make a delicious, satisfying, simple version of Mexico's big-deal *cochinita pibil* for an everyday dinner. You just have to scale back the normal party-size portions, use prepared *achiote* seasoning and employ a slow-cooker (or a Dutch oven, for oven-braising). Using a bone-in pork shoulder roast offers a rich flavor reminiscent of the whole-pig version, and slow-cooking equals delicious satisfaction. Fried black beans, a salad and warm corn tortillas are my favorite accompaniments. A final note: Hot yellow chiles (such as Hungarian wax) are commonly cooked with the meat in Yucatán. If that appeals, split them in half, take out the seeds and lay, cut side down, over the meat.

Serves 6

Half a 3.5-ounce package *achiote* seasoning (I like Yucateco brand *adobo de achiote*, available in Mexican grocery stores and through internet sites)

3/4 cup fresh lime juice (divided use)

Salt

Half a 1-pound package banana leaves (available in Mexican or Asian markets), defrosted if frozen (optional)

A 3-pound bone-in pork shoulder roast

1 large white onion, sliced about 1/4 inch thick

1 large red onion, thinly sliced

About 1/2 cup Roasted Fresh Chile Salsa (page 158), preferably made with habanero chiles, or bottled habanero hot sauce (such as Yucateco and Frontera brands), for serving

Place the *achiote* seasoning in a small bowl. Pour in *1/2 cup* of the lime juice and 2 teaspoons salt, then use the back of a spoon to work the mixture into a smooth, thickish marinade.

If you have banana leaves, cut two 2-foot sections and use them to line a slow-cooker—lay one down the length, the other across the width. Lay in the pork and pour the marinade over and around the roast. Scatter the white onion over the meat.

Pour 1/2 cup water around the meat. Fold up the banana leaves (if using) to roughly cover everything. Cover and slow-cook on high for 6 hours, until the meat is fall-off-the-bone tender (the dish can hold on the slow-cooker's "keep warm" function for 4 more hours or so).

While the meat is cooking, combine the red onion with the remaining *1/4 cup* lime juice in a small bowl. Sprinkle with about 1/2 teaspoon salt, toss and set aside to marinate, stirring from time to time.

Use tongs to transfer the meat (it will easily break into delicious-looking pieces) and onions to dinner plates. Spoon off any rendered fat that's floating in the juices. If there is a lot of brothy sauce—2 cups or more—tip or ladle it into a saucepan and boil it down to about 1 cup to concentrate the flavors. Taste the sauce and season with salt if you think it needs it, then spoon it over the meat. Top with the lime-marinated red onions and serve with the salsa or hot sauce—and plenty of hot tortillas, if that appeals.

No Slow-Cooker?

In a large (6- to 8-quart; at least 12-inch-diameter) heavy pot, preferably a Dutch oven, assemble the dish as described—including dribbling the water around the meat. Set the lid in place and braise in a 300-degree oven for about 2 1/2 to 3 hours, until the pork is thoroughly tender. Complete the dish as described. If there isn't much juice in the bottom of the pot, remove the meat and add about a cup of water. Bring to a boil, scraping up any sticky bits, and season with salt, then pour over the meat.

A Few Riffs on *Cochinita Pibil*

The most common variation on *cochinita pibil* in Mexico is made with chicken. You can simply replace the pork, pound for pound, with chicken thighs; pulling off the skin before cooking will mean less fat to spoon off at the end (the broth won't be quite as rich, however). The chicken breast version is a little more involved: Smear bone-in, skin-on chicken breasts in the *achiote* mixture. Brown them in oil in a large skillet over medium-high; remove them to a baking pan, lined with the banana leaves, if using. Add the onion to the skillet and cook quickly until golden brown but still crunchy; strew over the breasts. Cover with more banana leaves, if you have them. Cover with foil and bake at 325 degrees until just cooked through, usually 20 to 30 minutes, depending on the size of the chicken breasts.

Though I love *cochinita pibil* with black beans, you can easily scatter some quartered small red-skin boiling or Yukon Gold potatoes or cubed sweet potatoes around the meat to soak up all the delicious flavors.

7

Desserts

Here's my philosophy of dessert: if you have a sweet tooth (which I certainly do), feed it. But feed it with a good amount of thought. A bowlful of sweet strawberries with a big spoon of vanilla yogurt will fill you up faster and stay with you longer than a low-fat double-chocolate hot fudge sundae made with chocolate flavoring and Splenda. The same goes for a piece of really good dark chocolate or a freshly picked sweet-tart apple or a super-sweet tangerine.

But some days, having strawberries or a small piece of dark chocolate for dessert, even a simple *everyday* dessert, won't satisfy like something cooked, something in which several flavors mingle. Rather than going all the way to bakery or ice cream shop desserts, which typically rely on the wonderfully luxurious, special-occasion thrill of sweetness, flavorings and richness, I'm offering you three super-simple, easily varied recipes that focus on fruit—a fruit crisp, a fruit upside-down cake, a fruit ice. Plus plantains roasted in their skin and topped with a drizzle of Mexican caramel and toasted nuts. And my most flexible shortbread cookie recipe—*polvorones* in Spanish—which welcomes practically any nut or seed you throw its way.

PINEAPPLE SKILLET UPSIDE-DOWN CAKE

Pineapple (or Other Fruit) Skillet Upside-Down Cake

Volteado de Piña (u Otra Fruta) en Sartén

◎✿◎✿◎✿◎✿◎✿◎✿◎✿◎✿◎✿◎✿◎✿◎✿◎✿◎✿◎✿◎✿◎✿◎

I don't keep rich desserts around during the week—I'd eat them, one little forkful at a time, until they were gone. But this simple upside-down cake, made with a lean muffin-batter and a bunch of fruit, is a different story. It's as good (and appropriate) for breakfast as for dessert after a weeknight dinner. My daughter likes a slice in the lunch she takes to school. And it couldn't be simpler, since the fruit is sautéed in the same skillet the cake is baked in.

I'm always looking for ways to work whole grains into my cooking, but not if it means compromising great flavor. (Everybody runs for the Häagen-Dazs if dessert doesn't taste good.) Here whole wheat flour works, especially if the fruit you've chosen is blackberries. A final tip: If you want to use cranberries for the fruit, increase the brown sugar to 3/4 cup. If you're going for apples, choose one that cooks up soft, like McIntosh.

Serves 8

3 ounces (6 tablespoons) butter, preferably unsalted

1/2 cup packed brown sugar (I prefer the dark brown variety)

3 cups 1/2-inch cubed, cleaned pineapple (you'll need about three-quarters of a medium pineapple)

OR 3 cups (about 1 pound) fresh or IQF (individually quick frozen) raspberries, blackberries, blueberries or pitted cherries

OR 3 cups 1/2-inch cubes apple, pear, peaches, nectarines or mango

3/4 cup all-purpose flour

3/4 cup whole wheat flour (or additional all-purpose flour)

1/2 teaspoon salt

1/4 teaspoon baking soda

1 teaspoon baking powder

3/4 cup white sugar

1 "large" egg

3/4 cup buttermilk or plain yogurt

Turn on the oven to 375 degrees and position a rack in the middle. Melt the butter in a large (10-inch) skillet, with an ovenproof handle, preferably nonstick, over medium heat. Swirl the butter in the skillet until it turns nut-brown, then pour it into a medium bowl. Without wiping out the skillet, sprinkle the brown sugar evenly over the bottom. Top with the fruit in an even layer.

In a large bowl, whisk together the flours, salt, soda and baking powder. Add the white sugar to the browned butter and whisk until thoroughly combined. Whisk in the egg, then the buttermilk or yogurt. Pour the wet ingredients into the bowl with the dry ones. Whisk to thoroughly combine.

Pour the batter evenly over the fruit in the skillet. Slide the skillet into the oven and bake about 35 minutes, until the cake is golden brown and springy to the touch at the center. Remove and let cool 10 minutes.

Invert a plate over the skillet, then, holding plate and skillet firmly together with towels or pot holders, invert the two in one swift movement. Remove the skillet, and the cake is ready to serve. It's best right out of the oven.

PINEAPPLE SKILLET UPSIDE-DOWN CAKE

Skillet Fruit Crisp

Cazuela de Frutas Empolvoronadas

◎✻◎✻◎✻◎✻◎✻◎✻◎✻◎✻◎✻◎✻◎✻◎✻◎✻◎✻◎✻◎✻◎✻◎✻◎✻◎

This is one of my favorite desserts, weekday or weekend. Tender fruit infused with browned butter, topped with a crispy, nutty, shortbread-like crumble. (The name for this dessert in Spanish refers to the shortbread cookies called *polvorones*.) I sauté the fruit, bake the crisp and serve the dessert in the same skillet—making the preparation very easy. If you want a more elegant serving vessel, make the crisp in a paella pan, an enameled cast-iron gratin dish or a Mexican *cazuela*—just make sure it can go from stovetop to oven. I love the play between salty and sweet, but if the nuts you're using are salted, reduce the amount of salt in the topping. Or forget the fruit altogether and bake the crisp topping, crumbled into large chunks on a baking sheet, to serve over ice cream.

Serves 6

4 ounces (1 stick; 8 tablespoons) butter, preferably unsalted, softened (divided use)

2 pounds apples or pears, cored, peeled if desired, and cut into 1/2-inch slices (see Riffs for other fruit options)

1/2 cup plus 2 tablespoons white sugar (divided use)

2/3 cup flour (all-purpose flour is good, but whole wheat or whole-grain spelt flour adds a delicious nuttiness)

1/4 cup packed brown sugar (I prefer the dark brown variety)

1/2 teaspoon ground cinnamon, preferably Mexican *canela*

1/2 teaspoon salt

3/4 cup (3 ounces) toasted *pepitas* (pumpkin seeds) or practically any toasted, coarsely chopped nuts

Turn on the oven to 400 degrees and position a rack in the middle. Set a large (10-inch) skillet with an ovenproof handle over medium heat and add *2 tablespoons* of the butter. When it begins to brown, add the fruit. Sprinkle with *2 tablespoons* of the white sugar. Cook, stirring regularly, until the fruit is soft, most of the juice it has exuded has evaporated and it is beginning to brown, about 10 minutes.

While the fruit is cooking, stir together the flour, the remaining *1/2 cup* white sugar, the brown sugar, cinnamon and salt (use only 1/4 teaspoon salt if you have salted *pepitas* or nuts) in a medium bowl. Add the remaining *6 tablespoons* butter, working it in with a wooden spoon until a homogeneous mixture is formed (you can do this step with a mixer or in a food processor). With a spoon, stir in the *pepitas* (or other nuts).

Crumble the streusel topping evenly over the cooked fruit mixture. Slide the skillet into the oven and cook for 10 to 15 minutes, until the topping is crispy. Serve warm or at room temperature.

Riffs on Skillet Fruit Crisp

You can replace the apples or pears with peaches (peeled and pitted) or nectarines (peeled, if desired, and pitted): the fruit is so juicy it won't really brown with the butter, but you should cook it long enough for the juices to reduce. If you'd like to make the crisp with plums (pitted, not peeled), I suggest coupling 1 pound with a pound of apples or pears for body, because the plums' juiciness causes them to disintegrate in the cooking. Ditto for berries: I suggest using 1 1/2 pounds of apples or pears along with 8 ounces berries.

FRESH LIME ICE WITH BERRIES

Fresh Lime Ice with Berries

Nieve de Limón con Moras

This is one of the simplest, most refreshing, most satisfying desserts in the world, with or without the berries. A tablespoon or two of chopped mint leaves makes a wonderfully aromatic addition. And cubed mango or papaya makes a deliciously tropical replacement for the berries.

Serves 6

5 to 6 large limes (or enough to make 3/4 cup lime juice)

1 cup sugar

1/3 cup corn syrup

2 to 3 cups fresh raspberries, blackberries or strawberries (you'll want to slice or quarter strawberries), for serving

Grate the zest (colored part only) of 2 of the limes and scrape into a large bowl. (If the zest is in large pieces, finely chop it.) Juice the limes, measure 3/4 cup and pour it in with the zest. Add the sugar, corn syrup and 1 3/4 cups water. Stir until the sugar dissolves.

Pour the mixture into the canister of your ice cream maker and freeze according to the manufacturer's directions. The ice will have the best texture if you transfer it from the ice cream maker into a container and let it firm up for several hours in the freezer. The ice is best eaten within 24 hours. Scoop it into small dishes and sprinkle with the berries.

No Ice Cream Freezer?

Pour the mixture into a 13 × 9-inch baking dish, slide it into the freezer and "still-freeze" the mixture—stir it thoroughly after 45 minutes, then twice more at 15-minute intervals. It's that easy.

◎ **LIME ICE WITH CUCUMBER AND MINT:** Combine the lime zest, lime juice, sugar, corn syrup, 1 1/3 cups water, and 1 medium peeled, seeded, roughly chopped cucumber in a blender. Blend until smooth. For the smoothest texture, pass the mixture through a fine strainer. Pour into the ice cream maker's canister and freeze according to the manufacturer's directions.

◎ **ORANGE OR TANGERINE ICE:** One of my daughter's favorites. Make the ice from 2 1/2 cups fresh orange or tangerine juice, 2/3 cup sugar, 1/3 cup corn syrup and 3 tablespoons fresh lime juice.

◎ **CREAMY MANGO ICE:** One of my favorites. Make the ice from 1 1/2 cups pureed fresh mango pulp (peel and pit the mangoes, then puree in a food processor or blender), 1 cup water, 2/3 cup sugar, 1/3 cup corn syrup and 1/3 cup fresh lime juice.

◎ **JAMAICA ICE:** In a saucepan, combine 3 cups water, the sugar and corn syrup. Bring to a boil, then add 2 cups (about 2 ounces) dried jamaica "flowers" (available at Mexican markets and gourmetsleuth.com). Remove from the heat, cover and steep for at least 20 minutes (or as long as 2 hours—the longer, the stronger).

Pour the mixture through a strainer, pressing firmly on the jamaica to extract as much liquid as possible. Add 3 tablespoons fresh lime juice. Pour into the canister of your ice cream freezer and freeze according to the manufacturer's directions.

Roasted Plantains with
Mexican Goat Milk Caramel and Nuts

Plátanos Machos Asados con Cajeta y Nueces

I always keep a jar of *cajeta*, Mexico's extraordinary goat milk caramel sauce, in the refrigerator. A spoonful may be just enough to keep the sweet-tooth wolf at bay; but drizzled over roasted plantains and toasted nuts, *cajeta* turns fantasy into long-term satisfaction. At a Mexican market, I buy *cajeta* that's made from 100 percent goat's milk because I like its full, rich flavor. There are versions of *cajeta* made from cow's milk as well, which is basically the same as the well-known *dulce de leche*. For this dessert, the plantains need to be completely ripe—what I call "black" ripe. Plantains are much darker than regular bananas when their typical "potato" starchiness has been completely transformed into beautiful, bright sweetness. Two tips: When berries are in season, they are wonderful sprinkled over the plantains. And roasted-ahead plantains can be successfully rewarmed in the microwave.

Serves 4

4 small to medium black-ripe plantains

About 1 cup (3 ounces) pecan or walnut halves or whole almonds

About 1/2 cup *cajeta* (Mexican goat milk caramel, available at well-stocked groceries and Mexican markets)

Heat the oven to 450 degrees and position a rack in the middle of the oven. Cut the pointed ends off each plantain, exposing a small amount of the flesh. Make a shallow slit through the skin on the inner curved side of each one. Lay the plantains on a baking sheet and roast until completely soft and any exposed flesh has richly browned, about 20 minutes.

While the plantains are roasting, pour the nuts into a medium ungreased skillet and set over medium-low heat. Stir frequently until fragrant and very lightly browned, about 5 minutes. Remove from the heat.

Pour the *cajeta* into a small saucepan and warm over low heat. (Or heat in a microwave.)

When the plantains are ready, remove them from the oven and let cool slightly. One by one, peel back the skin and slice the flesh into roughly 1/2-inch pieces, slicing directly on (but not through) the plantain skin. For a rustic presentation, pile the pieces into an irregular mound on the skin, then lift the whole affair onto a small deep serving plate. Drizzle each plantain with a portion of *cajeta* and sprinkle with nuts.

To Grill-Roast the Plantains

If you're grilling and want to make these plantains for dessert, simply lay them on a medium-hot section of the grill and turn them occasionally until thoroughly soft and richly browned, 5 to 8 minutes.

To Replace the Plantains with Other Fruit

Increase the temperature of the oven to 500 degrees. Choose 1 large apple, pear, peach or nectarine per person, peel (if you wish), halve and core or pit them. Lay the halves cut side down on a baking sheet, spray or brush lightly with vegetable oil and sprinkle with a little sugar. Roast until soft and richly browned, usually about 20 minutes. Transfer to small deep serving dishes and top with the warmed *cajeta* and roasted nuts (almonds go particularly well with peaches and nectarines).

You can take the same tack with apricots (you'll need 3 or 4 per person; no need to peel), figs (4 or 5 per person; leave whole), mangoes (1 medium fruit per person; peel, cut the flesh from the pit and cut into large spears) or pineapple (a medium one will serve 4 or 5; peel, core and cut into thick slices).

Mexican Shortbread Cookies

Polvorones Mexicanos

◎✠◎✠◎✠◎✠◎✠◎✠◎✠◎✠◎✠◎✠◎✠◎✠◎✠◎✠◎✠◎✠◎✠◎✠◎

My favorite part of *polvorones* is the way they so gently crumble in your mouth—tiny, buttery morsels that appeal to folks everywhere. In fact, a vast majority of the world's cultures has learned how to combine pastry's three foundation ingredients (flour, sugar and butter) into melt-in-your-mouth satisfaction, into *polvorones* or shortbread or Chinese almond cookies or Greek kourabiedes or *sablés* or bikkies, as my Irish friends call them. In fact, it's a recipe from Ireland's most famous cook, Darina Allen, a recipe she calls Two-Four-Six Bikkies, that gave easy structure to my version. The toppings can go in a world of directions.

Makes twenty-four 2-inch cookies

4 ounces (1 stick; 8 tablespoons) butter, preferably unsalted

1 1/4 cups flour—all-purpose white or whole wheat flour works well, as does 1 1/3 cups white or whole-grain spelt flour

1/4 cup sugar

1/2 teaspoon salt

Optional toppings—1/4 to 1/3 cup of any one of the following: finely chopped Mexican chocolate, finely chopped nuts (I love pecans), pumpkin or sunflower seeds, sesame seeds, chopped dried or candied fruit, sprinkles (*grajeas* in Spanish), whole currants, crumbled banana chips, even oatmeal or a sprinkling of anise seeds

Cut the butter into 8 pieces, scoop into a bowl and microwave for 45 seconds at 25% power just to soften a little.

Measure the flour, sugar and salt into a food processor. Pulse several times to mix thoroughly. Add the butter and pulse until completely mixed (usually 10 to 12 times) but not homogeneous. Dump the crumbly dough onto your work surface and press into a ball. Cut a 12-inch piece of plastic wrap, lay the dough in the center and cover with a second piece of plastic wrap. Use your hands to press the dough into a disk that's 1/2 inch thick. Use a rolling pin to flatten it evenly to 1/4 inch. Refrigerate 30 minutes.

Heat the oven to 350 degrees and position a rack in the middle. Peel off the top piece of plastic from the dough. Use a cookie cutter or knife to cut out cookies; gather the scraps and roll them between plastic to cut more cookies. (If it appeals, roll the dough into a square and simply cut into square, rectangular or diamond shapes.) Transfer the cookies to an ungreased baking sheet, spacing them about 1 inch apart. Sprinkle one of the optional toppings evenly over the cookies, then gently press it in.

Bake 15 to 17 minutes, until lightly browned, turning the baking sheet once halfway through. (They will be a little soft when they come out of the oven but will crisp when they cool.) Cool 2 minutes, then use a spatula to transfer the cookies to a wire cooling rack. If you chose no toppings, you can sprinkle the cookies with powdered sugar or cinnamon sugar while they're still warm. Store in a tightly sealed container.

Index

Note: Page numbers in *italic* type refer to photographs.

S

V